Revised and Expanded Edition
The Chippewa and Their Neighbors

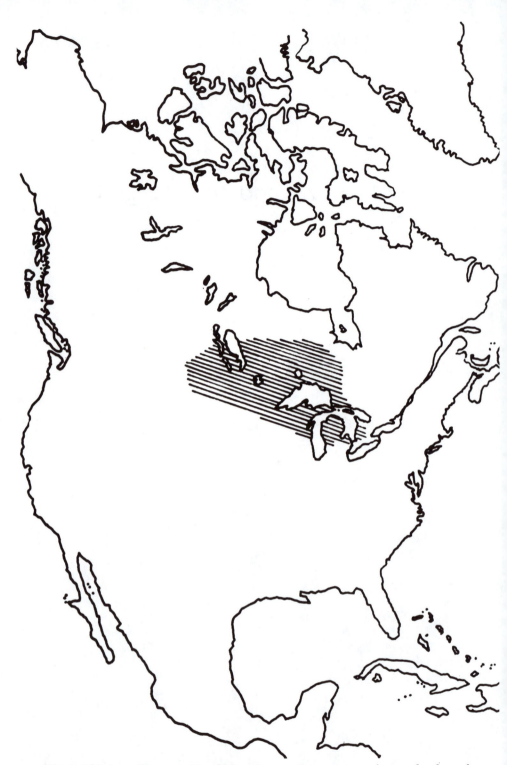

Map 1. Chippewa Country—North America: maximum extent of range by the early nineteenth century

Revised and Expanded Edition

The Chippewa and Their Neighbors

A Study in Ethnohistory

HAROLD HICKERSON

Foreword by Charles A. Bishop
Review Essay and Bibliographical Supplement by
Jennifer S.H. Brown and Laura L. Peers

WAVELAND

PRESS, INC.

Prospect Heights, Illinois

For information about this book, write or call:

Waveland Press, Inc.
P.O. Box 400
Prospect Heights, Illinois 60070
(708) 634-0081

For Polly

Waveland Press, Inc. gratefully acknowledges Helen H. Tanner, The Newberry Library of Chicago, and University of Oklahoma Press for their assistance with and support for this revised and expanded edition.

The color fold-out map has been reproduced from *Atlas of Great Lakes Indian History*, edited by Helen Hornbeck Tanner, Copyright © 1987 by the University of Oklahoma Press, and has been used with permission.

ISBN 0-88133-330-1

Printed in the United States of America

7 6 5 4 3

ABOUT THE AUTHOR

Harold Hickerson was professor of anthropology at Simon Fraser University in Burnaby, British Columbia, and held a Ph.D. from Indiana University. He did fieldwork in Guiana, British Honduras (Belize), and in several New York and Canadian Iroquois communities. Most of his archival studies of the Chippewa were done while he was researching Indian land claims at Indiana University. Besides serving as editor of the journal, *Ethnohistory*, Hickerson wrote numerous articles and monographs on the historical Chippewa. His last publications, three volumes on the ethnohistory of the Chippewa in the upper U.S. midwest, appeared in 1974.

ABOUT THE CONTRIBUTORS

Charles A. Bishop is professor of anthropology at the State University of New York at Oswego. Besides his major book, *The Northern Ojibwa and the Fur Trade: An Historical and Ecological Study* (1974), he has published many articles on Northern Algonquian ethnohistory, and most recently on native trade and social stratification in the interior of British Columbia. He also has been editor of *Ethnohistory*. He earned his Ph.D. at the State University of New York at Buffalo, working under Harold Hickerson.

Jennifer S.H. Brown is professor of history at the University of Winnipeg, Manitoba. Her publications include *Strangers in Blood: Fur Trade Company Families in Indian Country* (1980); *The New Peoples: Being and Becoming Metis in North America* (1985, co-edited with Jacqueline Peterson); and *The Orders of the Dreamed: George Nelson on Cree and Northern Ojibwa Religion and Myth, 1823* (1988, co-authored with Robert Brightman); and numerous articles on fur trade and native history.

Laura L. Peers is an independent researcher who has published on Northern Algonquian ethnohistory and on the nineteenth-century Quakers of southern Ontario. Following an Honours degree in anthropology and native studies at Trent University, she earned a Master's degree at the University of Winnipeg in 1988. Her thesis, "An Ethnohistory of the Western Ojibwa, 1780-1830," is being revised for publication.

CONTENTS

Foreword
by Charles A. Bishop

Harold Hickerson died on January 8, 1987 after a lingering illness dating to 1974. *The Chippewa and Their Neighbors: A Study in Ethnohistory*, which appeared in 1970, was one of his last publications, and it appears that his thoughts on ethnohistory and on the Chippewa subsequently changed little. Despite the passage of time, most of his conclusions about the historical past of the Chippewa have stood up under closer scrutiny and additional research although some topics were controversial at the time and have remained so.

This is a "how-to-do-it" book written by one of the first pioneers in ethnohistorical research. While a graduate student at Indiana University, Hickerson was involved in the Indian land claims research being carried on by the Ohio Valley — Great Lakes Research Project at that institution. It was thus no accident that scholars at Indiana played an important role in defining the field of ethnohistory and founding the American Society for Ethnohistory and its journal, *Ethnohistory*, in the early 1950s. Hickerson was editor of the journal in the late 1960s, and both it and the society continue to flourish.

A basic tenet of anthropology is that cultures, the lifeways of various peoples, change over time. Hickerson believed, as do most cultural anthropologists still, that the central task of the profession is to study changes in particular cultures in order to compare them with others. By doing so, anthropologists hope to attain general conclusions about the nature of change. This interest in the processes of cultural change and evolution has remained strong; witness the numerous studies of egalitarian, ranked, and stratified societies and the varied explanations of their development. In order to achieve understanding of general (nomothetic) evolutionary processes, Hickerson argued (chapter 1) that it was necessary to establish aboriginal baseline conditions for the societies used to illustrate these processes and to establish valid cross-cultural generalizations. But he also argued, as do many ethnologists today, that the processes of change among those small-scale societies which experienced prolonged direct contact with complex state societies (particularly European) were qualitatively different from those which had occurred prior to such contact. Consequently, another purpose of anthropological research is to document and explain post-contact developments. This gets scholars further into the subject matter of ethnohistory, since the assessment of historical change requires the employment of a variety of types of data as well as careful analysis of their meaning and validity. The particular theoretical orientation of the ethnohistorian is also an important variable, because it can influence the selection of data thought to be important and their interpretation in historical research.

In chapter 2, Hickerson discussed the various approaches employed in reconstructing past cultures and the changes that they have undergone. His warning that scholars should not read into past relationships those of the present, no matter how suggestive the evidence, unless they have a solid empirical basis for doing so, remains a cardinal rule. A corollary would be that accounts written at or near the time period being discussed should be employed. Historians would add that the reliability of the writer, the nature of the intended audience, and the extent to which the records represent firsthand or eye-witness reports must be assessed. Hickerson was especially concerned with the degree to which anthropologists had projected ethnographic information derived from the memory of living informants back to an assumed aboriginal past, without comparing it with archival sources.

More recently, some scholars have successfully combined data derived from recent fieldwork with the documents to flesh out past changes and events. In turn, the archival evidence takes on new meaning in light of the field materials. Other types of data such as old photographs, museum pieces, or artifacts from archaeological sites may serve to jog the memory of informants. New developments in ethnoarchaeology, historical archaeology, and anthropological linguistics offer new means of assessing and linking different categories of information and thereby bring fuller understandings of the past. In sum, those interested in the study of culture change employ an increasing variety of techniques to interpret historical events and conditions. It is this use of a wide range of analytical tools and information combined with a general scientific and humanistic interest in peoples of the past that distinguishes ethnohistory from other forms of historical research.

In chapters 3 to 8, Hickerson illustrated how ethnohistorical techniques could be employed to shed light on several little known or controversial aspects of Chippewa culture history. Chapter 3 focuses on the question of clans. Hickerson argued that the protohistoric Chippewa near the upper Great Lakes were characterized by corporate patrilineal totemic clan organization. Although the evidence for such organization among the earlier historic Chippewa is not great, there are later data supporting it and Hickerson's interpretation remains convincing. Indeed it has been supported by additional historical research (Bishop 1974, 1976, 1978). Still, however, a few scholars, in particular James G.E. Smith (1974) disagree, arguing that animal-named groups in the seventeenth century records were bilateral on the grounds that unstable ecological conditions would have inhibited the development of corporate clans. Later forms of patrilineal totemism are explained in terms of postcontact geographical movements. But given the disruptive effects of European contact, it seems unlikely that patrilineal totemism could have emerged after contact. Further, comparative evidence suggests that unilineal organization does not require stable ecological conditions to develop, but, rather, structured exchange relations between groups (see Bishop 1986). This is not the place to elaborate on competing paradigms, but readers should be aware that not all agree with Hickerson's and my arguments.

In chapter 4, Hickerson took up the elaborate ceremonial known as the Midewiwin. He argued that it was a creative nativistic movement that blended old ideas and customs with new elements that gave it meaning in terms of post-contact events. By inference from negative evidence (a lack of evidence), he suggested that the Midewiwin arose some time after 1680. As with Chippewa clans, the historical provenance of the Midewiwin remains controversial, although in my view Hickerson's skillful use of the sources to support his interpretation again remains convincing.

Chapters 5 to 8 trace the expansion of the Chippewa from locations along the south shore of Lake Superior westward into Minnesota at the expense of the Dakota Sioux. Hickerson masterfully documented the ecological and social implications of this expansion by drawing correlations among vegetal zones, game densities (particularly deer), and warfare. He provided a sound historical basis for subsequent more detailed studies by ethnohistorians and archaeologists, some of which are cited in this new edition.

In addition to describing the different kinds of evidence that can be used in historical reconstruction and illustrating how they can be employed in a particular case study, Hickerson demonstrated that records don't simply "speak for themselves." They require interpretation. Interpretation, in turn, involves a sound knowledge of general anthropological theory, comparative data, and training in how to extract the most information from incomplete evidence. This text, with the emendations added in this new edition, provides students with some of the basic knowledge and techniques needed to undertake ethnohistorical research on their own.

Preface and Acknowledgments 1988

The Chippewa and Their Neighbors appeared in 1970 as a volume in the series entitled Studies in Anthropological Method, under the general editorship of George and Louise Spindler. The Spindlers and their publisher, Holt, Rinehart and Winston, were pioneers in making anthropological texts readily available in paperback form; more than a generation of scholars and students has benefited from these readable, accessible volumes.

Harold Hickerson's volume made him a central figure in bringing recognition to ethnohistory as a growing and important field of study. He did not have the opportunity to engage in much graduate-level supervision; Charles Bishop, whose foreword opens this new edition, was his only Ph.D. student. But this book, for the nine years it remained in print, initiated several thousand undergraduates into some of the basic skills and problems in doing ethnohistory, and into the study of the Southwestern Chippewa in particular.

Several impulses have stimulated the rise of ethnohistory as a field from Hickerson's days at Indiana Universiy to the present. The last decades have seen anthropologists examine their profession increasingly critically. Its methods, theoretical underpinnings, relationships to other disciplines, and the ethics and political relevancy of the anthropological enterprise have all undergone increasing scrutiny, often at the hands of scholars (including some non-anthropologists) who find themselves attempting ethnohistorical syntheses (see, for example, Axtell 1981, chapter 1). The lengthening of historical perspectives on anthropological data has brought growing awareness of the limitations of the "ethnographic present" — that timeless moment of encounter which the older ethnographers preserved and constructed from their (quite historical) periods of participant-observation in the field (Stocking, ed., 1983). Hickerson helped to redirect anthropologists toward the study of historical change and process as essential contexts in which to situate their ethnographic data, and demonstrated how documentary sources, the usual preserve of the historian, could be enlisted to address anthropological issues and questions. In turn, such writings as his have served as a bridge to those increasing numbers of historians who seek to incorporate histories of native peoples into their researches and curricula.

Writing in 1970, Hickerson rather downplayed the practical applications of ethnohistory to settle the legal issues of Indian land claims; such uses of data, he observed in chapter 1, became of secondary importance to him and "in every sense a byproduct." Since he wrote, however, dozens of ethnohistorians have found a new political relevancy in their work, whether as researchers and witnesses in the burgeoning numbers of claims cases in courts across North America, or whether simply as generators of data and interpretations that are invoked by one or another of the legal adversaries. If Hickerson had been revising this book for reissue, he might have added some interesting perspectives on the evolving potentialities and pitfalls of ethnohistory as an applied social science.

There are two major reasons for republishing *The Chippewa and Their Neighbors*. First, it remains one of the relatively few brief, readable texts that explicitly address the methods and contributions of ethnohistory. Second, as a synthesis of some key facets of Chippewa historical processes and change, it has had wide influence, setting forth interpretations that, along with the ten or so articles Hickerson had previously published on the Chippewa, placed their history in a distinctive perspective that is still subject to debate and revision. As time goes on, it becomes possible (and useful) to situate Hickerson's own work in the historical stream of scholarship on Northern Algonquians, and to review its approaches and conclusions in the light of other thinking and newer researches.

This edition does not modify Hickerson's own text in any way. It adds, however, a new retrospective review at the end, to place the book in the broader context of ongoing scholarly inquiry. A bibliographic supplement is also appended to Hickerson's Recommended Readings and References (which themselves are reprinted unchanged). Our textual citations, if they are not already cited in Hickerson's References (and most are more recent than his list) will be found there. The supplement is by no means exhaustive; it merely samples a large literature with particular emphasis on items pertinent to *The Chippewa and Their Neighbors*.

A comparison with the 1970 edition will reveal that certain illustrations have been changed, in favor of images that seemed more representative of the periods and people discussed in the text. We are fortunate, as well, to have the permission of Helen Tanner and the University of Oklahoma Press to reprint a color plate from the *Atlas of Great Lakes Indian History* (Tanner 1987) illustrating tribal distributions and villages, ca. 1768, for the Chippewa (read "Ojibwa" on the map) and their Great Lakes neighbors. See the foldout in the back of the book.

Numerous colleagues assisted us with advice and suggestions drawn from their recent researches, and contributed perspectives on Hickerson's work. We list them, with warmest thanks, in alphabetical order: Charles A. Bishop, Mary Black-Rogers, James A. Clifton, Thor Conway, Bruce A. Cox, Tim E. Holzkamm, Victor P. Lytwyn, Edward S. Rogers, Donald B. Smith, James G.E. Smith and Leo Waisberg. It has not been possible to incorporate all the ideas they have offered us; to do so would have involved rewriting the book, or writing a new one. But we have benefited greatly from their help, as will those readers who pursue the varied perspectives and source materials that they have contributed to our text.

One point should be made clear at the outset, especially for newcomers to the field of Chippewa (Ojibwa) ethnohistory. Hickerson's interpretations of Chippewa culture, of clans, of the Midewiwin ceremony, of resource use, and other topics are, as Charles Bishop has noted in his foreword, controversial — in some instances more so than they were in 1970. Our colleagues' responses to the reissuing of his book ranged from enthusiasm to comments on the utility of bonfires. The review essay and supplemental bibliography that follow the text serve, we hope, to identify the major debates and to guide readers toward their own explorations of the issues and the source materials.

Jennifer S.H. Brown
Laura L. Peers

Introduction

THIS BOOK ILLUSTRATES the use of ethnohistoric methods to describe cultural organization and to analyze factors of culture change among the Chippewa at various periods in their history. Because the Chippewa were not at any time after their first contacts with Europeans isolated from other peoples, both Indians and Euro-Americans, they cannot be viewed except in terms of their relations with their neighbors. Hence the title of the book. Although a number of diachronic approaches lie at the background of this specific ethnohistorical study, the methodological emphasis is on the use of *primary documents* and their interpretation. By primary documents we mean accounts of people and the events affecting them, written by men who were eyewitnesses to those events, and who participated in them, either as interested observers or as role players. For the most part they were traders, officials, explorers, travelers, and missionaries. Many of the accounts have been published, some edited and annotated by professional historians, some more rarely by anthropologists. Others remain unpublished in archives, libraries, museums, and other repositories. Most, if not all, were the works of men not trained in the social sciences or history, indeed, men who existed, acted, and wrote in the period before the social sciences had assumed the dignity of academic disciplines.

However, some early observers, despite their lack of specific training, were remarkably observant and objective. Such men were rare, but they show up often enough to confirm or refute in concrete terms what the anthropologist has inferred from the analysis of other sources. Thus, the Scottish-Canadian fur trader, Duncan Cameron, in 1804, in his description of the Chippewa living north of Lake Superior, left no doubt that the practice of cross-cousin marriage and clan affiliation, both extremely intricate cultural phenomena, were important among that people. So, too, the descriptions of the seventeenth century French trader-official, Nicolas Perrot, are brilliant analyses of communal customs and the effects of French penetration among the Indians of the Great Lakes region.

The work of the anthropological ethnohistorian must be highly interpretive. He is inclined to find clans in societies in which they were not described as such

1

(see Chapter 3); he discovers causality in warfare from a confusion of scattered and unsynthesized data indicating warfare to be anything but rational (Chapters 5–8). He must be prepared to conjure up formal structures where none seem to exist; in other words, he must be ready to discover order where only disorder seems to prevail. As in other sciences, he is always on the watch for the simplest explanation for apparently complex relations.

In order to pursue his aims, he must have some acquaintance with historiographical as well as anthropological techniques. Some leads to this material are given below. Let us say here, however, that he must avoid becoming so engrossed in methodology that he loses sight of his primary objective, the explication of cultural organizations and of culture change among specific groups, and eventually, through comparative analysis, the statement of general laws dictating the direction of culture change in broadest scope. In this particular book, I prefer to stress that it is the *Chippewa and their neighbors* about whom I write; the historical techniques I employ are the implements with which I build an edifice.

Americanist anthropologists have been employing primary documents over a long period of time, beginning with H. R. Schoolcraft who, as Indian agent at Sault Ste. Marie and government ethnologist during the 1820s–1850s, wrote extensively on the Chippewa and others. Schoolcraft, who was himself a primary source for later anthropologists, used documents to lend perspective to his field studies. J. R. Swanton in his Southeastern studies (1946) is an example; A. L. Kroeber (1925) in his work on California tribes is to some extent another; A. I. Hallowell (1955) in his research into the Jesuit Relations and other primary documents on Woodland groups is yet another. Among others who have used documents is F. Eggan in his work on southeastern tribes (1966); outstanding in this regard has been the work of W. N. Fenton on the Iroquois (1940). Recently, work on Indian land claims has led the many Americanists involved to primary documents, to discover and verify occupation and migration patterns, and the make-up of social groups of numerous Indian peoples. Some valuable publication has come from this material, but much still remains in the obscurity of the United States Department of Justice files, and in the notes and reports which reside in the cabinets and on the shelves of those who participated. However, such work has served to quicken interest in ethnohistory and has been the prime mover in the founding and continuing publication of the journal, *Ethnohistory*, for many years under the editorship of the ethnohistorian of the Shawnee, Erminie Wheeler-Voegelin. This interest is also reflected in the inclusion of a chapter on ethnohistory by W. C. Sturtevant in a recent general text edited by J. Clifton (1968:450–475).

To illustrate ethnohistorical method, certain sections, especially the four chapters on warfare, are exhaustively documented, far more so than if the author were merely presenting the fruits of research indicated through a modicum of footnotes, but emphasizing results rather than procedures. If this involves a certain tedium in reading (it certainly did in writing), it is only because I wish to make a point: the ethnohistorian must be as assiduous in his work in the archives as the fieldworker is in the field. As one who has been in both places, I can say that the archival worker needs more patience and must be freer of frustration than the fieldworker, under ordinary conditions. There is little immediate reward in establishing rapport with a microfilm reader, and the most human relationship may occur when, at the end of his labors in a particular place, the worker in archives presents an especially helpful archivist with a box of candy.

This book, then, illustrates how documents can be used to supplement other methods in reconstructing the past of a tribe, and its career (or decay) under contact conditions. Not all experts in the area I discuss will agree with certain conclusions I derive from the data. Documents can be interpreted in different ways; only the events of history are objective. But at least those who disagree are presented with a corpus of historical materials upon which to base their disagreement. Much controversy in the past over the organizational status of Algonquians in general and the Chippewa in particular (cf. Hickerson, 1967a) has not been waged on the basis of exhaustive or even selected use of historical data, but rather on inferences drawn from observation of reservation communities, which at least one anthropologist of the Chippewa (B. James, 1961) has termed "marginal." I refer the reader at appropriate places to other works on the Chippewa which present points of view opposed to mine, without, however, stressing points of controversy.

I would suggest that the reader not trained in history look at certain recent historiographical works, especially the sections of them dealing with the subject of historical criticism. Of course, within history itself there are broadly varying points of view, not only in reference to philosophical foundations of history, but in reference to source criticism, and so on. There is, however, also much in common among the several approaches, especially in such matters as cross-checking references, chronology, validation, and other ideographic techniques. Among other works in historiography which can be readily located on university and public library shelves, and this is a highly selective list, is a work of the British diplomat-historian, E. H. Carr (1962), which presents a relativistic approach; that is, an approach emphasizing that history as written, as well as the primary sources upon which it is based, should be approached not in terms of absolute values, but rather of the values in force in the country, and during the age, in which the works appeared. This work is simply and humorously written, and because much of it has a social science orientation, is highly readable for professional anthropologists as well as for students.

The Cambridge historian, G. R. Elton (1967), takes a particularist position, emphasizing that specific historical studies serve to refute "overgeneralizations" indulged in by social scientists, especially those woven around the concept of "progress." Most valuable in Elton are the sections that deal specifically with historiographical method, including extensive passages on criticism of evidence and sources (Part II).

Somewhat earlier works valuable for their treatment of historiographical method are R. G. Colingwood (1946, especially Part V, Section 3, pp. 249–282) and F. J. Teggart (1960, but originally published in 1918). Teggart in Part 2, and Part 3, Chapter 14, makes extensive use of anthropological sources to indicate historical change through an analysis of wide-scale differences in contemporary human groups.

Another good source is W. H. Dray (1964), which, aside from its contributions in the philosophy of history and source criticism, contains a small, but highly relevant bibliography on historiography.

The great French historian, M. Bloch (1961), presents a readable and entertaining discussion of historical criticism to illustrate his own craftsmanship in going about his work.

Somewhat more grim are the essays by a number of eminent American historians, works resulting from Social Science Research Council seminars (1946; 1954) on the philosophy and methodology of history.

I should like also to recommend a simple and readable exposition of Marxian historical criticism, which, I believe, has not been superseded: the two essays written early in this century by the Russian, G. Plekhanov (1940), entitled "Historical Materialism," and "The Materialist Conception of History."

Although an abbreviated list, these works should provide the reader with a good concept of the way historians go about their specific tasks, and some of the philosophic basis, or rationale, for their labors.

On a practical level, I would suggest that, for the student of anthropology, whether beginner or a veteran, interested in the ethnohistory of a people, related peoples, culture areas, or even larger units, the beginning of document research is going to the library closest to the area of interest and following your nose from there. If you travel a trail long enough, material takes shape and begins to make sense in terms of consistency. Depending upon the scope of the problem, and assuming an adequacy of material, there is inevitably a point of diminishing returns reached, much as in fieldwork, and then research grinds to a stop. In fact, one should know *when* to stop digging and get down to work. One must, above all, avoid congestion where there is abundance.

I will now lay down a few ground rules for this present study:

Brackets within quotes are mine; parentheses are those of the original author. In nonquoted passages, brackets indicate the present name of locations referred to, by authors, by names now obsolete. Parentheses within nonquoted passages contain location names, given by original authors, that I have corrected to their modern forms.

It is not feasible to provide maps containing all the place names which appear in the text. These would be hopelessly cluttered. For those interested, road maps, atlases providing state maps in good detail, and, especially, geological survey maps are useful.

Quoted passages are given as closely to their original form as possible, with all the misspellings, grammatical aberrations, and abbreviations kept intact. I do not, therefore, use the word, *sic*, at all. There is no passage quoted, no matter how quaint, that will not be understood.

To most of the chapters I have appended a section on recommended readings. These are not meant to be exhaustive and, undoubtedly, I have omitted significant and relevant material, not by choice, but through ignorance or simple forgetfulness. The "Bibliography" covers only works I have cited in the text.

I should like to express my appreciation to Arthur Einhorn for arranging the plates and maps, including the cover, and to Dorothy Libby for help in the compilation of sources. My wife, Nancy P. Hickerson, read the manuscript and made helpful criticisms in matters of both style and organization.

1

Ethnohistory and the Chippewa

What is Ethnohistory?

ANTHROPOLOGY is both a natural and a social science. The boundary line has become indistinct with the new emphasis placed on looking upon culture as an adaptive mechanism distinguishing man from other primate genera. The study of social primatology and the social life of early man has utilized concepts of natural selection. Physical anthropology, as a branch of human biology, is no longer primarily concerned with the description and classification of racial types. The introduction of genetics in anthropology has shifted emphasis from viewing men as *racial types* to viewing men as populations, and to the way they adapt to changes in environment. Human populations have always been changing in their relationships with each other, and through fragmentation, with resulting modifications in gene pools.

As a social science, anthropology is concerned with the description of the cultures of peoples and the culture of man. I prefer to apply the term *ethnology* to this discipline of study, and it is with this discipline that we are concerned here. Ethnology views cultures as changing, even though techniques have been devised to study a single culture as if it were frozen at a given point in time, past or present. Those who make synchronic studies do not deny the importance of change in culture; it is only that they are primarily interested in how the different categories of culture—economic, social, political, and religious—function together within a social behavioral system, a society. It is a complex problem to see how these change together through time.

When we speak of change, whether in the genetic structure of populations or in various aspects of human culture, we refer necessarily to *history*. The entire course which mankind has followed, from its proto-human beginnings to the present (and presumably beyond into the future) is a grand history indeed. So great have been the changes that have taken place in the organization of the human physical form and in culture, that anthropologists and others have often been induced to use the term, *evolution*, to characterize them. With respect to culture, some ethnologists have even found it convenient to separate the concept of *evolution* from that of *history*, by considering the former as the definition of general change affecting the development of human life and institutions as a whole, and the latter as the definition of changes that occur in single cultures or momentarily discrete sets of cultures related organically or in geographical proximity.

In its most technical aspect, the one to be illustrated in this book, *ethnohistory* consists of the use of primary documents—library and archival materials— to gain knowledge of a given culture as it existed in the past, and how it has changed. Many tribal cultures of the past have survived in one form or another to the present, and although altered, continue to maintain distinctive technological and social systems and ideologies.

In its broadest sense, ethnohistory employs a number of research techniques to see in what way the present-day culture is similar or dissimilar to ancestral cultures; to what degree, in other words, the culture has changed, and what the distinctive historical factors were in determining such change. For example, many of the Chippewa Indians of today do not practice *cross-cousin marriage*, that is, marriage between children of opposite-sexed siblings. Yet, three centuries ago, when the forerunners of the modern Chippewa were first contacted by Europeans, and for a short time after, cross-cousin marriage was widespread, and indeed, may have been required. This does not mean, of course, that each person had a convenient *first* cross-cousin to marry, but, at that time Chippewa social groups were structured in a way to permit the classification of a large number of affinal relatives living in different (*exogamous*) communities as cross-cousins, whether they were actually first cross-cousins or not. Today cross-cousin marriage not only does not occur among many of the Chippewa, but is strictly forbidden to at least the fourth degree of relationship.

The historian of culture is not content merely to know that cross-cousin marriage existed at one time and exists no longer. He is interested in the total cultural situation in which *prescription*, then *proscription*,[1] occurred. What were the relevant historical factors? Can he discover in the remnants of the history of the people the precise or the approximate time at which this shift took place? Can he relate this shift to other changes in the culture? When we discuss this and other features of Chippewa organization we can apply, among other techniques, the use of *documentary* material, of which there is a relative abundance, not only for the Chippewa but for certain of their Algonquian and Siouan neighbors as well. There is material to be harvested from the time of their earliest contacts with the French who first began describing them in the mid-seventeenth century.

When I say "relative abundancy" I mean that seldom in the early documents, published or unpublished, on any people, do we find definitive statements on the organization of the people we are interested in. Rather, depending on the area, we have varying amounts of scattered, often fragmentary, source material, in

---

[1] A *prescriptive* rule narrows the choice in marriage by specifying persons who are marriageable according to relationship. A *proscriptive* rule narrows the choice by specifying persons who are *not* marriageable according to relationship.

which there are indirect references to features of social and economic life, often as they relate specifically to the experience of European missionaries, traders, travelers, or officials with Indians, in the pursuit of their own, their company's or their country's interests. From these indirect references describing episodes of contact, we try to piece together a picture of what the organization of the people was like; lacking *explicit* material to a great degree, we must rely for our picture on the *implicit* material gleaned from scattered sources.

Ethnohistorians, then, apply the methods of *historiography* to the cultures in which they are interested in the light of their general anthropological experience; to gauge change that has taken place in them and to comprehend the historical factors involved in and determining change. By grasping the content and dynamics of *aboriginal* cultures, that is, tribal cultures as they existed before contact with European and other civilizations, we begin to encounter the problems of development and change on an evolutionary level. At this level the anthropologist has no alternative but to direct his energies to the solution of general laws of culture change. Ethnohistory, then, is that sub-branch of ethnology which employs historiographical methods to lay a foundation for the formulation of general laws: in a word, *ideographic* means to *nomothetic* ends.

The Ethnohistorian Introduces Himself

Before coming to the Chippewa and their neighbors I must digress to place our study in another perspective, that of its background. I do this because, as in other disciplines, the scientist, no matter how objective he may think he is, cannot be separated conceptually from his work. This is perhaps especially true for the social scientist, whose every conscious thought is determined most immediately and pressingly by relationships within the society of which he is a part. Aside from questions of theory and "pure" history, what relevance might such an ethnohistorical reconstruction, such as I am attempting, have to the real world? To answer this, with respect to my own work, I became interested in Chippewa social organization as a result of participation in Land Claims litigation. Very simply, Chippewa, as well as virtually all other recognized Indian communities in the United States during the last two decades, have been bringing claims against the United States government to recover money due them from land cession treaties of past centuries dating virtually back to the end of the American Revolution. Actually, the money was not "owed" in the sense that the government did not fulfill most of its treaty obligations; rather, the Indian communities and their attorneys have contended that payments made for Indian lands by the government were inadequate in terms of their real value at the time of cession. The suits, then, are to recover the difference between what was paid and what should have been paid, plus accumulated per annum interest. Most of the claims so far settled have been, for the most part, successful for the plaintiffs.

Now, because this represents outlays on the part of the government running to hundreds of millions of dollars, and for each tribe or reservation community involved the possibility of compensation involves millions or even tens of millions, the litigation has become very complex. A claims commission of three distinguished and usually elderly men was set up by Congress to adjudicate the claims argued by batteries of attorneys of the Department of Justice on one side, and those representing the Indians on the other, with both sides employing bevies of experts; economic historians and land appraisal people to estimate the value of given lands at the time of cession; frontier historians to determine whether specific tribes held occupancy over relevant lands; anthropologists to help with that and also to indicate how specific social groups, tribal or otherwise, made use of the land—for example, as farmers, as gatherers of wild foods, or as hunters, and, if hunters, gatherers, and/or farmers, what kind of produce, when it was gathered or taken, how done, and so forth.

It was stipulated that specific Indian claimants as communities had to prove they were in occupancy of the entire cession area at the time of the ratification of the treaty by the Senate, at the time of the establishment of United States sovereignty over the lands, (which occurred in most of the country east of the Mississippi on July 4, 1776, in most of the country [save Texas] west of the Mississippi in 1803), and moreover, from "time immemorial," which meant in effect the time of first European contact.

For example, several Chippewa bands ceded land in northern Minnesota in 1855 in excess of 10,000,000 acres, presumably for less than the land was worth. To settle the claim, some idea of the value of white and Norway pine per board-foot in 1855, and how many harvestable board-feet there were in the cession area had to be decided. The Masabi iron range, part of which was within the area, was not known to exist at the time, and therefore does not enter into the computation of value; pine was considered virtually the only source of value. In addition, the modern Chippewa claimants had to prove that their ancestors actually occupied the land they ceded in 1855. Because the cession area lay on both sides of the Mississippi they had to prove occupancy as of 1776 *and* 1803, as well as in 1680 when first European contact was established (this criterion gradually came to be abandoned, because in many areas there was great difficulty in proving continuous occupancy by the same group from "time immemorial"). Also, it had to be known what parts of the area were productively occupied to the exclusion of all other tribes.

As an anthropologist employed by a research project under contract to the Department of Justice, and housed in a great midwestern university, my job was to write reports on the organization and occupancy of the Chippewa and others in the area of the western upper Great Lakes and the country intervening to the Red River of the North, which forms the boundary between Minnesota and the Dakotas before flowing north into Lake Winnipeg. These reports would then form the basis of my testimony on the cases as an expert witness before the Claims Commission. To do so, I had to ascertain what kind of social groups occupied which lands within the treaty cessions. To get at this material I and colleagues working on peoples living in contiguous areas had to examine all kinds of documents, published and unpublished, to find answers to these problems.

The Chippewa problem was especially acute, because they had been amply described in their reservation setting by anthropologists employing various field techniques, in Canada as well as the United States. Although the writing was extensive, very little was of service in clarifying the nature of the organization of social groups a century ago and more when the treaties were made, much less their organization at the time of first contact, that is, from "time out of mind."

In fact, the Chippewa have usually been described as "atomistic," a term connoting *lack* of organization above the primary family level. But in my early researches I quickly became aware of many instances of united action in hunting, fishing, war, religious ceremonials, diplomacy, and trade. The atomistic profile, if descriptive of reservation descendants, did not fit the early people. The question of change arose, involving the breaking down of groups. But my task would be to try to put together a picture of how Chippewa peoples organized their activities and then to explain how Chippewa society, once corporate and intensely cooperative, had been broken down. Thus, a quite practical question—who occupied what land and when?—began to take on theoretical interest, and my work more and more assumed the complexion of what scientists so ardently like to call "basic research," in this case, the nature of aboriginal social groups. Almost imperceptibly, specific project research directed toward the solution of legal problems came to be of secondary importance, eventually merely the excuse to solve what had become more important sociocultural problems, hence, in every sense a byproduct. . . .

The Chippewa and Their Neighbors

A few decades over a century ago, the Chippewa had achieved their greatest expansion, comprising many different villages and bands separate and distinct from each other, but sharing a common tradition of language and culture. Chippewa occupied, by the fourth decade of the nineteenth century, a region stretching from the lower peninsula of Ontario to the plains of Saskatchewan and eastern Montana. As you see on Map 1, their country comprised part of the eastern, northern and western shores of Lake Huron, including some of the larger offshore islands, the entire Lake Superior region, the upper peninsula of Michigan, parts of northern and western Wisconsin, the northern half of Minnesota, the entire country of the Red River of the North below (north of) the present Grand Forks, North Dakota, parts of southern Manitoba, southeastern Saskatchewan, and adjacent prairies and plains in North Dakota and eastern Montana. In addition, Chippewa occupied almost the entire region of Lakes Winnipeg and Manitoba, and a great part of the country lying east of Lake Winnipeg and north of Lake Superior, extending almost to the swampy region south and west of James Bay.

In the southeastern section around Lake Huron, their communities were interspersed with those of closely related and friendly Ottawa and Potawatomi. South of Lake Superior, especially in the country toward Lake Michigan including the Green Bay region, their country was adjacent to that of more distantly related and usually friendly Menominee. Toward the southwest of Lake Superior in western Wisconsin and Minnesota, and in the upper Red River country, Chippewa villages were separated from those of the eastern (Santee) and prairie (Yanktonai, Yankton) Dakota by large tracts of unoccupied or sparsely occupied country. This tract constituted a kind of "no man's land," a buffer between them and the Dakota with whom they carried on almost endless warfare. (This warfare provides the subject matter for Chapters 5–8.)

In the Red River country and west, Chippewa bands were scattered among Cree, Assiniboin and the famed Gens Libre, or Métis, so called because of their mixed Indian (mainly Cree) and European (mainly French) ancestry, and the fact that they were descendants of old fur company employees, *free people*, having been released from their status as indentured servants.[2] Chippewa often accompanied Métis on their semi-annual buffalo hunts, sharing with them the hazards of the hunt and encounters with their mutual enemies, the Plains Dakota.

In the region of northern Lake Manitoba and northern Lake Winnipeg and east toward the Hudson Bay swamp, or *muskeg*, the trapping and fishing grounds of the Chippewa interpenetrated with those of their close northeastern congeners, the Cree, with whom they were normally, but not always, on good terms. North of Lake Huron Chippewa bands merged into those of other even closer congeners, the Algonquin, who occupied hunting grounds in the east.

In this immense area only in the Lake Superior region and in the interior of that lake north, south and west were the Chippewa exclusive occupants. In other areas they were but one of two or more groups. Either they maintained discrete communities interspersed with those of Algonquian congeners with whom they maintained friendly relations, or, in rare cases, shared communities with closely related Algonquians, especially Ottawa and Potawatomi.

Within this vast territory Chippewa, in historical times, engaged in a variety of occupations. In general, south of the upper Great Lakes in Michigan and Ontario they grew maize and squash to supplement a basic hunting and fishing economy. North of the Lakes where cultivation of crops was difficult due to poor soil and cold climate Chippewa were primarily hunters and fishermen, also using maple sugar and to some extent wild rice to supplement the basic meat and fish subsistence. In Wisconsin and Minnesota wild rice was quite important as a subsidiary activity, hunting and fishing again taking first place. In the western plains, bands of Chippewa hunted buffalo on horseback and, like other plainsmen, scorned the more sedentary pursuits of fishing and farming. Everywhere, except on the plains, Chippewa throughout the historical period were greatly reliant on trapping for the fur trade: their movements and, to a great extent, their organization, as we will see, were geared to their participation in this activity that was introduced and sustained on a large scale by Europeans.

Of course, today, Chippewa occupy reservations within this area as a minority people scattered among Euro-Americans, Métis and other Indians. Only in parts of Canada east of Lake Winnipeg and north of Lake Superior do they com-

---

[2] This occurred on the occasion of the merging of the Northwest Company and the rival X. Y. company in 1804–1805. The concentration of posts resulted in a superfluity of interpreters, voyageurs, and so on, who were mainly mixed-bloods. These folk, inured to frontier conditions, came to form a self-conscious group, in every sense a distinct society with a distinctive culture, specializing in hunting buffalo on the northeastern plains and selling the meat to the Hudson's Bay Company. Their most famed contribution to Americana was their use of the two-wheeled cart. There is one on exhibit at the Hudson's Bay Company building in Winnipeg.

prise the basic population. Even there, however, they are dependent on the Hudson's Bay Company and the Canadian government for trade goods, food and money subsidies, schooling, medical care and other things which have become integral to their present way of life.

In this study I am primarily, but not exclusively, concerned with the Chippewa who, in historical times, came to occupy the region interior to southern and western Lake Superior, chiefly in the present states of Wisconsin and Minnesota. However, as we move back in history, we find that the total area occupied by the

This drawing done by Seth Eastman in 1850 shows Chippewa women harvesting wild rice, an important food for many Chippewa. Women were responsible for the harvesting, processing, and storage of the rice; their male relatives assisted by slowly poling the canoes through the rice fields so the women could remove the rice from the stalk. (Courtesy James Jerome Hill Reference Library, St. Paul, MN. Used by permission.)

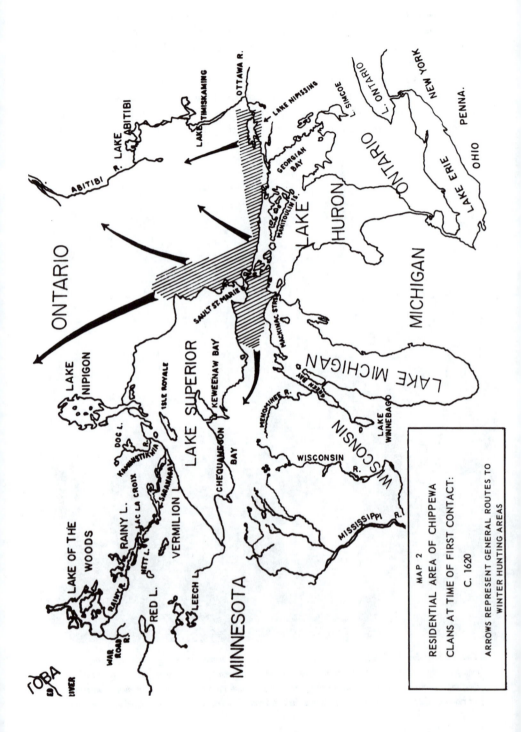

MAP 2

RESIDENTIAL AREA OF CHIPPEWA
CLANS AT TIME OF FIRST CONTACT:

C. 1620

ARROWS REPRESENT GENERAL ROUTES TO
WINTER HUNTING AREAS

Chippewa becomes less and less, shrinking from its greatest extent in the nineteenth century to a rather limited region around northern Lake Huron and eastern Lake Superior. The center was at Sault Ste. Marie on the St. Mary's River connecting the two upper lakes. There they gathered for ceremonials during the summer, and there they were first contacted by the French in the mid-seventeenth century. Indeed, contrary to the often expressed notion of the shrinkage of Indian groups due to European encroachment, the Chippewa in the long run, underwent great expansion through their contact with Europeans, largely due to their energetic participation in the fur trade leading to the occupation of new trapping grounds, and, at times when groups of them were acting as middlemen, new tribal contacts. Some of this expansion was peaceful, some of it occurred in the face of military opposition from entrenched populations. The expansion of the Chippewa was arrested only by the advance of the frontier in the United States during the second third of the nineteenth century. In Canada north of Lake Superior, where Chippewa continue to occupy immense tracts of land, the government came to take an active role in the lives of the Indians, starting in the 1870s when treaties were made and reservations established. The Chippewa, taken as a whole, were already splintered before confinement to reservations, and, of course, this fragmentation of social groups has continued under reservation conditions.

As I carry this study back in time it becomes, therefore, more and more comprehensive of the Chippewa as a whole, until when I write of the proto-group (pre-1640) in Chapter 3, I am including as many of them as are known to history.

The Precontact Chippewa

Very little is known about the Chippewa before European contact. It is known that they had a stone-age culture adapted to a mixed deciduous-coniferous forest region with many lakes and streams. This region is centered in the northern upper Great Lakes (see Map 2, which also includes territory south and southwest of Lake Superior for places often mentioned in the text). They lived in groups of perhaps 100–150 and made their living chiefly by fishing and hunting. Their manufactures were simple: containers and utensils fashioned from birch bark, stone, and animal horn, with a goodly amount of simple ceramic ware; to catch fish and game, spears and arrows tipped with flint or bone; fishing nets made of plant fibers; to process hides, scrapers and knives of flint, bone awls, and similar items.

They wore skins of moose, deer, and caribou, and pelts of beaver and otter, roughly tailored. Their houses were built by covering sticks and small poles bent to form a dome or arc with birch bark and matted grass. These could be quite large and house several families. They made canoes of birch bark reinforced with the gums of spruce or pine, with which they navigated the Great Lakes and tributary waters in the summer time. In winter they crossed the snow to reach their hunting grounds and to track game on raquettes whose frames were ash laced with thongs made from moose hides. To transport heavy goods they dragged wooden toboggans across the snow; they carried their infants in wooden cradle boards strapped to the back of the mother or an older child.

Cradle Board: The love of Indian parents for their babies is never more graphically demonstrated than when one views the lavish ornamentation devoted to a cradle board bunting. A child spent only its first year in this confinement, viewing the fantasy of charms, bells, and other playthings suspended from the bumper guard and continually swaying before the baby's eyes. (Courtesy Buffalo Museum of Science)

Quilled Birchbark Containers: Porcupine quill work was an aboriginal precontact decorative trait practiced by many North American Indians. It was applied to clothing, accessories, and utilitarian items like weapons and tools. From the mid-nineteenth century to the present, many Chippewa have highly developed the art for the tourist trade, as evidenced by these fine examples. (Courtesy Buffalo Museum of Science and A. and S. Einhorn Collection)

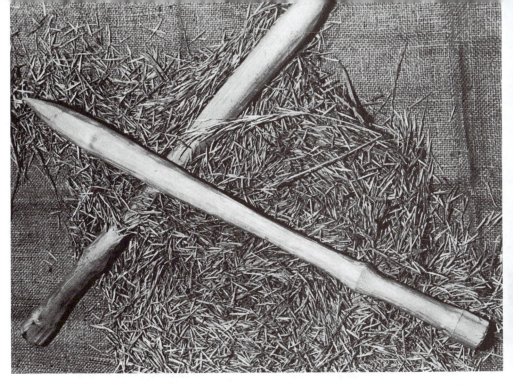

Wild Rice and Harvesting Sticks: Ricing sticks collected in 1965 from a Central Minnesota Chippewa family. The form is of a type that seems to have been in use from precontact times. The grain in the photo is freshly harvested wild rice. (Courtesy A. and S. Einhorn Collection)

Snow Shoes: For most northeastern woodland Indians the snow shoe was as essential to winter survival and hunting as was food and warmth. The wooden frame was generally made of ash; the netting was produced from deer, moose, caribou, or horse hide kept in a semicured rawhide state, which the French called babiche. (Courtesy A. and S. Einhorn Collection)

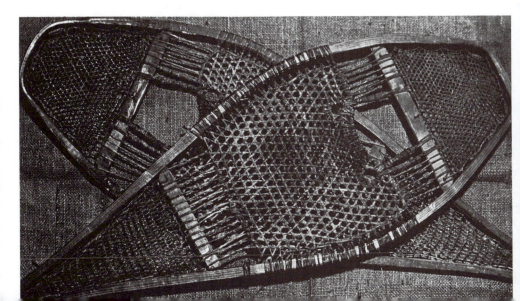

All the essential articles they used they made themselves, and all members of the group could perform the requisite tasks. Although they perhaps carried on some small trade, exchanging hides of moose and caribou for corn with neighboring farming peoples like the Iroquoian Huron, they were primarily self-sufficient and self-contained, shunning close contacts with all but near neighbors to whom they were related by marriage.

In their ceremonial and religious life, as far as it is known, they emphasized direct relations with objects in their immediate surroundings. Religious leaders were men and women who had magical ways to ensure that game animals and fish would be available to the people. These *shamans* also had special medicines, mainly herbs and powders of various kinds, and other procedures, magical and practical, to prevent and cure sickness, to repair wounds, and to set broken bones.

Their belief system centered in establishing and maintaining close and friendly relations with spirits, investing and giving animation to animals and plants and even to such "nonanimate" things as stars, stones, storms, hills and lakes.

The industrial and ideological systems, then, were geared to the simple needs of small communities whose members exploited a rather difficult environment without using artificial means to produce animal or plant food. Artifactual and belief systems are known in general through archeological and ethnological data garnered through fieldwork, not only on precontact and postcontact Chippewa, but on contiguous societies and on farflung societies on a similar level of cultural development. But what of the social system or the sociopolitical system within which technological and ideological systems took root and were maintained? Little is known about this from archeological and ethnological research. We may assume minimally that the prehistoric Chippewa peoples had an equalitarian political system founded in kin relations, with each group of relatives, no matter how large or small, acting as a semi-autonomous unit maintaining ties of hospitality with similar neighboring units to whom they were invariably related through marriage. Beyond this I can say very little, and perhaps I have already said too much, for I have been anticipating some of what follows.

The Chippewa Today

How does such a society (or societies) organize its political system to cope with the problems involved in assuring a livelihood for its members? Furthermore, how does such a society change its organization to cope with new relationships accruing from contacts with Europeans? It is here that there is great difficulty, for we can scarcely recognize, in present-day Chippewa social organization, mechanisms enforcing the cooperative and communal behavior which must necessarily have dominated their relations in the past.

Indeed, nowhere today do the Chippewa rely chiefly upon goods of their own fashioning. Some clothing, including moose hide moccasins in particular, snow shoes, toboggans, cradle boards, and a few household accessories made of birch bark, are among the items surviving from aboriginal times. Even the birch bark canoe which reached its most perfect form among the Chippewa and some of their northern Algonquian neighbors, has all but disappeared, replaced by imported canvas or aluminum canoes powered by an outboard motor.

Much of the material culture, then, has been lost, or rather replaced and enriched by the introduction of mass-produced commodities from outside. Great changes have occurred also in community organization. The reservation is a far cry from the autonomous community of the past, and even in wilderness parts of Canada where Chippewa continue to form the main population, reliance on the national government and schools, and on Euro-American commodities is virtually complete. This is of course even more the case in the United States, where the reservations are completely surrounded by the Euro-American population.

In terms of the aboriginal past, Chippewa culture is a shambles, so much have the people everywhere had to accommodate to the new conditions imposed by their relations with Euro-Americans. It is the task of the ethnologist to start with this shambles, and working backward with all the resources he can command, reconstruct the aboriginal culture and the factors which caused it to change. In the process of accomplishing this (he can never quite do so), he is enabled to see stages of change at various points during the contact period. A recognition of the dynamics of such changes affords him a glimpse of culture process, but here I express a very ambitious aim and again get ahead of the story.

A Survey of Historical Approaches in Cultural Anthropology

Introduction

HOW SHOULD THE AMBITIOUS GOAL expressed in the last chapter be approached? Let ethnohistory be viewed here as the employment of one of a number of historical techniques for the purpose of reconstructing given cultures of the past, the relationship of environmental factors to socio-cultural change in such cultures, and the reconstruction of the movement and location of identifiable populations. Before reconstructing the culture of a proto-historic tribe, it is necessary to establish first who the original tribesmen were, the limits of their occupation, and the locus and direction of their migrations. This is not always a simple matter, if only for the reason that the terms used by early writers for tribes and locations often differ quite sharply from those we use today, and at times are not even consistent within given time periods.

Cultural anthropologists interested in reconstruction employ a variety of historical techniques assuming, as is most often the case, that they cannot find in the debris of the present culture, severely modified as it normally is, a real picture of the past. There are several paths available to them; documentary research is but one of these. In this section I will survey briefly some of the historical approaches most widely used by anthropologists, to reconstruct the cultures of the past and the dynamics of culture change. I will confine this to a discussion of cultural approaches, and will ignore techniques developed in physical anthropology as being generally outside the scope of this essay.

Archeology

It is hardly possible to discuss historical approaches without at least a brief mention of archeology. Archeologists attempt to reconstruct culture history through the analysis of cultural remains that they extract from, or see in, the ground. The artifacts and other manifestations of human activity and habitation that archeologists are able to infer by inspection of the ground, such as the post-holes of houses and stockades surrounding settlements, provide the archeologists with insights into certain aspects of the organization of old communities.

Archeologists are concerned almost entirely with the chronologies of *prehistoric* cultures and culture systems. In the New World, with the notable exception of the civilizations of Meso-America and the Andes, archeologists deal exclusively with old traditions and cultures, which, before the coming of Europeans, were entirely without written history. Much of the material unearthed by archeologists, covering as it does the entire sweep of human habitation in any area, is remote from the specific interest of the ethnohistorian, who wishes to articulate the most recent prehistoric past with the earliest historic past. The ethnohistorian is concerned with the point at which these two eras merge in a single continuum, and in what immediately precedes and follows. Archeology can bring to light a great deal about cultures as they existed shortly before there were Europeans to describe them in writing, and thus provides not only a check on such early descriptions, but also a means to gauge the degree and nature of change in material and other aspects of culture after contact.

In the northeastern woodlands. a portion of which we are concerned with in this study, there has been a great deal of archeological work done covering the entire period from pre-agricultural Archaic times to the beginnings of the contact era. This work indicates, in some instances, the beginnings and development of farming, changes in settlement patterns, the building of earth structures such as burial mounds, pottery sequences, house types, military activities, death cults, and so on. It is obvious from comparisons of recent prehistoric and early historic settlements that European trade items, such as knives, axes and kettles, all made out of iron, quickly replaced comparable items manufactured in precontact times from native bone, flint, and clay.

Death cults, indicated by the burial of articles of value with the deceased, and mass burials (represented by ossuaries), perhaps in many places in the context of a Feast of the Dead, a ceremonial widespread among Iroquoians and neighboring Algonquians in early historic times, were also practiced widely in much of the same area in prehistoric times. But whereas in prehistoric times, except during one or two brief flamboyant eras, the goods buried with the dead, almost everywhere, were modest in amount and value, after contact, when the fur trade introduced by Europeans had come to absorb the interests and energies of the eastern Indians, the final resting place of the dead was in great pits accompanied by large amounts of peltry, glass beads, iron kettles, and other European goods which had great value in the trade. The contrast between the mass burials of prehistoric and historic times serves, among other things, to indicate the enormous enrichment in the material culture of North American tribesmen, as a result of the introduction of the fur trade, and, at the same time, a continuation of old communal practices, relating, perhaps, to values respecting the disposition of the dead, and the social organization of such values.

It may be seen, then, in certain instances, through comparison of archeological and ethnohistorical data, continuities and discontinuities in cultural practice and cultural tradition. Although the significance of such processes is not always apparent in the specific context of a given cultural tradition, the accumulation of such data will have its impact on the general field of culture change, especially that change resulting from the contact of Indian with European sociocultural systems.

George I. Quimby's archeological work (1966) in upper Great Lakes historical sites has been fruitful in establishing a continuous culture tradition from Archaic times through Woodland stages into the historical period. Quimby has developed techniques for dating historical sites through the analysis of glass beads and other trade wares. Such continua are rare, however, and archeological-ethnohistorical analysis as an approach, even in such potentially fruitful areas as the southern United States, is still in its infancy.

Space and Time

In astronomy, the history of the motion of stars and star systems within a single galaxy is rather complex for the observer, if only because the period of movement of star systems around a galactic center is greater as the distance between the system and the center increases. The astronomer sees a peculiarly skewed history in the images of the light-reflecting and light-producing bodies that he observes. The segment of the universe he brings within the range of his telescope has no present reality; it simply reflects a series of stages relating to the position and movement of a vast number of spatial objects at an equally vast number of points in the past. On the basis of analysis of the positions and migration paths of spatial entities, whether of the order of stars, star clusters, or even galaxies, the relative position and direction of such entities at the moment of viewing are theoretically predictable. Astronomy, which concerns itself with the evolution of the universe as a whole, as well as with the history of discrete space systems, is also a science in which the relations of the present not visible to the contemporary observer may be inferred only from the recognition and analysis of past events linked in historical sequences. In the process of inference-drawing, space and time become but two aspects of a single continuum. It is significant, with regard to this, that the distance between celestial units is conventionally expressed in terms of the time it would take for a light wave to travel between them, hence in *light years* and *parsecs*.

If astronomy is the most notable discipline in which space and time are viewed as twin parts of a continuum, such a continuum was first applied in the earth and natural sciences. Unlike astronomy, present relationships are not "predicted" on the basis of the analysis of past events; rather, understanding sequences of past events is predicated on the basis of analysis of present formations. The geologist, for example, under the principle of uniformitarianism, and by applying mechanics and chemistry, is able to uncover the events which led to present earth formations through the analysis of the juxtaposition of rock and soil strata, as well as the shape of the landscape.

Natural historians have fossils to help them in their reconstructions of the history of species. However, naturalists also interpret events in the history of species, through the observation of contemporary relationships among living species. For example, the reptiles are both contemporary with and, in terms of evolutionary sequence, prior to, the birds. Comparison of the characteristics of contemporary species of the two classes provides insights into the processes of modification of certain species of the former, to produce the latter. The fact that the fossil record discloses forms which appear to be intermediate between the two classes is a happy coincidence reinforcing what has already been inferred, on the basis of the evidence derived from the comparison of morphological traits among living representatives, within the theoretical context of evolution.

Thus, while in the science of astronomy, present relationships of bodies in outer space may be inferred only from the analysis of events and relationships of the past, in both the earth and natural sciences, past events are inferred chiefly on the basis of analysis of relationships of the present. Like astronomy, however, temporal sequences are inferred from spatial distribution; hence, in these sciences as well, space and time merge at certain conceptual levels to form a continuum. The *evolution* of life and matter is the focus toward which all scientific analysis converges. In the social sciences, general procedures of research in the natural sciences have been adapted with variable success to problems in culture history. Ethnology, with which I am concerned here, is both a descriptive and historical science, but because ethnologists have emphasized studying cultures without written languages, as well as the entire spectrum of culture history, the ethnologists have been forced to develop techniques to infer historical and chronological sequences without the benefit of the kind of documentary material available to historians.

One such technique I refer to as the *space-time continuum*, because, as in the other sciences I have mentioned, temporal sequences are inferred from spatial distribution.

There are three main ways in which the space-time continuum has been employed in cultural anthropology. One of these is *age and area*. The other two I call *space-time equivalence in evolution* and *space-time equivalence in history*.

1. The *age and area* method concerns the inference of time sequences from the spatial distribution of individual culture traits or complexes (trait clusters). The crucial point of age and area theory is that culture traits accumulate at a center and spread out ripplelike to margins retaining their original shape as they spread, while undergoing elaboration and development in the original locus. This spreading from a zonal center may be arrested by geographical features—mountain ranges, bodies of water, or even sharp changes in biome—or channeled by others—river valleys, trade routes, and so on—so that the shape of the area of distribution of a series of traits may be uneven. Nevertheless, according to age and area theory, the tracing of the trait or complex from the edge of its distribution back to the center is, in effect, tracing the history of its development. Sequence

of development, then, is reflected in the aspect of its distribution. Conversely, the center of distribution of a trait may be inferred from the relative degree of complexity of its development, thus the history of its diffusion, assuming again that it appears in its most elaborate form at the original locus from which it spread.

The age and area hypothesis is parallel to the idea in biology that older orders survive on the margins of the distribution of a class, an example being the survival of those primitive mammals, the marsupials, at the very edge of the distribution of mammalian forms. Here again, the older forms exist at the margin of distribution, while the younger, more advanced forms predominate around the original loci of mammalian radiation.

The history of the diffusion of such culture traits and trait clusters as the sinew-backed bow, matrilineal descent, pottery forms, the Plains Sundance, military societies, and the horse and maize complexes, were traced through analysis of factors in their spatial distribution. Some of these studies, examples being those of Lowie (1916), on military societies, and Spier (1919), on the Sundance, were marvels of detailed analysis of similarities and differences in the arrangement of the traits within those complexes among the several tribes concerned.

The age and area method absorbed a great deal of the attention of some of the most notable anthropologists during the first three decades of this century, especially of those interested in reconstructing the culture history of the American Indian. Emphasis was placed by such scholars, not on the history of whole cultures, but on culture traits, and not on the character of the evolution of culture, but on processes of the diffusion of discrete cultural elements. The age and area method stressed the study of the history of traits, and not that of peoples.

Age and area in cultural anthropology is a logical construct, which does not necessarily take into account differential rates of diffusion, selectivity in borrowing accruing from differences in the status of cultures in paths of potential diffusion, and modifying influences on elements accepted into existing ideological and technological systems. In other words, anthropologists cannot assume *uniformity* in change as do the natural scientists. These were matters actually understood and commented on by many of the anthropologists who used age and area method.

Kroeber and Sapir, among others, indicated the doubtful nature of the results of such analysis due to lack of corroborating documentary evidence. Kroeber (1931: 263) characterized age and area research:

> . . . method of inference, supplementary to the direct evidence of documentary history and archeological superposition; but, as such, it is warranted when it is desired to push beyond the confined limits of this sort of evidence.

Thus, the age and area method, confined to the study of the history of the diffusion of elements, is a last resort in instances when documents or prehistoric sites are not available for research. At present the age and area method applied to trait complexes has largely been abandoned, or rather survives surreptitiously, as interest in anthropology has shifted from studies of discrete traits to studies of whole cultures and the whole of culture.

2. The *space-time equivalence in evolution* is based on the idea that cultures

of the present represent, in the variation of their technological, social, and ideological development, stages of cultural evolution. Hence, hunting-gathering cultures still existing today in marginal areas would represent survivals from a period when all of human culture was at the hunting-gathering level (paleolithic-mesolithic). Somewhat less marginal farmers or herders who employ implements fashioned from wood and stone represent survivals from the next stage (neolithic), and so on, up to modern industrial society. In each stage survivors from previous stages remain on the outer peripheries, each group affected by the mainstream of later cultural evolution to some degree. (Here is another application of the age and area idea, the simpler cultures occupying the peripheries, the more developed and newer cultures occupying the centers of population distribution and cultural intensity.)

The great nineteenth century American anthopologist, Lewis Henry Morgan, in his classic work, *Ancient Society* (1963), viewed culture as moving in an orderly progression, beginning at a simple hunting-gathering stage, working up through agriculture and metallurgy, and culminating in industrial civilization. Morgan traced development in technology and forms of property ownership and social organization from their most rudimentary beginnings in the earlier stage, which he called *Lower Savagery*, up through succeeding stages of *Savagery* and *Barbarism*, to *Civilization*. Morgan cited contemporary cultures, Polynesian, Algonquian, Iroquoian, and others, as living representations of the several stages of cultural evolution. Thus, he viewed temporal sequence in terms of spatial distribution. Elman Service, one of the leading contemporary representatives of the "evolutionary" point of view, has pointed out the significance of classifications of present-day cultures into evolutionary levels, or stages, with regard to the evolution of human culture as a whole. Service (1963: xvi–xix) has met possible objections to his theoretical position, namely that individual cultures are always changing, (thus cannot be considered as true representatives of prototypical cultures), by arguing that not all cultures have always changed, a matter proven by the continuing existence of societies with theoretically limitless capacity to change still on a band or tribal level of organization:

> . . . the evolutionary perspective is useful in suggesting a kind of classification of contemporaneous primitive cultures which not only helps us to put them into an order based on significant similarities and differences, but also helps to account for the simultaneous presence of such disparate types of society.

Service points out the analogy between cultural and biological classifications, and, incidentally, the analogous application of the space-time continuum in both cultural and biological research:

> . . . the theory of evolution in biology had a similar significance, suggesting a classification of extant forms of life at the same time as it helped to account for how the differences arose among them in the first place.

This implies, among other things, great variation among contemporary cultures on a simple level of technological development and social integration such as *bands* and *tribes*, small groups organized around family and kin relations. Such simple groups are variably adapted to a broad range of specific environments—from arctic cold, as in the case of the Eskimo of the far North and the Yaghan of Tierra del Fuego, to tropical heat, as in the central Australian desert where live the Arunta, and the forests and islands of the Bay of Bengal, the home of the Andamanese. Such variations through adaptation also find their analogy in the variation of genera. . . .

The space-time equivalence in evolution, with the implication that the whole record of human history lies before our eyes, is fascinating but somewhat grandiose for this stage of the discussion. In the meanwhile, I am interested in more circumscribed problems relating to the specific history of tribes.

3. Immediately relevant is the *space-time equivalence in history*, which incorporates ideas similar to those in age and area and the evolutionary space-time equivalence, except that it is much less ambitious than either in scope. This method is geared to the analysis of changes within local regions which have occurred within the relatively brief span of the historical period, from the time of the first continuing contacts of indigenous tribal and peasant populations with incoming Europeans. The earliest recorded date for such contacts in the New World is 1492, but of course in many regions throughout both hemispheres contacts between natives and Europeans occurred at later periods roughly coincident with European exploration and discovery.

The formulation of the space-time equivalence in history received great impetus from the efforts of Robert Redfield, who applied it to a series of studies he carried out in the early 1930s in the Yucatán Peninsula of Mexico. Redfield (1965) described a culture in Yucatán that, although it contained elements from both Spanish and Maya civilizations in that region since the days of the Conquistadores in the early sixteenth century, was not precisely one or the other; rather, it apparently represented a kind of amalgam of the two. This hybrid folk culture, however, had changed quite radically in much of Yucatán since the first coming of the Spaniards, attested by the presence of such a modern center of urban civilization as Mérida, the capital of Yucatán. To gain some understanding of changes which had occurred relating to ever-increasing influences from outside the confines of the Peninsula, the rest of Mexico, and even such distant places as the United States and Europe, Redfield devised the plan of making simultaneous studies of a series of communities on widely varying levels of organization, and subject to influences from the outside of broadly varying degrees of intensity. The *city* of Mérida, a medium-sized *town* somewhat off the main roads and railroads, but not entirely isolated, and a small *village* located far in the bush in desolate Quintana Roo were selected as providing a suitable basis for developing a continuum from "tribal" to "folk" to "urban" level. (The spatially most remote community, I need hardly point out, is that which represents the oldest stratum in time, hence again the resemblance to age and area theory.) In Redfield's words (1965: 23), the comparison of these communities was "underlain by a fundamental assumption: that by means of it we shall be able to outline a process of culture change. . . ." This is a very succinct expression of the space-time equivalence.

Redfield did not assert that the bush village would in detail constitute a past representation of the town, but strongly implied that in broad outline such could be considered to be the case. Thus (23),

. . . we have frequently found the old people in the town recalling from their childhood customs and features of social organization which are today characteristic of the village. That is to say, one can go back either in time or in space, one can delve into memory or retreat into the bush, and reach the same set of facts.

As an example, he cites courtship and marriage customs still existing in practice in the village; however, it existed only in the minds of the older residents of the town, practiced in a way which the conservative aged look back upon with a feeling of nostalgia.

The space-time equivalence is well expressed in this passage (24):

The comparison of these three communities—city, town, and village—can therefore be expressed in terms of a process of transition. I think of this process as a shift from one type of society, which the most isolated village represents, toward another type, illustrated by the Yucatecan capital city but even better by our more mobile northern cities. But the process is also, as I have just indicated, in large measure an actual historical process, in that the sequential changes made manifest by the comparison are actual events that have taken place in the chronological development of certain members of the series.

Redfield continues by giving examples from the three type communities of comparable traits in which changes can be seen to have taken place.

Closer to the subject matter of this study has been the application of the space-time equivalence to the historical Chippewa. The foremost Chippewa scholar, A. I. Hallowell, has devoted a great amount of attention to the effect of Euro-American contact on the basic personality structure of groups of Chippewa living under variable conditions in the United States and Canada. Hallowell makes the assumption that Chippewa living in inland wilderness areas east of Lake Winnipeg, due to their isolation, have retained many features of aboriginal Chippewa life. They can be contrasted with Chippewa from the shores of Lake Winnipeg, who have had much more extensive contacts with Euro-Americans. In Hallowell's words (1955: 334; italics mine):

. . . it was evident that the people of the two Inland bands offered a striking contrast to those of the Lakeside band. The Inland people were undoubtedly much less acculturated. Thus, two levels of acculturation were identified. Besides this, from information obtained at the same period from Indians who had come in contact with Ojibwa[1] at more accessible inland points, such as Deer Lake and Sandy Lake, it was a still lower level of acculturation than that of the (Inland bands). It was equally clear that in eastern Canada and certain parts of the United States there were Ojibwa groups much more acculturated than the band at the mouth of the Berens River. *Thus the cultural gradient on the Berens River might be considered as part of a wider continuum of acculturation, the manifestation of an historical process which, under varying pressures and events and at different rates, has been transforming the lives of these American aborigines.*

Hallowell, on the basis of other evidence, including the analysis of Rorschach tests administered to Chippewa at several locales, inferred that modifications had occurred in the personality structure of the more acculturated groups. He also used

---

[1] Ojibwa is an alternate form to *Chippewa*.

early documentary sources to support other evidence for the continuum (1955: 334–335):

> I was . . . struck by the fact that the generalized psychological structure that I had independently pieced together from the seventeenth- and eighteenth-century accounts of the Indians of the Northeastern Woodlands . . . was fundamentally equivalent to the inferences I could make from the Rorschach protocols of the Ojibwa of Berens River. This was particularly true of the Inland groups. Hence it seemed reasonable to take the personality characteristics of the Inland group as a psychological base line from which to measure any changes.
>
> On the basis of the data available up to this point I assumed the following: (1) The personality structure of the Inland group of Berens River Indians approximated, if it was not identical with, an aboriginal type of modal personality structure which was not only characteristic of the Ojibwa, but of other Indians of the Eastern Woodlands.

It is not within the scope of this study to argue the pros and cons of the application of space-time continua to aspects of cultural analysis. Translation of spatial relations into temporal ones in anthropology is at best a construct resting upon certain logical or theoretical premises which, because of lack of written or other documentation, must stand essentially without empirical backing. This is not to say that such methods that have been developed should be entirely discontinued, only that a great degree of caution must be exercised in using them.

With respect to this, however, whether one agrees or disagrees with specific conclusions on Chippewa values and personality arrived at by Hallowell, and interpretations based on the historical record are often arguable, his use of documentary sources, especially the Jesuit Relations of the seventeenth century, in conjunction with comparative field studies, is a model of the type of scholarship which can lead to fruitful results in reconstructing the past and weighing the effects of contact on persistence and change in these and other aspects of culture.

Conclusions based on space-time equivalences without the benefit of solid empirical data, documentary where possible, suffer from modifications involving, on the specific historical level, disturbances caused by contacts between broadly different cultural systems, such as tribal systems confronting feudal or industrial systems, and on an evolutionary level, suffer from change occurring over great periods of time in surrounding ecosystems affecting the development of cultural systems.

With respect to the space-time equivalence applied historically, peoples who appear to be marginal today may have been more central in terms of their total surroundings in past times. Their very marginality, as in the case of Indians living on reservations, is the product of contact and of pressure, usually exploitative, exerted by dominating Euro-American culture systems; hence, their present cultural status cannot reflect an aboriginal condition, but one that is derived from relocations, migrations, and other disturbances in all or many aspects of life occurring entirely within the historical era.

I will conclude this all-to-brief discussion of space-time continua by again stressing that such procedures are best used in conjunction with other historical techniques, including archeological techniques, and that their application must avoid the cardinal historical fault of reading into past relationships those of the present, no matter how suggestive departures in the minority culture might be.

Structure and History in Linguistics and Kinship

In anthropological linguistics several techniques have been devised to discern historical relationships of various orders. In fact, a scholar who was primarily a linguist, E. Sapir, wrote the classic *Time Perspective in Aboriginal American Culture* (1916), a standard source of methodology for anthropologists of the so-called historical-geographical school, and still compulsory reading in most graduate survey courses. In this work Sapir employed age and area method in both ethnology and language to derive the relative age of elements in a given culture or among cultures, the history of cultural associations, as of elements, and the history of relationships among languages and linguistic stocks. Sapir used linguistic (morphophonemic and semantic) analysis to gauge the relative age of culture elements— traits and complexes—or the period of occupation of certain areas by identifiable culture groups. Thus, for example, certain words which cannot be broken down into separate morphemes or multiple stems, but are frozen, so to speak, in irreducible form, tend to be representations of ancient elements. Hence, the word, *cart*, which cannot be further broken down, represents an older culture element than the word *rocketship*, which can. About place names, in Sapir's words (1916: 56–57):

> The analysis of place names is frequently a valuable means of ascertaining whether a people have been long settled in a particular region or not. The longer a country has been occupied, the more do the names of its topographical features and villages tend to become purely conventional and to lose what descriptive meaning they originally possessed.
> Thus, it is by no means an accident that a considerable number of village names among the Nootka are incapable of satisfactory analysis, whereas the names of topographical features among such less settled tribes as the Paiute and Ojibwa are in practically every case readily interpreted.

Sapir gives as a case in point, the contrasting names for Mount Shasta among the Hupa and Yana, two California tribes. The Hupa term for the mountain is descriptive (literally "white mountain"), while the Yana term cannot be analyzed for meaning. This indicates a longer residency in the area for the Yana, and other evidence bears this out. Sapir was ingenious in suggesting the employment of such analytic tools to discern historical relations. Methods he suggested have been almost unconsciously incorporated in the work of ethnologists in tribal and areal studies where the focus is on specific historical processes, such as diffusion of elements or the elaboration of behavior with respect to certain definable elements. Sapir, acting within the framework of the research problems of his time, contributed nothing to evolutionary theory.

Another technique, *glottochronology*, using ground rules devised by linguists, M. Swadesh (1952), and R. B. Lees (1953), involves counting cognate words in related languages to state the point in absolute time at which they separated. The assumption is that change in basic vocabulary items (universal words, such as words for body parts, qualities of heat, colors, numbers, and generics for life forms) occurs in all languages at a predictable rate; thus, if two languages share 66 percent of their vocabulary of basic culture words, according to formulae worked out in glottochronology, they have been separate at least 1000 years, each having retained, as derived by equation, 81 percent of the vocabulary of the parent language. The rate of attrition has been found to be, from known instances of change in written languages, 19 percent/1000 years. Glottochronology, thus based on lexico-statistical analysis, has by no means been widely accepted by all linguists as a firm method to fix absolute scales of divergence within language families. The method is, however, generally considered to have validity for the relative chronology of separation.

With the refinement of methods of glottochronology and discoveries in the field of the nature of cognate relations will rest many major conclusions on gross population movements and, ultimately, the degree of antiquity and the center of radiation for modern man. In the meantime, this study must concern itself with historical analysis on a much more modest scale.

An important, and somewhat more modest, kind of historical reconstruction is based on comparative historical linguistics. Comparative analysis of kin terms among a number (preferably the entire sample) of linguistically and historically related peoples may lead to the formulation of a proto-typical terminological system, that is, an original system common to all their stock forerunners. Then, on the basis of the reconstructed early type of terminology, conclusions about the overall social organization may be made on the basis of general ethnological experience, and changes among modern descendants seen against that baseline.

The studies of H. Hoijer on the Athabascans of the MacKenzie drainage (1956) and the work of C. Hockett on Central Algonquians (1964) are examples of this type of research. Hoijer's study, however, suffered from the inadequacy of available material which would have enabled him to attempt the reconstruction of cousin terms, always an important criterion for the type of social organization. With the parts of the kinship system he was able to reconstruct he posited that the proto-Athabascan system was *bilateral*. There are, however, in contemporary reports on these peoples, many indications of a past matrilineal organization (cf. Hickerson 1967a) which probably did *not*, as has sometimes been suggested, occur as the result of contact with matrilineal tribes such as Tlingit and Tsimshian of the Northwest Coast, groups with which the more westerly Athabascans had extensive contacts. Rather, this may have resulted from the dynamics of their own social organization. Hoijer's conclusions must await confirmation from other historical data.

One important byproduct of Hoijer's study was his conclusion that the Navajo and Apache, Athabascan speaking peoples living in the southwestern part of the United States, had separated from their congeners of the MacKenzie drainage as part of a general drift of Athabascans southward from their northern homeland in aboriginal times. This conclusion serves to confirm a hypothesis long held but not proven on the basis of other historical and archeological research.

A more recent study is the work of Hockett on the proto-central Algonquian social system (1964). Hockett ventured a more complete reconstruction than Hoijer. On the basis of his discovery that terms for cross-cousin, cross-aunt (father's sister), cross-nephew (sister's son, male speaking; brother's son, female speaking), and cross-niece were but slightly modified terms for consonant in-laws (cross-nephew with son-in-law, and so on), he was able to posit a cross-cousin marriage system.

Hockett's kinship evidence led him to conclude that the cross-cousin marriage system was *matrilateral*, hence *asymmetrical*, which means that a man would be obliged to marry a person in the category of mother's brother's daughter, but would be prohibited from marrying a person in the category of father's sister's daughter. Hockett further proposed that this system existed in combination with *patrilocal residence*, under which the bride comes to live in the local group of her husband and his paternal relatives.

This is a refinement which seems to elude support from other historical data on these peoples, and one that has been challenged on structural grounds. Other data appear to point to *bilateral* cross-cousin marriage (Eggan 1966: 96; Hickerson 1967b). This is not, however, the place to argue fine points in historical analysis; it is sufficient to indicate that the road to reconstruction is by no means a smooth one, and there are many chuck holes and blind turns. Hockett, whose work on Central Algonquian kinship is particularly valuable because it confirms scientifically the historical provenience of cross-cousin marriage of *some* kind, well recognizes the pitfalls of such research (1964: 243).

> . . . when the methods of comparative linguistics have been applied to the fullest extent possible, reconstructed parental forms for sets of words are still only hypotheses. The point is that hypotheses have varying degrees of reliability, and that, in this particular context, hypotheses based on careful application of the comparative method have a far higher order of reliability than those based on impressionistic reactions. That the firmer conclusions should still be merely hypotheses is nothing unusual, since *all* inferences as to events or states of affairs in the past, made by any method available to the historical sciences, remain hypothetical. There are no time machines. We cannot do fieldwork in vanished communities, any more than a geologist can personally watch the glaciers at work forming the basins of the Great Lakes.

Similar to reconstruction on the basis of linguistic analysis is that work based upon analysis of surviving elements in kinship and other structural systems. Reconstructing history on the basis of analysis of such systems is as old as formal anthropology. The pioneer nineteenth century American anthropologist, Lewis Henry Morgan, was one of the first to attempt, in a challenging way, the reconstruction of stages in the development of social institutions through systematic examination of kinship terminology and other aspects of social behavior. For example, lack of distinction in certain kinship systems for the terms for siblings and cousins led Morgan to suppose a stage in human history in which marriage could occur indiscriminately (or promiscuously), no matter how closely or distantly related the people were. He saw in the absence of terms distinguishing affines and consanguines, then, a *survival* of an ancient group-marriage which no longer was actually in existence anywhere. Morgan proposed other stages in the organization of the family reflected in variant kinship systems and other social forms like the *clan* existing among contemporary primitive peoples. His purpose was to reconstruct the history of human society from its beginnings to the present, and he employed all ethnographic material available to him, much of which he himself gathered on field trips and through the circulation of questionnaires to missionaries and others, which would provide him with the necessary data.

The task of the ethnohistorian is parallel to this, if somewhat more modest. Inferences on behavior through analysis of structural forms can become fairly complex, however, even when applied in specific instances of tribal or areal history. A good example of historical reconstruction and analysis of change in a given historical and ecological area is the work of Eggan in his study of changes in the social structure of a number of southeastern tribes (1966).

Eggan noticed that the terminological systems of such important historical tribes as the Muskogean-speaking Choctaw, Chickasaw, and Creek, and the Iroquoian-speaking Cherokee were reminiscent, to varying degrees, of a kinship structure carrying rather striking features, known in anthropology as the *Crow* type. In this type (cf. Schusky 1965: 32ff) lineal descendants of a man's (male ego's) mother are separated sharply from those of his father's sister and members of her matriline. A "pecularity" of the system is the use of the term "father's sister" for all females in the father's matriline, and the term, "father," for all males in that line, regardless of generation. In essence, this terminology is of such a character as to simply divide those of ego's mother's (hence ego's) matrilineal descent line from those of his father's matrilineal descent line; other refinements in the system relate to this crucial dichotomy. Hence, the term "father's sister" and "father" mean respectively "female and male of my father's matriline," thus emphasizing *lineage* and playing down *generation* distinctions.

This emphasis placed on descent lines is highly suggestive of a *unilineal descent* type of social organization, in this case matrilineal, and, indeed, on the basis of broad samplings of ethnographic data, is known to occur in conjunction with it. Although most of the southeastern peoples, many of whom had long since been removed to the Oklahoma Indian Territory, no longer had corporate unilineal descent groups, Eggan was able to propose such groups as their forerunners on the basis of their retention of aspects of Crow terminology.

This general historical reconstruction was made possible, not only on the basis of surviving kinship elements, but also by analyzing variant degrees of Crow kinship survivals among the different groups. By doing this, Eggan was able to reconstruct steps in the history of change from an emphasis on descent groups to an organization based upon the socio-economic autonomy of the nuclear family. Thus, the Choctaw showed the greatest variation from the original Crow system, the Creek less, the Chickasaw even less, and so on. With the basic kinship material, Eggan proposed varying degrees of the impact of White contact on the separate groups occurring at somewhat different periods in their past.

It is of great interest for the purposes of this study that Eggan was not content to let his research rest at this point; instead, he set out to see if his conclusions were supported by other data. To do so he explored *documentary sources* and was fortunate enough to discover 1) documentary evidence from the mid-nineteenth century for the existence of a "pure" Crow kinship system among the very Choctaw who in more recent times had departed most broadly from it, and 2) evidence in secondary historical sources presenting extensive primary data on the southeastern tribes affirming the very degrees of differential acculturation guessed by Eggan on the basis of the relative degrees of departure in the kinship system from the Crow type.

A corollary conclusion was that kinship terminology changes at a slower rate, or lags behind, but is eventually consonant with, changes in gross aspects of social organization. This has great significance for historical research because of the potential in such studies for reconstructing earlier forms of organization which are highly suggestive of the types of societies existing in the past before they were disturbed by contact and, of course, before there were literate visitors to describe them.

Cross-Cultural Studies and Statistics

I mention at this point another approach which has implications for functional-historical analysis, the employment of statistics in cross-cultural studies. The use of statistics was developed in history and the embryonic social sciences in the nineteenth century and enjoyed a strong vogue toward the end of that century and in the early part of this one. One of the late nineteenth century pioneers of scientific anthropology, the Englishman E. B. Tylor, used statistical tables extensively in attempting, through enumerating the relative frequency of the association of cultural elements in a broad sample of societies, to derive laws of cultural development. After a long lull, interest in applying statistical analysis to cultural associations, and in establishing gradients of cultural complexity has been revived in recent years, partly at least, as the result of the wide dissemination of discrete cultural data derived from masses of textual material through the Human Relations Area File, in which many university libraries participate.

In theory, through comparing frequencies of the clustering of culture elements within defined cultural units—tribes, states, and so on—with the degree of clustering that would be expected on a random basis, generalizations concerning the functional relationship of element clusters may be derived. Hence, as a very simple example, if, in a broad sampling of societies on a tribal level of organization, it is found that inter-village warfare occurs with significantly greater frequency in sedentary cultures with matrilineal descent and avunculocal residence than in nomadic cultures with patrilineal descent and virilocal residence, this would be significant for the comprehension of the level of organization of the society and the degree of cohesion and integration of units within it.

On a nomothetic level, the amount of diversity of organization within cultures, in combination with the cohesiveness of constituent units such as clans, villages, ceremonial societies, military bodies, and so on, and the numbers of persons included in such social units provide indices of relative complexity. Analysis of the gradient set up on the basis of relative complexity would disclose steps in the development of culture and eventually lead, first, to the definition of processes of change, and ultimately, to the formulation of laws of change on an evolutionary scale.

On a more humble ideographic level, the results of comparative analysis may have certain advantages. For example, if it could be shown that certain elements tend to cluster within certain types of cultures, the ethnologist interested in reconstructing a historic culture of that type would be led to search in documents and in other evidence for elements missing from the cultural inventory of descendant communities normally associated with other elements which have survived. He might even assume the former existence of such missing elements without documentary support if the frequency of correlation derived from a large enough sample was very strong. Such conclusions, however, would be fraught with danger: there are always exceptional cases, and it occasionally occurs that an element may be diffused from one group to another without the other elements with which it is normally associated.

Up to now, as in other branches of historical anthropology, those who employ statistical cross-cultural analysis have been primarily concerned with working out methods, or formulae, involving such important problems as data control, including the definition of discrete cultural units to be used in the samples. For example, are two apparently autonomous clans to be counted as separate units of the sample, or as one unit because they habitually intermarry and meet together frequently for trade, common participation in ceremonies, and the exchange of news? In the final analysis, cross-cultural study based on statistics, if it is to have pretensions for significant reconstruction on all levels of cultural activity, will have to base itself, not upon descriptions of contemporary "tribal" and other cultures which have undergone distortion, or "contamination," from European and other advanced sociocultural systems, but upon material gathered painfully from studies of groups as they were before they were deeply disturbed by contact with systems outside, especially exploitative ones. Only when such studies are available in quantity, a matter which awaits a great deal of research, will statistical cross-cultural analysis contribute significantly to theoretical anthropology. This will involve as a first step the rather humble exercise of checking out, mathematically, generalizations made on the basis of direct and historical observation of a limited number of cases. Cross-cultural analysis, then, is, at present, dependent more upon discoveries made employing other diachronic methods, especially ethnohistory, than the other way around.

Memory

Two historical but nonstructural techniques which have been used by anthropologists to which I must also give brief mention are *memory ethnography* and *migration legends*. I lay aside *creation myths* and other material of frankly supernatural design as not properly within scope of this study. Oral traditions reflecting definite historical associations in the minds of members of cultures without written language may provide strong insights into existing cultural values and even the attitudes, mores and geographical movements of the recent past. But neither one nor both together normally provide adequate information to give an accurate notion of details of the life of more than two or three generations ago, perhaps at most 70–100 years. Such important elements as descent systems, subsistence specialties, religious concepts, and so on are often difficult to trace on the basis of oral statements and tradition alone, especially where European introduced ways of behaving have seriously disturbed old life ways. I do not mean to indicate that oral recitations are of little value: in fact, without field investigation, which is the lifeblood of anthropology, no ethnohistory would exist, and field work is primarily discussion with random informants. Also, certain cultures, even some in North America like the Hopi of the southwestern United States, have maintained old ways in various categories of organization over long periods so that oral accounts of ceremonies, clan groups, and so on do have value for general historical reconstruction within such tribes and the areas in which they continue to flourish.

Migration legends and other oral statements can at times be checked against archeological and documentary accounts, and are found at times to have a degree of accuracy. In Chapter 4, I will demonstrate in the discussion of the *Midewiwin*, how oral and documentary evidence complement each other to form a picture of Chippewa residence and migration in the early contact era, and how oral tradition, even with many inaccuracies, may still be used to shed light on historical events known in broad outline from other sources.

It cannot be said that oral techniques are not fruitful in piecing together history. Rather, as in the case of space-time continua, great caution must be exercised before placing trust in such data.

Comments and a Note on Cartography

In the foregoing I have made a survey of historical approaches in anthropology, including archeology (chiefly relevant to prehistory), and various techniques employed by ethnologists: space-time formulations of various kinds relating to different orders of cultural material; reconstructions based on structural and functional analysis, including statistics, in ethnology and linguistics; and oral tradition, or folk history.

One technique I have not discussed and one that aids ethnologists and archeologists in reconstruction, is cartography. This is a demanding and delicate specialty in history and in ethnohistory, like numismatics, interpretation of inscriptions, and so forth. Maps are the graphic reproduction of the knowledge that has come from discovery, and as such are invaluable sources on the distribution of peoples and the limits of contacts of all kinds—commercial, military, navigational. As one goes back in time maps can tell much about the distribution of tribes; as one comes forward, the territorial divisions of nation states are seen.

I include in this a facsimile of the Jesuit Relations map of the upper Great Lakes region, or as much of it as was known (JR 55: map facing p. 34) compiled in the late 1660s, as an example of the way maps provide information on tribal locations, and also the extent of knowledge on the part of the French about the country in which the specialist is now interested. It can be seen (and a French-

English dictionary may be consulted) that Green Bay, or *Baye des Puants*, on Lake Michigan, called *Lac des Ilinois*, was well known, but confluent streams less so, except for short distances from the Bay. However, upon one such stream was located the *Nation des outagami*, the ancestral group of the present Fox, or Musquaki Indians, and the *Mission de St. fr. Xavier* which had recently been established by the Jesuits. It may be assumed, of course, on the basis of these representations, that there was direct French contact, and that the locations were about the limit of French exploration, discovery and settlement at the time.

Observe also the relative accuracy with which Lake Superior, called *Lac Tracy ov{u} Svperievr*, is drawn. Tracy was the name of the French Governor General of Canada at the time; happily, to all intents and purposes he has been forgotten, Superior being in every sense a more appropriate name, translated from several Algonquian languages meaning simply a great expanse of waters. Important among other identifications, is the small written entry at the extreme west end of the Lake: *R. pour aller au Nadouaissi a 60 lieues vers le couchant*, that is, the River (St. Louis) leading to the Sioux (Dakota) 60 leagues (150 miles, the French league being 2.5 miles) toward the west. The location of the Dakota was known to the Jesuits from hearsay from other Indians, or perhaps from French *coureurs de bois*, or illicit traders, since official French exploration had not yet reached the Dakota country in the interior of Minnesota.

Other information indicating discovery and contact is available on this map, and it indicates quite clearly where the French had been and where they had not been, and also the location of many peoples, general or specific, with whom they were coming into contact in that very alien country.

I will not dwell here on the question of the authenticity of maps. This is in itself a discipline rivaling, in some respects, the science of the validation of works of art. Authenticity ascertained by the experts, maps provide part of the sinew for ethnohistorical research on some of the questions and problems I have indicated.

All major branches of historical anthropology make use of documentary records where possible, or at least express regret for the lack of such documents. (Needless to say, such lack is often more the result of not looking for them than their not being there.) Even archeology, which is characteristically concerned with prehistoric material, employs documents—stelae and other sources of inscriptions, for example—where available. In areas utterly unlettered, archeologists find documents of aid in covering the period when prehistory verges on history. These, of course, are the productions of people from lettered cultures early in the area, and can be invaluable in determining whether there was continuation or interruption in given cultural traditions, as, for example, material available in Spanish and French sources connecting the prehistoric and historic periods in the lower and middle Mississippi valley.

I have touched upon certain techniques developed by linguists such as glottochronology and the reconstruction of kinship systems in proto-cultures, and cross-cultural studies; these and other historical techniques are in a stage of incubation. Certainly, one of the main assumptions in doing the culture history of nonliterate peoples is the employment of several methodological devices simul-

Map 3. Jesuit Relations, map of c. 1670.

taneously to test the validity of the findings based on any one of them. I cited the instance in which documents were found on southeastern tribes confirming conclusions reached on the basis of structural-functional analysis of kinship systems. In given instances, does the archeological record verify conclusions on the period of separation of peoples arrived at through the application of glottochronological analysis? Does oral tradition confirm inferences derived from the examination of primary documents, texts and maps, for the time of the beginning of the practice of a certain ceremony? Or vice versa?

It has been seen that anthropologists who have used various techniques in their research into the cultural past have stressed the value of documentary source material as an aid to their study, not to mention its use as a basis for their formulations of culture change in general and in specific. When such material is missing, history itself becomes, to a great extent, a matter of guess-work and the conclusions drawn must be expressed as hypotheses demanding proof. As Hockett has so well stated, however, this should be no deterrent to "historicizing." Anthropologists who have concerned themselves primarily with history, I am sure, would agree that the greater amounts of information on general culture process that continue to accumulate, despite shortcomings in method and the availability of material, renders the past more and more susceptible to analysis, and so, justifies speculation.

I now leave speculative history and turn to documentary history, or *ethnohistory* in the strictest sense, and its application to specific research problems involving the Chippewa and their neighbors. I define these as falling under the general rubrics of: 1) the identification and definition of proto-historic social groups (Chapter 3); 2) the origin of a tribal ceremony and its political implications (Chapter 4); and 3) war and its ecological base (Chapters 5–8). In presenting these essays I hope incidentally to elucidate some of the modes of operation of practicing ethnohistorians.

3

The Clan: An Evolutionary
Problem

S I HAVE STRESSED, no reconstruction of a past culture or any of its elements—
social organization, warfare, religious ritual—can be achieved without
employing a number of historical techniques, including searching documentary sources where available. In this chapter I piece together important features of the social organization of those peoples, living in the vicinity of eastern
Lake Superior and northern Lake Huron, who form the ancestry of the widespread peoples of today known as Chippewa. My reconstruction should be valid
for the period roughly between 1640 and 1670, when Chippewa first came
into wide scale contact with the French, who called them "People of the Sault,"
from their center at Sault Ste. Marie. This period is referred to as the *proto-contact
era*, because it was at that time that Chippewa culture was undergoing adjustment
to new conditions, imposed by contact; yet it retained significant features of the
precontact or *aboriginal* organization.

The proto-contact era comprises two general periods, the period of *direct
initial contact* with French traders, soldiers, and missionaries, following a period
of *indirect contact* with European economic systems through trade of furs for
goods of European manufacture carried by Indian middlemen. It is not known
as yet when European trade goods first began coming into the country of the
Chippewa, but at latest it must have been very early in the seventeenth century
when the Iroquoian Huron from south of Georgian Bay of the lake which bears
their name were first carrying French goods over old trade routes established in
aboriginal times. These were the routes over which Huron corn and ceramic ware
had passed to the north and west in exchange for hides and perhaps birchen containers, raquettes, and other commodities produced by the Chippewa and their
Algonquian congeners: Algonquin, Nipissing, and the cluster of peoples—Sinago,
Kiskakon, and others—who later became known as Ottawa, or *traders*.

Sources of Reference

How does one get at the early organization of the Chippewa? First, there are large compendia of published material, most of which represent gleanings from great masses of unpublished documents mostly in French from the seventeenth century, scattered in archives from Paris to Ottawa to Montreal to Albany, and in numerous other sources that in one way or another were connected with the fur trade, and with mission and government affairs. This material covers multiform relations in the entire St. Lawrence River system and large sections of the drainage areas of the Mississippi River and Hudson Bay. A glance at the map will show what a large area this was, for French trade, long before the turn of the eighteenth century, had penetrated as far south as the country of the Illinois, and even to the Arkansas tributary of the Mississippi on the west side; after the establishment of the Louisiana Colony in 1700, French trade tentacled east through the valley of the Tennessee and expanded west to the middle reaches of the Missouri, perhaps as far as eastern Montana.

It was, at the time I did my basic research, impractical to search the primary archival sources (Paris would have been a pleasant place to *cherchez les documents*), but very valuable material was available in the following records: the Jesuit Relations, that great collection of reports by Jesuit missionaries working in the Great Lakes and upper Mississippi regions from the 1630s right into the early eighteenth century; historical society volumes, or sections thereof, from such states as New York, Michigan, Illinois, Wisconsin, and Minnesota, containing great amounts of official correspondence on Indian affairs collected, translated, and annotated by excellent historians; the six volumes of French exploration and discovery compiled in the late nineteenth century by the historian, Pierre Margry. Also helpful were such one- or two-volume works as the translation by E. H. Blair of original manuscripts descriptive of French-Indian relations and Indian "customs" by the seventeenth century trader-official, Nicolas Perrot, and his later historian amanuensis, Bacqueville de La Potherie; and the strange and wild account of the trading and military adventures of the fantastic Pierre Radisson and his brother-in-law, Médart Chouart des Groseilliers written by the former in the quaint English of the period of the Stuarts. Radisson had an enormous capacity for leaving one in the dark as to precisely where he was at any given time, but he threw out many useful leads on Indian customs and behavior.

These are the main primary sources for the proto-Chippewa of the 1640–1670 period, all, except the Margry volumes, available in English translation. The Jesuit Relations happily have the original French (and occasionally Latin) on the left, or even-numbered pages, and the English translation on the odd pages. Although there is little direct information in these sources on precise factors of social organization, it will be seen how such factors may be inferred from the mass of material. This study is helped by writings from the nineteenth, and even the twentieth century that cast light on interpretations of material from the seventeenth. This will be, then, an exercise in extrapolation.

The Early Saulteur and Their Ceremonies

I will begin as if nothing is known of seventeenth century Chippewa organization. My only information is that certain people called, by the French, *Saulteur*, or, in English translation, People of the Sault, were living at least part of the year in the vicinity of Sault Ste. Marie, on the St. Mary's River, which not only divides Ontario from upper Michigan, but also carries the clear glacial water of Lake Superior over the rapids (the Sault, or Soo), into Lake Huron. This is known from looking up *Chippewa* in the Handbook of American Indians North of Mexico (Hodge 1907–1910 1:277).

In fact, the Handbook directs one to the Jesuit Relations as the first great source on these people. Volumes 72 and 73 comprise an index with references to peoples mentioned throughout the first 71 volumes. Under *Chippewas* the listings are *Ojibwas*, and also *Sauteurs, Saulteurs*, and *people (nation) of the Sault*, all variant terms for the same people, the ancestors of the modern Chippewa. These are supplemented with the accounts of Nicolas Perrot, cited above, who traveled and traded in the upper Great Lakes and contiguous regions from 1665 to 1695, and Radisson, who was in the Lake Superior region and adjacent areas at various times from about 1654 to about 1660.

I will turn to some of the material concerning the community life of the People of the Sault. Throughout the 1640–1670 period the center for these Saulteur was Sault Ste. Marie where the Jesuits eventually came, in the 1660s, to establish an important mission. The Indians from earliest times engaged in the fur trade, which preceded the missionaries there, as it invariably did. The Indians, as well as others in the area, were transporting great amounts of peltry to French depots like Montreal and Quebec on the lower St. Lawrence. It is true that at times the trade was interrupted by marauding Iroquois from the south side of Lake Ontario, but even in the worst of times, attempts were made to keep trade channels open.

There are five features of life which stand out in the Jesuit and other descriptions of the Saulteur and related peoples during the period:

(1) The Saulteur not only engaged in the fur trade, but had come to rely upon it for their very existence, acting both as trappers and as middlemen to tribes which had less access to trading entrepots.

(2) They engaged in periodic warfare as allies of other upper Lakes—Algonquians against Iroquois to the east and Dakota and others to the west.

(3) They and their Algonquian neighbors, Nipissing and perhaps one or more of the tribal divisions of the Ottawa, conducted frequent joint ceremonials centering in the Feast of the Dead, which had as its main function the establishment and maintenance of alliances based on fur trade relations and common cause against common enemies.

(4) Sault Ste. Marie, aside from ceremonial activity as such, during the summer months was a gathering place for members of many groups who normally lived to the north and south, more or less close congeners of the local people. These were variously Potawatomi, Cree, and Algonquin, and perhaps the Siouan-

speaking Winnebago were occasional visitors as well. Such groups, swelling the summer population of the Sault to well over 1000, came to feast on whitefish which were abundant in the rapids of the St. Mary's. They were often described as refugees from warfare, and also, as in the case of those who spent the winter in the inhospitable region of the Canadian Shield to the north, from periodic famine.

(5) Many of the peoples who gathered at Sault Ste. Marie were hunters and trappers, but it is emphasized that the dwellers there, and their closest kinsmen (various groups who together make up the ancestry of the Chippewa) maintained abundant fisheries at various river mouths, bays, and inlets along the adjacent shores of the two lakes connected by the St. Mary's, where they carried on seasonal village life.

There are numerous passages in the Jesuit Relations, supplemented by other general descriptions by Perrot and Radisson, of forest diplomacy, trade, warfare, ceremonials and subsistence modes covering 1640–1670, in which tribal life is portrayed, including extensive intertribal and Indian-French relations. These leave an impression of intensive cooperative relationships. The stereotype of Chippewa and other northern Algonquians as highly individualistic, hence noncooperative, begins to crumble under the force of the descriptions of the period. I give here two sets of quotations, the first from the Jesuit, Jérome Lalemant, who visited Lake Nipissing east of northern Lake Huron during the summer of 1641 at the time of the annual Feast of the Dead. He described the arrival of visiting groups in enthusiastic terms (JR 23:211):

> Those of each Nation, before landing, in order to make their entry more imposing, form their Canoes in line, and wait until others come to meet them. When the People are assembled, the Chief stands up in the middle of his Canoe, and states the object that has brought him hither. Thereupon each one throws away some portion of his goods to be scrambled for. Some articles float on the water, while others sink to the bottom. The young men hasten to the spot. One will seize a mat, wrought as tapestries are in France; another a Beaver skin; others get a hatchet, or a dish, or some Porcelain beads, or other article,—each according to his skill and the good fortune he may have. There is nothing but joy, cries, and public acclamations, to which the Rocks surrounding the great Lake return an Echo that drowns all their voices.
>
> When all the Nations are assembled, and divided, each in their own seats, Beaver Robes, skins of Otter, of Caribou, of wild Cats, and of Moose; Hatchets, Kettles, Porcelain Beads, and all things that are precious in this Country, are exhibited. Each Chief of a Nation presents his own gift to those who hold the Feast, giving to each present some name that seems best suited to it.

There are several indications in this description of features of social organization which are important, even if their significance in a broad cultural context is not yet understood. These are the mention of *Nations*, the mention of *chiefs*, and the exchange of *gifts*.

Lalemant goes on to describe festivities including dances and games, more gift exchanges, the perpetuation of alliances, and rites of the transport of the bones of the dead.

The second set of quotations is from Perrot, who has the following to say about the ceremonial (Blair 1911 1:86–88). The hosts prepare

. . . a large cabin, stoutly built and well covered, for lodging and entertaining all those whom they expect. As soon as all the people have arrived, they take their places, each nation separately from the others, at the ends and in the middle of the cabin, and, thus assembled, they offer their presents. . . .

They

. . . lavish all that they possess in trade-goods or other articles; and they reduce themselves to such an extreme of poverty that they do not even reserve for themselves a single hatchet or knife. Very often they keep back for their own use only one old kettle. . . .

So now there are added elements; communal housing in great houses probably made from bark mats thrown over bent poles to form long domed structures. It is known from other descriptions that these could house as many as 200–300 persons (JR 55:139); the separation of the "nations," one from another; and, perhaps most important, the utter impoverishment of the hosts as a result of their outlay of gifts.

In another passage Perrot indicates the amount of *communal* activity which was necessary to conduct the ceremonial (Blair 1911 1:86):

If the savages intend to celebrate the feast of their dead, they take care to make the necessary provision for it beforehand. When they return from their trade with the Europeans, they carry back with them the articles which suit them for this purpose; and in their houses they lay in a store of meat, corn, peltries, and other goods. When they return from their hunting, all those of the village come together to solemnize this feast. After resolving to do so, they send deputies from their own people into all the neighboring villages that are allied with them, and even as far away as a hundred leagues or more, to invite those people to attend this feast. In entreating them to be present at it, they designate the time which had been fixed for its solemnization.

Again there are mentions of: trade; hunting (apparently communal); and alliance, as prominent traits in the ceremonial complex.

From these descriptions I believe one gets a sense of vigor, and in the preparation and conduct of the rites a *joie de vivre*, which perhaps seems to some of us out of keeping with the solemnity of the occasion: after all, one of the main features was mass burial. But part of the ceremonial involved the "resurrection" of the names of dead chiefs now bestowed upon living descendants "elected" to the office. This, if the forms observed virtually everywhere among North American Indians were observed there, was done by the unanimous consent of the participants, a matter which quite naturally invited universal acclamation.

By this time it has been discovered, through a cursory reading of eyewitness accounts by intelligent French observers, that there was intensive group activity going on during the period of initial direct contact of Great Lakes Indians with French, activity that by that time had apparently become traditional. One must then ask the question: what was the *nature* of these groups; in a word, what structure did they have permitting such relations, within "nations," and among them. Clues now must be found in these and other writings of that and later periods, to lend refinement to this analysis.

Saulteur Social Groups: Clan Structure

To do so I must first turn, as usual, to the Jesuit Relations. One passage in particular is of overriding interest; in fact, it is of such special magnitude that it provides a terminal date for the proto-historical period. This passage is from a report of 1670 by the Jesuit, Claude Dablon, on the progress of his mission at Sault Ste. Marie. Dablon gives a sharp picture of conditions at the Sault; the passage also represents a summary of some of the pertinent material presented thus far (JR 54:133–135):

> The principal and native Inhabitants of this district are those who call themselves *Pahouitingwach Irini*, and whom the French call *Saulteurs*, because it is they who live at the Sault as their own Country, the others being there only as borrowers. They comprise only a hundred and fifty souls, but have united themselves with three other Nations which number more than five hundred and fifty persons, to whom they have, as it were, made a cession of the rights of their native Country; and so these live here permanently, except the time when they are out hunting: Next come those who are called the Nouquet, who extend toward the South of Lake Superior, whence they take their origin; and the Outchibous, together with the Marameg, toward the North of the same Lake, which region they' regard as their own proper Country.
>
> Besides these four Nations there are seven others dependent on this Mission. The people called Achiligouiane, the Amicoures, and the Mississague fish here, and hunt on the Islands and in the regions round about Lake Huron; they number more than four hundred souls.
>
> Two other Nations, to the number of five hundred souls,—entirely nomadic, and with no fixed abode,—go toward the lands of the North to hunt during the Winter, and return hither to fish during the Summer.
>
> There remain six other Nations, who are either people from the North Sea [Hudson Bay], as the Guilistinous . . . [Cree] . . . and the Ovenibigonc [?], or wanderers in the regions around that same North Sea,—the greater part of them having been driven out of their Country by famine, and repairing hither from time to time to enjoy the abundance of fish there.

I have presented the English translation of this passage as it appears in the standard edition of the Relations, but I must, for the sake of accuracy, rerender part of one sentence of the foregoing quotation in French and then retranslate it to make better sense of a difficult construction. The phrase that begins,

> . . . and so these live here permanently, except the time they are out hunting: *Next come those who* [and so on; italics mine],

in French, after the word *hunting*, reads:

> *Ceux qu'on appelle les Nouquets* [and so on],

that is,

> Those who are designated Nouquet [and so on] . . .

so that there now are three new affiliates of the Saulteur, all of them named, and not three unnamed affiliates plus three other named folk only there as temporary summer guests, but with permanent villages elsewhere. This is important, because, as I will indicate later, the names of the three affiliates have great significance in terms of the dynamics of the social organization of the time.

But here, for the moment, I must rest content with the idea, so graphically set forth by my Jesuit friend, that peoples of yet indeterminate origin and linguistic and cultural provenience were flocking to the Sault where a *people* resided, and in some instances attaching themselves to this people as *confederates*, not simply allies, and trading partners, clients, and so forth. I may be so bold here as to suggest that this confederation ended one era of social history and initiated another, but I incur, with broad statements of this kind, the risk of anticipating the data, of indulging in what the Germans somewhat architecturally call *unbegrundete Verallgemeinerungen*, baseless generalities.

It must be assumed that, having become confederated, or even merged, at a given time, the relevant peoples theretofore had been separate, each with rights to an extent of country, or territory, each presumably politically autonomous. I suspect that further search will indicate more about such groups and their relations with each other. One highly relevant question is, what did the Jesuits mean by "nation"? A passage from the Jesuit Relations of 1640 referent to the late 1630s, virtually at the beginning of the period of direct initial contact, and its interpretation seem apropos to this question (JR 18:229–231; brackets mine):

> Let us return now to the fresh-water sea [Lake Huron]. This sea is nothing but a large Lake which, becoming narrower in the West, or the West Northwest, forms another smaller Lake, which then begins to enlarge into another great Lake or second fresh-water sea [Lake Michigan].
>
> I have said that at the entrance of the first of these Lakes we find the Hurons. Leaving them, to sail farther up, in the Lake, we find on the North the Ouasouarini; farther up are the Outchougai, and still farther up, at the mouth of the river which comes from Lake Nipisin [French River which flows into Lake Huron], are the Atchiligouan. Beyond, upon the same shores of this fresh-water sea, are the Amikouai, or the nation of the Beaver. To the South of these is an Island in this fresh-water sea about thirty leagues long [Manitoulin Island of northern Lake Huron], inhabited by the Outaouan; these are the people who have come from the nation of the raised hair [Ottawa]. After the Amikouai, upon the same shores of the great lake, are the Oumisagai, whom we pass while proceeding to Baouichtigouian,—that is to say, to the nation of the people of the Sault, for, in fact, there is a Rapid [Sault Ste. Marie], which rushes at this point into the fresh-water sea. Beyond this rapid we find the little lake [actually Lake Superior, the Jesuits being ignorant at that time of its size], upon the shores of which, to the North, are the Roquai [*Sic*: Nouquet]. To the North of these are the Mantoue, people who navigate very little, living upon the fruits of the earth.

Again, even with the imperfect knowledge the French had at that time of the upper Lakes area, a number of "nations" is clearly perceived, *each occupying its own territory.* An interesting aspect is that few of the peoples mentioned in the Jesuit writings exist today, nor have they existed as independent cultural units for the past one-to-two centuries. The question is, who were those peoples, and what became of them?

I must turn to later sources to answer these. Still relatively early, in 1697, a French fur merchant, Aubert de La Chesnaye, listed the residence of several Saulteur groups living on both shores of Lake Superior, among them: *Ouchipoë*, *Macomilé*, *Ouxeinacomigo*, *Mikinac*, and *Malanas*, or *gens de la Barbue* (Margry 1886 6:6). (All these are pronounced according to the French orthography.) There were other groups also mentioned by La Chesnaye, but they appear to have been Cree or Algonquin groups, so-called *gens de terre*, or People of the Land, and outside the compass of this study.

One feature that is striking about these "nations" listed by the Jesuits and others of early vintage is that the majority of them bear the names of animals, or referent to animals, some in the form of nicknames. This I conclude by comparing the early terms with names for local and clan groups recorded by later authorities, such as the Handbook (Hodge 1907–1910 1:279, and in both volumes under notices of the several groups; also see list of synonymies, vol. 2, pp. 1021–1178); Landes' *Ojibwa Sociology* (1937); Warren's history of the Chippewa (1885); and a list of Saulteur and other peoples compiled by Michel Maray, Sieur de La Chauvignerie in 1736 (NYCD 9:1053–1054). Some of the comparisons take a bit of acrobatic orthographic maneuvering, but, by and large, correlations seem to hold up. I have discussed at greater length some of the parallels (1962a: 78–79), but would have preferred to have had more linguistic material available. I point this out mainly to indicate how a concordance of historical, ethnological, and linguistic research can elucidate problems of synonymy significant for the analysis of social forms, even if the example here is far from perfect.

Thus, Nouquet, and also Macomilé is Bear (cf. Landes 1937: 40); Marameg, or Malanas (in French *barbue*) is Catfish; Mikinac is Snapping Turtle; Ouxeinacomigo refers to Birds in general (see Landes 1937: 40; Hickerson 1962a: 79); Amicoures, or Amikouai, is Beaver; Ouasouarini, or Auwause[e], is Fish (NYCD 9:1954; Hodge 1907–1910 1:279); Mantoue, or Mundua, is Marten (Warren 1885: 50); Outchibous, or Ouchipoë, is probably derived from Ojeejok (Hodge 1907–1910 1:279) plus the suffix /bwa/ connoting "voice" and referent to the Crane, hence *Voice of the Crane*; Achiligouan and Outchougai refer perhaps to Heron; and Oumisagai, or Mississague, perhaps to Eagle, as their crests, that is, the symbolic drawings they would affix to official documents, would indicate (NYCD 9:1053). But Heron and Eagle are called by somewhat different terms given in the Handbook following Morgan (Hodge 1907–1910 1:279), as *Mooshkaooze* and the vaguely redolent *Omegeeze* respectively. I almost run out here, and admittedly my last three efforts to relate tribal terms to animals might not stand up in court.

But still, there *does* exist a battery of correspondences, and when you add to the rest a term used by Perrot for another people, or "nation," the Nikikouek, or Otter (Blair 1911 1:153; Hodge 1907–1910 2:70–71), the list becomes that much more formidable.

Why this preponderance of animal names? The first thing that enters the head of an anthropologist is that animals might signify *totems*, a kind of mystical wellspring of *clans*. Indeed, the very word, totem, is Algonquian, and especially Chippewa, denoting a *local group of consanguines*. Hence, one is tempted to look upon those early groups, once separate from one another politically but linked through ritual practice and common stores of legends and myths (see Hickerson 1963), and in many instances prone to confederate, as at Sault Ste. Marie in 1670, as *clans*. I will not at this point go into detail on the eventual fate of many of these groups, which I may now suggest were quasi-independent totem, or clan groups, except to say that, with a few notable exceptions, namely the Missisauga and perhaps some Amikwa (Amikouai), they gradually became absorbed through a process of merging that began on a large scale in 1670 by the Saulteur, later called Chippewa. By the nineteenth century all but the Missisauga had lost independent status.

The Saulteur themselves, from earliest proto-historic times a community that had no particular totemic or clan organization, apparently comprised an amalgam of members of many clans; they existed, perhaps in some sense, as a symbol of the unity based on common language, culture, and traditions of all of them. In socioeconomic terms, the Saulteur proper formed the nuclear settlement for annual ceremonials, trade, renewal of alliances, and, to some extent, fishing, and this status may well have reached back to aboriginal times.

There is a parallel for this. Among the related Central Algonquian Illinois who comprised a number of kindred semi-autonomous tribal divisions (perhaps originally matrilineal clan groups), one village, Kaskaskia, located on the shores of Lake Peoria in central Illinois, during the 1680s a central location for trade, diplomacy, and war, was unique in that it contained members of all other divisions: Cahokia, Peoria, Tamaroa, Moingwena, and several others, all of these also maintaining separate villages and territories elsewhere and normally following independent pathways. The Kaskaskia, originally only one of the Illinois divisions, were designated as "the real Illinois" (cf. Blasingham 1956: 198–199), due to their focal position. As among the Chippewa groups, the Illinois peoples gradually lost their separate identity, all of them eventually becoming subsumed under the generic term *Illinois* before becoming virtually extinct in the early nineteenth century.

But I have strayed somewhat. I have not yet sufficiently demonstrated that the groups forming the basis of the Chippewa, or Saulteur, who did *not* become extinct, were indeed clan groups. By clan, in the context of the tribal proto-Chippewa, I mean a corporate unilineal descent group with a fictitious ancestor.

This can be approached along two main avenues—analysis of surviving forms, and inductive reasoning. First, in a purview of present and nineteenth century literature it is discovered that most of the names of the proto-historical semi-autonomous Saulteur communities have survived as designations for groups of consanguines which are still referred to as clans (or synonymous terms such as *gentes* or *sibs*). These groups are no longer local, nor have they been for two centuries and more; but scattered among multifarious village, band, and reservation communities the length and breadth of the vast Chippewa area, they still, in most places, maintain exogamic relations. Hence, a Bear boy from Red Lake, Minnesota would not be inclined to marry a Bear girl from Emo, Ontario, even though they could not trace actual common descent. In 1640, those Bears would have been living in the same village on the southeastern shore of Lake Superior, and referred to each other as "brother" and "sister," that is, "member of my descent group of my generation," male and female respectively.

Clan organization today, of course, is not a potent factor in political life, and it is true that even exogamic structures are beginning to break down in many places, chiefly where common descent cannot be traced, but it persists as a mere fiction. But a century and more ago, such structures were still maintained. In the mid-nineteenth century, William Whipple Warren, a Chippewa historian and spokesman, himself half-Chippewa, described, in detail, ritual, political, and other functions of clans, which he also called "totems." In writing about important men he invariably gave their clan affiliation, and even referred to "principal men" of the clans, or rather, of phratries, which he called "grand clans," there being four or five linked clans in each of the five grand clans.

Other primary published source material from the early to mid-nineteenth century helps in this reconstruction. Henry R. Schoolcraft, the Chippewa agent at Sault Ste. Marie from 1819 to 1840, and a scholar of Indian life, had this to say about the Chippewa living on the south shore, and inland to the south and west, of Lake Superior (1834: 146):

> The most striking trait in their moral history is the institution of the Totem—a sign manual, by which the affiliation of families is traced. . . . And this institution is kept up with a feeling of importance, which it is difficult to account for. An Indian, as is well known, will tell his specific name with great reluctance, but his generic or family name—in other words, his *Totem*, he will declare without hesitation, and with an evident feeling of pride.

Elsewhere Schoolcraft wrote about the "ruling power . . . exercised by certain totemic families, who claimed the right by descent" (1851–1857 6:385). . . . With respect to this, Warren (1885: 336–337) recorded an incident in which a fur trader invited Chippewa to a council to urge them not to go to war against enemy Dakota,

> . . . and after stating to them his wishes, he presented some tobacco, and a small keg of liquor to each head, or representative chief, of the several grand clans, or totems.

The clans, then, as functioning units appear to assume more importance as one goes back in time. There are clear expressions of this in earlier nineteenth century sources. Recognition of clan exogamy is indicated by a Hudson's Bay Company fur trader and surgeon, Dr. John McLoughlin, in an unpublished report of 1822–1823 (WHS Mss.):

> . . . it is unlawful for a man to marry a woman of the same tribe or Mark, and children are Reckond in the fathers tribe.

Here *tribe* and *Mark* refer to *clan* and *totem* respectively.

Another trader, Duncan Cameron of the Northwest Company, wrote in 1804 that Chippewa living north of Lake Superior were divided in *totems*, and that totem mates considered themselves related even when blood relationship could not be traced (fictitious ancestor), and thus could not marry. Moreover, in a quarrel, a man would side with an "unrelated" clan mate against a closely related [cross] cousin, the cousin being, due to the rules of exogamy, a member of a different clan (Masson 1889–1890 2:246–247).

There is continuity in maintenance of the clan from the present going back into the past, and I have established that the clan was of great importance in Chippewa social, political and ritual organization, even though, by the turn of the nineteenth century, clans did not form local groups. Also it has been seen that the names of modern clans (see Hodge 1907–1910 1:279) like Ahmik (Beaver), Auwausee (Fish), Noka (Bear), Mikonoh (Snapping Turtle), and others, had their parallels in the local groups of the proto-historic past.

Before turning to very early observers for further confirmation of this, I will present more evidence for this proposed locality of clans, from more recent authorities. Schoolcraft, who was a student of Chippewa language as well as culture, wrote that the very word, *totem*, was a derivation of *Do Daim*, the Chippewa term for village, that is, local group. Hence, clan equals local group. This is all the more interesting because there is confirmation, undoubtedly independently arrived at, in a communication from the linguist, Truman Michelson, cited by the contemporary anthropologist, Ruth Landes, to the effect that *dodem* [totem] is derived from *ode.na* which means *village* (1937: 33–35). These statements are highly suggestive of a condition in force at one time, but no longer, that the totem, or clan, was indeed the village, or local group, and vice versa.

What evidence might there be for this in the writings of the earliest authors? Very little. There are, however, four statements, two by Perrot and two by the flamboyant Radisson, strongly indicating the local autonomy of the clan. Perrot flatly states (Blair 1911 1:37; brackets mine):

> You will hear [the Indians] say that their villages each bear the name of the animal which has given its people their being—as that of the crane, or the bear, or of other animals.

This statement is relevant to several peoples living in the Great Lakes region, including Saulteur. Another statement by Perrot concerning totemic practices of the Amikwa, who later were absorbed by the Saulteur, and were linguistically and culturally indistinguishable from the generality of the Saulteur peoples, leaves little doubt as to the clan nature of their society (Blair 1911 1:62–64):

> . . . when any stranger or poor widow is in need near the Amikouäs or any one of their clan, they see a branch that has been gnawed at night by some beavers, the first person who finds it at the entrance of his tent picks it up and carries it to the head of the clan, who immediately causes a supply of food to be collected for the poor person, who has a memorial of their ancestors.

Here, then, is indicated the Amikwa (or Beaver) *clan*, a clan leader who is also the headman of the village, and the clan-village itself. I cannot help, in the light of Perrot's general statement cited above, proposing that Crane, Bear, Catfish and others had *their* clan-villages as well.

Radisson's statements are not as direct as those of Perrot, but they serve, in the light of other material, to strengthen my hypothesis. Radisson described a Feast of the Dead ceremonial in which he participated, held in 1660 in the interior south of Lake Superior among Saulteur, Dakota and others. After feasting and exchanging gifts according to the usual patterns, and during the bestowal of

gifts on the several parties by Radisson and his French companions to encourage
the establishment of trade and alliance, Radisson remarks, with respect to the gift-
giving (Scull 1943: 217; brackets and italics mine):

> The 3rd [gift] was to oblige them to receive our propositions, likewise the
> Christinos [Cree], to lead them to ye dance of Union, wch was to be celebrated
> at ye death's feast and *banquett of kindred*. If they would continue the warrs, yt
> was not ye meanes to see us againe in their Countrey.

"Banquett of kindred" refers to the feasting and gift-giving among the
participants, and indicates strongly interlocking relationships among them, which
can be inferred to be consanguineal and affinal relationships. This supposition is
supported in another passage describing the ritual of the Feast. I give this at some
length to provide some of the color of the ceremonial (at least as Radisson saw
it), emphasizing with italics the passage most relevant to the specific interest of
this study. Understand that the battle described is a ritual or mock battle, its
purpose being to allay possible hostilities among peoples speaking diverse languages, the Saulteur peoples on one hand and Siouan Dakota on the other (Scull
1943: 218–219; brackets and italics mine):

> The feast was made to eate all up. To honneur the feast many men and women
> did burst. Those of that place coming backe [Dakota], came in sight of those
> of the village or fort, made postures in similitud of warrs. This was to discover
> the ennemy by signs; any that should doe soe we gave orders to take him, or
> kill him and take his head off. The prisoner to be tyed (and) to fight in re-
> treating. To pull an arrow out of ye body; to exercise and strike wth a clubbe,
> a buckler to theire feete, and take it if neede requireth, and defende himselfe, if
> neede requirs, from the ennemy; being in sentery to hearke ye ennemy that comes
> neere, and to heare the better lay him downe on the side. These postures are
> playd while the drums beate. This was a serious thing, wthout speaking except
> by nodding or gesture. Their drums weare earthen potts full of watter, covered
> wth staggs-skin. The sticks like hammers for ye purpose. The elders have bomkins
> [not a small bom, but a knob] to the end of their staves full of small stones, wch
> makes a ratle, to wch yong men and women goe in a cadance. The elders are
> about these potts, beating them and singing. The women also by, having a nosegay
> in their hands, and dance very modestly, not lifting much their feete from the
> ground, keeping their heads downewards, makeing a sweet harmony. We made
> guifts for that while 14 days' time. Every one brings ye most exquisite things, to
> shew what his country affoards. The renewing of their alliances, *the marriages*
> *according to their countrey coustoms are made*; also the visit of the boans of their
> deceased ffriends, ffor they keepe them and bestow them uppon one another. We
> sang in our language as they in theirs, to wch they gave greate attention. We gave
> them severall guifts, and received many. They bestowed upon us above 300 robs
> of castors [beavers], out of wch we brought not five to the ffrench, being far
> in ye countrey.
> This feast ended, every one retourns to his countrey well satisfied.

The italicized phrase must be interpreted as an endemic feature of the
Feast of the Dead, which attracted related peoples living separately for most of the
time, to a central location where they encamped as separate units. Although
non-related allies, in this case Dakota and French, in other cases such peoples

as Huron and Cree, would be invited to sanctify alliances, these outsiders would not normally be expected to intermarry with the hosts. Rather, such marriages "according to their countrey coustoms" would be precisely those occurring between members of the separate but related "kindred" groups congregating. This suits perfectly a situation in which those groups were local clan-villages with strict rules of exogamy. Without going into detail, there are parallels to this type of activity in kinship-based societies ye worlde over.

Two Conclusions

I have applied specific anthropological techniques to the solution of the problem of the social organization of proto-Chippewa groups. I relied heavily on primary sources covering parts of the period between 1640 and the present era, all of which are published except one, the statement from an unpublished manuscript by Dr. McLoughlin of the Hudson's Bay Company for 1822–1823, which lives in a box in the archives of the State Historical Society of Wisconsin at Madison.

Most important in this reconstruction was the discovery that clans that survive in highly fragmented, and I might say, decadent, form at present, were of great importance in the past. Only ethnohistorical research could have provided the empirical basis for this hypothesis, itself derived from a combination of preliminary casual reading in early documents and awareness of the broad distribution of clan societies elsewhere in North America and other parts of the world where socioeconomic relations are direct and simple.

Other factors, too, involving general anthropological knowledge, play a part, so much so that it is often difficult to state all the ingredients that go into such reconstructions as this. For example, surviving kinship terms in some areas in which Chippewa continues to be spoken indicate the equivalence of cross cousins and affines, and it may be assumed that that was universally so in the past. Although cross-cousin marriage, implied by this, no longer occurs among most Chippewa, especially those living in the United States, it must be assumed that cross-cousin marriage was a widespread practice in the past (cf. Hickerson 1962a: Ch 6). Although cross-cousin marriage is not necessarily functionally linked with clan organization, it is congruent with the type of clan relations proto-Chippewa and, no doubt, aboriginal Chippewa, had. In fact, it was with the breakdown of the local clan in many areas that cross-cousin marriage ended, although some of the terminology, always slow to change, survived.

There are two very general conclusions:

1) The existence of local clans is indicative of a stage of sociocultural integration which has evolutionary significance. It fits a widely held idea that aboriginal primitive society was *clan society*, with implications for intensive communal patterns, these in turn becoming disturbed by contacts, especially trade contacts, with more advanced socioeconomic systems (in this case European systems). One cannot, at this point, tell whether the local clans were matrilineal or patrilineal, although this too would have significance for possible evolutionary reconstruction.

This and related questions will eventually be answered by the development of techniques of reconstruction of proto-linguistic forms, especially kinship terms, and refinement, through inductive reasoning, of methods permitting an appraisal of the types of social organization which has given birth to such proto-forms. There are not as yet such means for reconstruction.

2) The clans, and communal behavior in general, broke down under the weight of contact. The genesis of this is a complex problem which will be touched upon in the next chapter, again through primary use of documentary evidence. (Also see Hickerson 1966.) In brief, the demands imposed by the fur trade and military and other conditions engendered by it resulted in the need for the permanent mobilization of much larger village groups than existed in pre-trade times when lake fishing and woodland hunting, with some limited trade with Indian neighbors, provided the means of subsistence. The large villages of the eighteenth to nineteenth centuries were made up of members of many clans who unified under village *tribal* councils. At first there were only a few large villages, but these later split into numerous smaller villages, not along clan lines, as might be expected, but in such a way that each daughter village contained all or most of the kinship elements—a replica, so to speak, of the mother village. But this is a different story, and not to be dealt with here.

4

Origin of the Midewiwin:
A Historical Problem

Introduction

I N THIS CHAPTER I again employ early sources, chiefly from the pens of the old French priests and traders, but including later authorities like School-craft and Warren, and also an unpublished source or two from the nineteenth century to help in solving a problem which, if at first blush might appear trivial, still has its significance. The problem is discovering when the *Midewiwin* began, and why. Unlike the last chapter, when reconstruction involved only peoples who formed the ancestry of the modern Chippewa, this chapter must use ethnohistorical material on neighboring peoples as well to marshal evidence for the central thesis— that the Midewiwin was postcontact. I would suggest at the outset that when, later in the chapter, such peoples as the Central Algonquian Fox, Miami, Mascou-ten, Menomini, Potawatomi, Illinois, and others are mentioned, such standard sources as the *Handbook of Indians North of Mexico* and the *Glossary* of the latest edition of the *Dictionary of Canadian Biography* should be consulted. Also, the latest editions of the *Encyclopædia Britannica* contain useful, if somewhat encapsulated, information on many of the tribes.

In this chapter I rely heavily on logical constructions of culture history relevant to material presented in the last chapter, on analysis of written documents, on historical criticism, and on that most tenuous and difficult of all historiographic techniques, appraisal of *negative evidence*, which amounts to concluding something did not exist because it was not mentioned.

The Midewiwin as a Nativistic Movement

But first, what was the Midewiwin? In briefest terms, the Midewiwin was a set of ceremonials conducted in many of the Central Algonquian and Siouan tribes by an organized priesthood of men and, among the Chippewa at least, women as well, who had occult knowledge of "killing" and "curing" by use of herbs, missiles, medicine bundles, and other objects which had medicinal properties. Among Chippewa, and to varying degrees among other tribes, members of the Mide society were repositories of tribal traditions, origins, and migrations integrated in *systems* of myth and legend, that is, folk-history, much of the lore being transcribed in pictographs on birchbark scrolls considered sacred. The society also owned songs and dances that would be performed ritually on the occasion of the meeting of the society. A characteristic of the Mide society was limited membership. Initiation could be achieved only after a long period of instruction in its mysteries provided by one or more members of high standing, often in exchange for articles of value. Another characteristic was the ranking of members in "degrees," somewhat reminiscent of sodalities like the Masons.

As with other aspects of Great Lakes Indian culture, the Midewiwin has undergone changes since the beginning of its existence at about the turn of the eighteenth century; it survives in some reservation groups as a refuge organization for the most conservative tribal members, in others as a still vital force in community affairs, and has completely disappeared in some others. In some contemporary communities Mide priests are looked upon by the majority as dangerous sorcerers, in others as benevolent doctors and carriers of tribal lore, in still others as anachronisms. Of course, in any case today opinions would be divided among the members of communities in which the Midewiwin is still practiced.

Historically, the Midewiwin belongs to that class of ceremonials that, in the anthropological literature, has been called "nativistic," and includes among others in North America the Sundance of the Plains tribes, the Ghost Dance of the western tribes, the Handsome Lake religion of the Iroquois, the Pontiac conspiracy, and the cult of the Shawnee Prophet, in the west. A feature common to these movements is the transmutation of ancient ritual practices and beliefs to new ideological and ritual contexts that also tend to incorporate material from outside cultures, especially if these cultures exert a dominating socioeconomic influence. (This merging of the old and the new is often not realized in the consciousness of practitioners.) Another common feature of such cults is that the ritual is supernaturally revealed to one or more persons who then disseminate it to the masses. It may be said here that there is no such specific data on the origin of the Midewiwin. Such cults arise during periods of social stress, when old patterns of behavior are threatened, and culture forms adapted to traditional modes of life are in a state of breakdown. Often anthropologists have viewed such movements in terms of wholesale disintegration of the old culture, as the Ghost Dance of the 1880s–1890s, which had as its main purpose the restoration of the early nineteenth century Plains culture involving the magical disappearance of the Whites and the reappearance of the buffalo herds. So also the cult of the Shawnee Prophet, who with his military brother, Tecumseh, during the first decade of the nineteenth century, at a time of rapid expansion of the White frontier into Ohio and Indiana, urged destruction of all goods introduced through trade by the Whites and a return to "pure" Indian ways. Interestingly enough, in certain areas Indians were urged by emissaries of the Prophet to destroy their dogs, under the illusion that they too were a European introduction! These movements, unlike Christianity, for example, itself originating as a "nativistic" movement, were doomed to failure for politico-historical reasons.

But there were nativistic movements that did not seem to be negative, violent, or "revivalistic" in their content, that indeed seemed to spring spontaneously from new states of affairs not involving the wholesale destruction of old ways of life, but rather serving to lend vigor and meaning to innovations in social and political organization stemming from changing relationships with the outside world. The early contact period (1640–c.1700 among the Chippewa) was one characterized by the distribution of new goods through the fur trade and new means of acquisition, the opening up of new resource areas for primary and secondary exploitation through the hunt and trade, and new contacts with different and challenging ideological systems—Christianity, for instance. In a strong sense one may refer to this type of response as "creative," rather than negative.

I left the Chippewa in the last chapter in a state of reorganization of communities, and implied that old patterns were breaking down. I referred at length to the breakup of the local clan groups and their coming together to cluster in new large village centers. This reorganization involved, among other things, the end of the celebration of the Feast of the Dead, and this occurred, as seen in historical perspective, for two main reasons: 1) with increasingly heavy competition in the fur trade as a result of overexploitation of accessible fur regions, furs were in short supply, and it was no longer feasible for local groups to impoverish themselves through the giveaways; 2) the groups that once lived apart as separate semiautonomous socio-political units in the relationship of close allies were now establishing joint residence through confederation, merging at a few prominent central locations, and forming new offshoot communities at places strategic for trade; these new communities were structured by an entirely new canon of organization, the *multiclan village*, which with the possible exception of the community of Sault Ste. Marie, were nonexistent, except on the most temporary basis, in the pre- and proto-historic past.

These shifts resulted in total realignment of old political groups and profound changes in leadership systems. Properly speaking, when the clan was the local unit, as is usual where the local clan forms the society, leadership was exercised by elders who, by virtue of their superior experience, attested to by the attainment of the very status of *elder*, quite naturally influenced, most strongly, decisions affecting the welfare of the group: where to hunt, when to fish, whether to trade, and so forth. They were, in a sense, very much like heads of large families. But when several such units amalgamated, who was to make the decisions that now involved diplomacy, trade, war, and other relations of much greater compass and delicacy than had ever existed in precontact times when the social units were simpler?

Now the Midewiwin enters the scene. Let me approach the question of the function of the Midewiwin by saying first that in the Jesuit Relations covering the period 1640 to 1700 there is not one reference to anything called, or referent to, *Midewiwin* among any upper Great Lakes peoples. This sets one wondering, since in later times, authors, whether missionaries, traders, or officers of government, frequently mentioned, and even in some cases, described, the rites of the Mide lodge, or "Grand Medicine," as they often called it.

Functions of the Midewiwin

The first statements on the Chippewa Midewiwin are found indirectly through a process akin to what the ethnohistorian of the Iroquois, William N. Fenton, called "upstreaming." It is known from recent and late nineteenth century literature on the Chippewa and related peoples such as the Menomini and Fox that the Midewiwin holds a prominent place in tribal practice and tribal lore. There are extensive descriptions of the ritual, the pictographs, the dances and songs, the ritual killing and resuscitation of initiates, and other elements. But this material is not entirely satisfying, because nowhere in the modern descriptions (save Hickerson 1963) is it indicated what the historical function of the ceremonial was, nor what its origins were. I suspect that the ceremonial was *not* aboriginal for several reasons: for one, certain symbolic representations included the use of a cross as a distinguishing mark for one of the degrees; for another, there was payment in goods of non-Indian production as fees for instruction and initiation; for yet another, there were occult practices in its performance; and for a fourth, the very existence of an organized priesthood seems improbable as an aboriginal institution.

The first detailed lengthy description of the Chippewa Midewiwin was by W. J. Hoffman and published by the Bureau of American Ethnology in 1885–1886; this description was based on personal observation and interviews by the author. Hoffman (p. 155) assumed that the ceremonial was aboriginal. Before Hoffman, still in the nineteenth century, there are references to the ceremony by Warren and Schoolcraft who were cited in the preceding chapter, and also by various missionaries and traders, chiefly the American Board missionary, William T. Boutwell, who observed several ceremonies during the mid-1830s at Leech Lake and the present site of Duluth, Minnesota (MHS mss. 1832–1837), and Peter Grant, a trader, who gave a brief account of the ceremonial in 1804 (Masson 1889–1890 2:361–363). The descriptions by Boutwell and Grant are in strong agreement with modern descriptions. The former is interesting because it is in manuscript form in one of the journals Boutwell kept, detailing his missionary activities in Minnesota in 1832–1837. That and other missionary journals were found by the author and colleagues in the Minnesota Historical Society at St. Paul, and these, along with reports of fur traders and Indian agents on deposit at the same society and also in the St. Louis County Historical Society in Duluth, provide invaluable material on Indian activities, including ceremonials, in that "wilderness" region at the time. The Grant manuscript, on the other hand, has been published along with journals of other fur traders of the old Northwest Company, in a two volume compendium by the French Canadian historian, Louis R. Masson (1889–1890).

However, Boutwell's description, although containing most of the highlights recorded by later trained observers, are rather colored by his Presbyterian bias against "heathen" practices, and he made no real sense of it. As an example, in describing ritual killing of an initiate, he wrote (MHS mss. 1832–1837: 105; brackets mine):

> The old Chief Maozid, i.e. Loon's Foot, took a charge of powder in his hand upon the top of which he placed a ball painted with vermillion, carried it round the lodge, exhibiting it to all present, after which he took his musket, and loaded it with the same powder and ball. One of the strong Medicine Men made a circle on his breast and took his position at the other extremity of the lodge, for a mark. The chief discharged the musket, aiming at the mark. The man fell as one dead. The drums now beat, the rattles shook, the potent sacks [of medicine] were applied and the man rose up, the ball dropping at the same time from the man's bosom, while about a gill of blood was found, but the man entirely unhurt. . . . Mr. Aitkin a trader related to me in the evening that some of the Indians at Lac Court Oreille [Sawyer County, Wisconsin], once tried the same trick, but being more honest, put in the ball, and *killed his man*, in spite of drums, rattles, sacks, medicines, and what not.

I believe there can be detected in this some suspicion on Boutwell's part that trickery was involved, and one would not be at all surprised to discover in some way that the *killing* at Lac Court Oreilles was apocryphal.

But it is in Boutwell's accounts of transactions he had with the Chippewa at Leech Lake, Minnesota, among whom he labored, in which he mentioned only in passing the "Grand Medicine," that one finds material relevant to its function as a tribal ceremonial, especially when viewed in relation to published statements by Schoolcraft and Warren. I will come to this directly.

First, far from being just a medicine cult ceremonial, the Midewiwin was described by Schoolcraft (1851–1857 5:416) as a "grand national society devoted to the mystical arts." Elsewhere (1851–1857 5:434) he remarked that the Chippewa expressed "national pride in these fêtes." His use of the term, *national*, in both instances is significant because of the implication of much more widespread participation than cult members alone. The national character of the ceremonial is symbolized in the use of a small white sea shell called in Chippewa *megis*. According to Warren (1885: 77–80), perhaps the outstanding authority on the Midewiwin, writing in the early 1850s when the Minnesota and Wisconsin Chippewa were still largely independent of direct government authority, the *megis* symbolized tribal unity. This shell appeared and disappeared to the Chippewa as they moved by stages ever westward in mythical times. The "rays" of the *megis* were said by Warren to "reach the remotest village of the wide spread Ojibways."

A significant point in Warren's account, which was based not on documentary material but rather on tribal myth and legend, is his statement that it was at *Chequamegon* that the Midewiwin was celebrated "in its purest and most original form." Although Warren believed that this dated from before the coming of the French, it is known from extensive survey of such documentary source material as the Jesuit Relations, Radisson, Perrot, and the fur trader-explorer, Daniel Greysolon, Sieur Duluth (Margry 1886 6:19ff.), that Chippewa did not permanently occupy Chequamegon (La Pointe), the peninsula jutting out into Lake Superior on the south shore in Bayfield County, Wisconsin, until about the year 1680, long after initial French contact, when Duluth succeeded in negotiating a peace between them and the Dakota to the west (cf. Hickerson 1962a: 65–66). Following good ethnohistoriographical method, that is, not trusting the testimony of Duluth alone, one discovers, in a passage by the very knowledgeable Perrot, support for the notion of the arrival of Chippewa at Chequamegon in *historical* times (Blair 1911 1:277; brackets mine). Perrot wrote that part of the Chippewa had remained at Sault Ste. Marie, but

> . . . the others have gone away to two localities on Lake Superior [Chequamegon and Keweenaw peninsulas], in order to live on the game which is very abundant there. Those who left their natal soil made an alliance with the Nadouaissioux [Dakota], who were not very solicitous for the friendship of any one whomsoever; but, because they could obtain French merchandise only through the agency of the Sauteurs, they made a treaty of peace with the latter. . . .

One must attribute credence to Warren's statement on the status of Chequamegon as a center for the Midewiwin, even though it is known that he was wrong in considering this as the center of the Chippewa in aboriginal times. Indeed, Chequamegon in the nineteenth century was looked upon as the traditional center of Chippewa polity. According to Schoolcraft, who visited Chequamegon in 1831 (1834: 270):

> . . . Chegoimegon . . . is the ancient seat of Chippewa power in this quarter. It is a central and commanding point, with respect of the country lying north, and west, and south of it. It appears to be the focus from which, as radii from a centre, the ancient population emigrated; and the interior bands consequently look back to it with something of the feelings of parental relation.

A lengthy quote from Warren tells more about the importance of the ceremony and of Chequamegon (1885: 99–100):

> . . . some of their old men affirm that there was maintained in their central town, on the Island of La Pointe, a continual fire as a symbol of their nationality. They maintained also, a regular system of civil polity, which, however, was much mixed with their religious and medicinal practices. The Crane and Aw-ause Totem families were first in council, and the brave and unflinching warriors of the Bear family defended them from the inroads of their numerous and powerful enemies.
> The rites of the Me-da-we-win . . . was [sic] practised in those days in its purest and most original form. Every person who had been initiated into the secrets of this mysterious society from the first to the eighth degree, were imperatively obliged to be present on every occasion when its grand ceremonies were solemnized. This created yearly a national gathering, and the bonds which united one member to another were stronger than exist at the present day, when each village has assumed, at unstated periods, to perform the ceremonies of

initiation. Tradition says that a large wigwam was permanently erected in the midst of their great town, which they designated as the Me-da-we-gun, wherein the rites of their religion were performed. Though probably rude in its structure, and not lasting in its materials, yet was it the temple of a numerous tribe, and so sacredly was it considered, that even to this day, in their religious phraseology, the island on which it stood is known by the name of Me-da-we-gaun.

The element of nationality is again stressed, and although one knows from other sources that the Mide priesthood was separate from the civil leadership (although individuals performed dual functions) (Schoolcraft 1851–1857 5:188–189; 434), the ceremonial, like the Sundance among Plains tribes, provided the setting for the gathering of tribesmen from near and far.

I suggest, then, on the basis of the inspection of a number of diverse documents, that the Midewiwin attained its pinnacle of importance among the confederated Chippewa clans who had flocked to Chequamegon, or La Pointe, in about 1680, and remained in a large village there (as well as a smaller subsidiary village, Keweenaw, to the east on the south shore of Lake Superior) until the second-third of the eighteenth century, when many of them began moving inland south and west of Lake Superior to found new villages (cf. Hickerson 1962a: Ch 5). How soon after 1680 the Midewiwin was originated is not known, nor the precise circumstances of its origination, whether on the basis of rites revealed to a person, or as the result of the gradual integration of several clan myths into a single body of tribal myth. The "killing" and "curing" practices were undoubtedly ancient, the knowledge the property of individual practitioners, or *shamans*, and these practices were incorporated by the new priesthood into their now formalized and complex ritual.

I have so far, however, only presented general statements on the significance of the Midewiwin for tribal, or "national" cohesion. I turn for further information to two statements, one by Schoolcraft, the other by Boutwell, to indicate how the Mide ceremony in specific instances played its role in the unfolding of events affecting the tribal polity. Schoolcraft in the following passage refers not to the Midewiwin itself, but to a related ceremonial, the *Madodiswon*, or medicine rites of the sweat lodge (1851–1857: 425–426).[1]

The madodiswon is sometimes practised by a chief who has something to ask of his nation, and who, having no right to ask or demand it as chief, shelters himself under the rites of medicine to accomplish his object. He invites first, four *medais*, for the vapor-bath, and communicates his wishes to them; these invite afterwards a great many others, conformably to the ideas suggested by the chief.

---

[1] It has come to my attention that Schoolcraft appropriated this passage almost in its entirety from an as yet unpublished manuscript in French by the French explorer, engineer, and cartographer, Joseph N. Nicollet, and refers to the year 1836 when Nicollet visited Leech Lake. Schoolcraft was at Leech Lake only in 1832, and in the narrative account of his visit there, written in 1832–1833 and published in 1834, mentions no such ceremonial. Such are some of the hazards of ethnohistorical research. Fortunately, it does not affect the sense of the passage that Nicollet, who was a most acute observer, rather than Schoolcraft, was the real author of it, nor that the statement applies to 1836 rather than 1832. For the Nicollet manuscript in her translation I am indebted to Dean Melva Lind of Gustavus Adolphus College who rediscovered it, and who I hope will publish it along with other Nicollet materials.

They depute the *Oshkabewis* throughout the whole country, carrying little sticks painted of different colors, a foot long, of which he delivers one to each individual invited upon a day assigned. The sticks which could not be delivered because the persons to whom they were destined were absent, are brought back to the bath-lodge. These are the sticks which are used to beat time in the songs employed upon these occasions, in which the drum is not admitted. The day arrives, and the persons invited enter into the vapor-lodge, where they receive the communications, upon which they deliberate afterwards among themselves, without the intervention of the inviter. The baths are succeeded by the feast—a great feast—*wikondiwin*. The guests retire, the faculty only remaining, when around the stones which were employed to produce the vapor, are arranged all the little sticks of those who were not able to comply with the invitation. These sticks are witnesses that they were invited, as they stand in lieu of the consent of those for whom they are destined. When I arrived at Lake Leech, the chief, Flat Mouth . . . had been gone for two months to visit the English, to ask from them munitions for projects which he wished to execute, and which he had not yet abandoned. Before his departure he had given such a fete. I saw the madodiswon which he had constructed, and about thirty or forty sticks which were witnesses of those who had been invited, but who could not be present. Nevertheless, a great many savages had participated, for the ceremonies had lasted nearly a week.

Boutwell, who had his mission (but, alas, no converts) at the large Chippewa village at Leech Lake in 1833–1837 records in his journal an incident which took place in 1834 requiring serious negotiations with the Chippewa regarding his status at Leech Lake. Boutwell had just "purchased" a part of a maple sugar grove from an old woman who happened to be the sister of a leading civil chief, appropriately named Elder Brother, for a place to erect his mission dwelling and plant a garden, a matter which incensed many of the men of the village who were away trapping at the time when the "transactions" occurred. When Boutwell was told of their displeasure he set about to call a council, which he initiated through the time-honored procedure of giving tobacco to the chiefs. He also wished to read to the assembled Chippewa a letter from Iroquoian Seneca Indians in New York advising their "brothers" to undergo religious instruction and give up liquor. These topics were reserved for discussion on the occasion of the annual celebration of the Midewiwin in which the entire population of the Lake, about 800 strong, was involved. The climax of the council, held in the great Mide lodge, occurred when a Mide and civil leader, Maji Gabowi (MHS mss. 367–369)

. . . made several inquiries in the course of our interview, such as, how long I expected to stay, how large I should make my garden, and whether other white people would come and make houses. My answers I intended to convey no dubious or doubtful meaning, and led to the query on his part, "what will the consequences be, if we should all tell you to go on." I replied, you may all tell me to go on, but it is not you that can send me away. Here they stopped their queries, and thus concluded the interview. . . .

During the course of the proceedings of the council Maji Gabowi, acting as spokesman for the Chippewa, made it clear that: 1) Boutwell was contributing little to the welfare of the people, but always bargained or traded; 2) he was using village lands for his own ends; and 3) by building a house and planting a garden on "purchased" land, he represented a threat to their occupancy of the lake. These, of course, were matters of serious moment to the entire populace, fittingly discussed at a time when communal participation was at its height, namely on the occasion of the holding of the Midewiwin.

History of the Midewiwin

Despite the fact that the Midewiwin was believed to have reached its "purest" form at Chequamegon, presumably after 1680, I have not as yet uncovered any references to its being practiced there from documents of the time. This is not surprising, however, for there is a general lack of information on the Chippewa of the Chequamegon village except for wars, trade, and hunting reported by one or another of the French traders and military commandants located there. In fact, before the brief description of the Midewiwin of 1804 by Peter Grant one has to go all the way back to 1718 for another mention of it, and that not even for the Chippewa among whom it unquestionably originated, but for the Potawatomi, a related people who at the time were inhabiting the area near and westward from Detroit. This reference was by Jacques de Sabrevois, commandant at Detroit from 1714 to 1717, who made the brief statement (WHC 16:367): "Often the old men dance the medelinne; they look like a band of sorcerers."

Before 1718, there is a description by a Canadian official, Antoine Denis Raudot, written in about 1709 or 1710 (Margry 1886 6:9–10), but perhaps referent to a decade or so earlier, of what appears to be a Saulteur cult suggestive of the Midewiwin. Raudot wrote of the way in which Saulteur "jongleurs" (jugglers, or magicians) impressed and frightened members of other tribes with their ability to "kill" and revive with medicine:

> Ces Saulteurs trouvent le secret de se faire craindre par leurs discours, et, pour en persuader davantage les autres, ils conviennent avec une ou plusieurs personnes qu'elles feront le personnage du moribond, de mort et de vivant, suivant que cela leur sera nécessaire pour prouver leur puissance.

Also, "on y dansera la médicine, et que les jongleurs y feront voir des effets prodigieux de leur science et de leur pouvoir." Other statements in Raudot's description also indicate cult as well as individual shamanistic practice, and, as the central theme, always the death and rebirth of victims.

Before Raudot, there is nothing, and I here must conclude that in his simple French Raudot was sketching out the rudimentary beginnings of the cult and the mystery of the Midewiwin.

As I have indicated, modern anthropologists have generally assumed that the Midewiwin was an aboriginal institution. An exception was the excellent anthropologist, Felix M. Keesing, a student of the Menomini, close neighbors of the Chippewa living in the region between Green Bay and eastern Lake Superior;

Keesing stated flatly that the *Mitawin* did not exist before European contact (1939: 44ff.), but, rather, it incorporated old shamanistic practices within the framework of a new cult.

In fact, at a time when I had just completed an article which had the post-contact origin of the Midewiwin as its main point, I was severely jolted when a well-meaning colleague pointed out that at least two authors, both highly respected, had stated, on the basis of "evidence" from the Jesuit Relations, that the Midewiwin was precontact! I had labored diligently over my Chippewa material and was certain of my conclusions when this blow was struck. W. J. Hoffman (1885–1886: 155) and V. Kinietz (1940: 215) used the same passage from the Relation of the great Jesuit missionary explorer, Jacques Marquette, to prove that the Midewiwin was aboriginal. Marquette, with the geographer and mapmaker, Louis Joliet, on the way to discover the Mississippi in June, 1673, arrived at a Central Algonquian village on Fox River in Wisconsin where, in Marquette's words (JR 59:103), he was

> . . . Consoled at seeing a handsome Cross erected in the middle of the village, and adorned with many white skins, red Belts, and bows and arrows, which these good people had offered to the great Manitou (This is the name which they give to God). They did this to thank him for having had pity On Them during The winter, by giving Them an abundance of game When they Most dreaded famine.

Hoffman commented on this passage (1885–1886: 155):

> Marquette was without doubt ignorant of the fact that the cross is the sacred post, and the symbol of the fourth degree of the Midē'wiwin. . . . The erroneous conclusion that the cross was erected as an evidence of the adoption of Christianity, and possibly as a compliment to the visitor, was a natural one on the part of the priest, but this same symbol of the Midē' society had probably been erected and bedecked with barbaric emblems and weapons months before anything was known of him.

And Kinietz, without citing Hoffman, thus indicating that he had arrived at his own conclusions concerning this passage independently, wrote (1940: 215):

> The cross was undoubtedly a feature of the midewiwin or grand medicine society, and although this had a religious significance, it was certainly not in connection with the Christian religion, as Marquette assumed.

The assumption that the cross seen by Marquette had nothing to do with the Christian cross, but was an aboriginal "feature" of the Midewiwin, a matter of some importance, should not have been made without an exhaustive examination of sources. In fact, the Jesuit Relations alone provide information on activities in the region interior from Green Bay, but there are other sources as well. Suspicion should have been aroused by the fact that 1673 was a relatively late date for French trade and missionary activity in the Green Bay–Lake Superior area.

The two chief trading locales for the western Indians during the 1660s were

Chequamegon, where Ottawa and Huron refugees of the Iroquois wars had established a village, and Green Bay, where Potawatomi and perhaps others acted as middlemen carrying French merchandise inland to such central Algonquian peoples as the Sauk, Fox, Mascouten, Miami, and Kickapoo (Blair 1911 1:Ch 9; JR 55:161ff.; 56:115–117). Algonquians of various tribes living inland from Green Bay, who were going to Chequamegon for trade, heard the preaching of the famed Jesuit, Claude Allouez (JR 50:267, 273, 297ff.; 51:29, 43ff.). One reads in Perrot's account how avid Algonquians in the Green Bay area were for French trade goods (Blair 1911 1:321, 329–332, 344, 349). A quotation from La Potherie, who published a long account of Perrot's activities based on Perrot's own notes, this passage relating to the 1660s, indicates the influence French traders and missionaries were able to exert on Indian customs and beliefs (Blair 1911 1:332):

> That alliance began, therefore, through the agency of Sieur Perot. A week later the savages made a solemn feast, to thank the sun for having conducted him to their village. In the cabin of the great chief of the Miamis an altar had been erected, on which he had caused to be placed a Pindiikosan. This is a warrior's pouch, filled with medicinal herbs wrapped in the skins of animals, the rarest that they can find; it usually contains all that inspires their dreams. Perot, who did not approve this altar, told the great chief that he adored a God who forbade him to eat things sacrificed to evil spirits or to the skins of animals. They were greatly surprised at this, and asked if he would eat provided they shut up their Manitous; this he consented to do. The chief begged Perot to consecrate him to his Spirit, whom he would thenceforth acknowledge; he said he would prefer that Spirit to his own, who had not taught them to make hatchets, kettles, and all else that men need; and they hoped that by adoring him they would obtain all the knowledge that the French had.

Although Perrot preceded the missionaries at Green Bay, he was actively preparing the ground for their arrival. The advent of the Jesuits in the late 1660s, especially during 1669 to 1673, when Marquette and Joliet were "consoled" to see the cross, occasioned the distribution of numerous crucifixes in the Indian villages, and the erection of large crosses in many of them. There were also, at this time, many conversions among Indians in the western upper Great Lakes area (JR 52:201–207; 54:205–207).

Allouez' influence among Indians interior to Green Bay is well expressed in his account of a trip he made in April, 1670, to interior villages of Fox, Mascouten-Miami, and Kickapoo on the Fox River and its Wolf River tributary. In fact, in at least one village Allouez was invited to remain to establish a mission. The Indians were hard pressed through warfare with Iroquois to the east and Dakotan tribes to the west and badly needed trade goods, especially fire weaponry which they could only obtain through stable relations with the French. In some places the Indians, according to the accounts of the French, referred to Allouez as a *Manitou*, or god, a sobriquet he politely declined (JR 54:219ff.).

Late in 1670 Allouez and a brother missionary, Claude Dablon, visited the same interior Algonquian villages. An indication of the friendliness of their reception is found in the following passage. According to Dablon (JR 55:199–203):

They had conceived so high an opinion of the things of the Faith, and of those who published it, that they invited us to many feasts, not so much for the sake of eating as of obtaining, through us, either recovery from their ailments, or good success in their hunting and in war.

Further, in the Miami-Mascouten village, the same in which Marquette three years later saw the cross:

... a very peculiar ceremony was observed. It seemed to be a feast for fighting, and not for eating; for in place of a table, a sort of trophy had been erected, on which had been hung all a warrior's arms,—bow, arrows, quiver, and war-hatchet, —together with provisions, namely, a little meal and some tobacco; with other articles commonly carried on their persons by the Warriors of this country, to give them renewed courage for fighting.

No cross was mentioned in this passage, but rather an "idol," the kind perhaps to which Perrot in 1665 had applied the name *Pindiikosan* (Blair 1911 1:332), and also similar to one seen by Allouez at Chequamegon *ca.* 1666 (JR 50:287). These were, of course, medicine bundles.

In 1671–1672 Allouez visited various villages around Green Bay and showed religious pictures, one being Jesus on the Cross (JR 56:135–141). On the basis of Allouez' report to Dablon, the latter wrote concerning the Fox, called Outagami (JR 56:143–145):

The sign of the Cross is held in such veneration among those Outagami Peoples that the Father thought it time to plant a cross in the middle of their village, and thus take possession of those infidel lands in the name of Jesus Christ, whose standard he was erecting farther within the realm of the demon than it had ever before been planted.

At this point, one begins to see clearly the Christian cross assuming ritual properties among the Algonquians who had close relations with the French. In fact, it was reported that the Fox marked a cross on their shields and on one occasion at least made the sign of the cross when going into battle against the Dakota (JR 56:145–147).

In 1672 the French erected crosses in four villages near Green Bay (JR 58:41). In August, 1672, Allouez preached before great crowds and baptized 114 persons in the Mascouten-Miami village which by that time included some Kickapoo and Illinois Indians as well. On August 18, he erected "at the door of our Chapel a cross 22 feet high." Next day he noticed that the Miami had hung on the cross sheaves of Indian corn, belts, and red garters as a "mark of veneration." Allouez, at their request, erected another cross for their section of the village (JR 58:21–27).

In May, 1673, a year later, Allouez returned to the Mascouten-Miami village, and next day (JR 58:59),

... while passing by, with all the french [traders] who accompanied me, we adored the cross that we had planted there the previous summer.

It was in June, a month later, that Marquette and Joliet passed through this *same* village on their way to discovering the Mississippi. Marquette, after mentioning the attention the Indians had given Allouez (JR 59:101–103), was consoled by the

> . . . handsome Cross erected in the middle of the village, and adorned with many white skins, red Belts, and bows and arrows, which these good people had offered to the great Manitou. . . .

Conclusion

With the solution of the problem of the cross in the Miami-Mascouten village, I could rest easy again. The cross was not that of the fourth degree of the Midewiwin, as Hoffman and Kinietz had suggested, but the Christian cross. My theory on the post-contact origin of the Midewiwin among Chippewa and others had held its ground, on positive and negative evidence. The Midewiwin was in fact a nativistic movement, a reaction to contact with Europeans, and not aboriginal. The ceremonial represented and reflected new modes of organization, not ancient ones.

5

Warfare between the Chippewa and Dakota: Historical and Ecological Background

Introduction

I NOW TAKE LEAVE OF THE PERIOD of the beginning of the postcontact history of the Chippewa and their neighbors, and focus attention on inter-tribal relations during the eighteenth and nineteenth centuries. This is a lingering goodbye to the seventeenth century, however, because it is impossible to understand the relationships of one era without reference to the one preceding it. In history, an author writing on a certain period invariably prefaces his study with a resume of what he considers to be the most important events of the period before, to present a continuum, and at the same time to confront the reader with an idea of purpose. Hence, no history of the American Revolution can be written without reference to the relations of the preceding Colonial period, nor can a history of the Italian Renaissance be conceived without reference to the period of the rebirth of commerce in the Mediterranean.

In anthropology this task often imposes grave difficulties, if only because anthropologists are forever running out of documents, not only significant documents, but any and all. In addition, they are dealing with a multiplicity of small sociopolitical organisms whose interests have a tendency to coincide and conflict, to wax and wane, over very brief periods, not only among themselves, but with respect to their contact with Europeans, people of a very different culture, who were not always aware of the motives and purposes of "native" acts. It seemed foolish to many European traders, for example, for adjacent tribes to fight or raid each other for the apparent sole purpose of avenging past defeats, or to be able through a heroic action to wear the feather of a certain bird, or paint a stripe of a certain color across the cheek or brow. It was especially annoying to traders that Indians would embark on war parties for such apparently trivial reasons, at the expense of trapping for the fur trade.

One must assume at all times that warfare and other events, and relationships among "primitives" are as elusive of hasty analysis as the great events of world history. In this chapter I present a necessarily selected, but, I hope, representative, body of material to indicate the causality and effects of warfare among sections of the Chippewa and Dakota. In doing so, I hope to establish the method by which ethnohistorical research of a very detailed nature can illuminate relationships that, in the perspective of contemporary ethnology, might well have remained obscure.

Sources

To do so I employ not only primary source material, published and unpublished, but also other published material which is nonanthropological and in some cases nonhistorical as well. As I proceed in this discussion it will become necessary to rely on the publications of natural historians: conservationists, geographers, ecologists, and others, to illuminate material I derived from the usual type of research, the primary historical documents relating to Indians. In the first place, in the title of this chapter I used the term, *ecology*. In anthropology, ecology has come, over the past 20 years or so, to have a broad meaning in cultural studies. In brief, ecology is the ways in which peoples utilize given environments and interact within them, in terms of modes of production and distribution, including technology, trade, cooperation, and other facets concerned with primary and secondary exploitation. With groups who chiefly relied upon the collection of wild foods, including hunting, fishing, and gathering, ecology is concerned, among other things, with the habits of the game and plant life, and the relationship of those habits to human exploitation. Human ecology, then, which involves modes of exploitation, distribution, and exchange, relates integrally to the ecosystems of the products exploited, distributed, and exchanged.

Historical Background

First, some historical background. I have shown in Chs. 3 and 4 how the Chippewa established a tribal polity on the basis of the amalgamation of semiautonomous clan groups, following the introduction of the fur trade and all the intensive activity that the trade engendered. It was seen how a new ceremonial apparatus, the Midewiwin, was developed, to lend coherence and stability to the new assemblages, and also how tribal displacements in the upper Great Lakes area, involving Chippewa migrating in large numbers west from original locations around Sault Ste. Marie (chiefly along the south shore of Lake Superior) to found villages at prominent peninsular sites.

The main reason Chippewa were able to move westward was a peace and alliance they had made with once hostile Siouan Dakota tribes living south and west of western Lake Superior; the alliance involved the exchange of French merchandise by the Chippewa for fur and privileges of entry into the relatively rich hunting grounds of the Dakota. A statement by the French trader-officer, Perrot, quoted at length in the last chapter, will be recalled; also, there is extensive descriptive material from Duluth, which gives a blow-by-blow account of the peace made under his auspices between Chippewa and Dakota meeting at the place at the west end of Lake Superior which now carries his name (Margry 1886 6:20–34). Duluth and his confederates were most anxious for this peace, as were the Indians, precisely because previous warfare among Algonquians including Chippewa and Dakota, had rendered a large region west of Lake Superior unsafe for entry by anyone. According to Duluth (Margry 1886 6:30), only through peace could the country at the west end of Lake Superior, which was rich in beaver and had not been hunted for ten years past, be entered.

This sets a theme for this discussion, for I perceive here a relationship between warfare and hunting, the suggestion of a "no-man's land," an unoccupied zone within which valuable game had a chance to enrich itself undisturbed.

The peace was made, the land was trapped, and the Dakota and Chippewa, the former living in the Minnesota forest and prairie country, the latter with their main village at Chequamegon where they did a little farming, a lot of fishing, and a good deal of trading, remained at peace and as allies until the year 1736. During the 1730s, expansion of French exploration westward to the Mississippi and beyond, and into the Lake Winnipeg region to the north and the Missouri River region to the south, involved the establishment of direct trade with peoples like the Dakota who had earlier been dependent on Indian middlemen like the Chippewa (cf. Innis 1956: 84–118; Burpee 1927; Margry 1886 6:495–732; Hickerson 1962a: 69).

In effect, the Chippewa of Chequamegon, bypassed by the French, no longer had access to game areas and trade fur; hence, they were obliged either to try to survive on the meager game resources afforded by the barren boreal forest region surrounding western Lake Superior, in addition to the fish they took out of the Lake, or to attempt to expand into new areas, perhaps into the very areas they had been entering as allies of the entrenched Dakota population. As in other instances of the kind throughout recorded history, some of the people were more venturesome than others, and, aligning themselves with new-found allies to the west, chiefly Cree and Assiniboin, who were traditional foes of the Dakota, they embarked on a series of raids into the Dakota country in northern Minnesota, which, lasting over a period of approximately 50 years, eventually took great toll of the Dakota population and resulted in Chippewa occupancy of part of the old Dakota area. I will discuss this in some detail below, especially the later part of this movement.

I now begin a detailed account of Chippewa-Dakota relations in the present state of Minnesota as these relations developed during the middle years of the eighteenth century to pave the way for the stabilization of relations of war during the nineteenth century. Many of the Chippewa from western Lake Superior were trying with might and main to gain a foothold in the country to the south and west to provide fur and larger game. It should be mentioned that Chippewa at the same time were penetrating into western Wisconsin, where Dakota had also been living and hunting and where, on prominent lakes and streams, game, fish, wild rice, maple sugar, and other natural products were found. The focus is narrowed, however, chiefly to the northern Minnesota area, with the realization that the dynamics of such intertribal relations extended along a much broader frontier.

Chippewa Scalp Dance, from watercolor by Peter Rindisbacher. (Courtesy West Point Museum Collections, United States Military Academy. Used with permission.)

A narrative account of trading activities in the country northwest of Lake Superior for 1765 by Alexander Henry gives insight into tribal relations in northern Minnesota and adjacent areas at that time. Henry, one of the earliest British traders in the Great Lakes after the French and Indian War (1754–1760), and in partnership with a veteran French-Canadian trader, Jean Baptiste Cadotte, established a post at Chequamegon. Henry found 50 Chippewa "families" at Chequamegon and 50 families at more easterly locations along the south shore of Lake Superior, all in distress because of the absence of trade over the past several years due to the war. In Henry's words (1901: 186–188; brackets mine), he

> . . . [was] obliged to distribute goods, to the amount of three thousand beaver-skins. This done, the Indians went on their hunt, at the distance of a hundred leagues. A clerk . . . accompanied them to Fond du Lac [west end of Lake Superior], taking with him two loaded canoes. Meanwhile, at the expense of six days' labour, I was provided with a very comfortable house, for my winter's residence.

Henry does not mention where those Chippewa went to hunt. They probably entered the St. Louis River at the west end of Lake Superior, and went from there inland across well-known portages and along smaller streams. According to Henry's account (1901: 194–195), the women and children returned to Chequamegon on April 20 after the ice had broken up and they could use their bark canoes, and the men returned with their catch of fur on May 15, *after having been out on a war party against the Dakota.* During this war party many men on each side were slain, including 35 Chippewa. The Chippewa nevertheless were the victors. Henry mentioned a Chippewa "village" established in the interior and that the battle was fought along a river, which he did not name.

Although there are no indications in this account regarding the location of the Chippewa "village" (and that undoubtedly meant a large *encampment*), nor the location of the battleground, the large size of the war party would indicate the Mississippi, a natural waterway for so large a flotilla. The Mississippi as an important war road and battleground is suggested in the accounts of Warren, whom I cited in the last chapter. Warren (1885: 222, 227–232, 235–241) told about a series of battles described to him by old men whose "grandfathers" took part. Much of this fighting took place in the upper Mississippi, especially downstream from Sandy Lake [Aitkin County], where the Chippewa were said to have had a base camp. Warren's accounts were semilegendary in character, but his general notice of the severity of warfare must be taken seriously. The battle described by Henry may well have come down to Warren in legend, the details of it distorted through repeated telling.

An impressive aspect of Henry's account was the fierceness of the struggle waged between the Chippewa and the Dakota. The loss of 35 men is enormous when reckoned in terms of usual Indian warfare. One could conclude that after a period of depression brought on by severance of the fur trade during the French and Indian War, the Chippewa were spurred to take drastic action to gain ascendancy in a region which had become essential for their exploitation, at a time when the fur trade was returning to the upper Lakes. This was not the last battle fought on the upper Mississippi, but it no doubt served to give notice to the Dakota that Chippewa were attempting to gain permanent occupancy of lake sites in the northern Minnesota forests.

Except for a limited amount of material on the Chippewa west of Lake Superior for the years 1774–1775, there is a shortage of information on the Mississippi source region for the period between 1765 and 1783, especially during the time of the American Revolution.

In 1774–1775 Peter Pond, a trader among the Dakota along the Minnesota River, recorded the efforts of fur traders to assemble Dakota and Chippewa at Mackinac Island in northern Lake Michigan, where a major British depot and fort were located, to establish intertribal boundaries and make peace in the interest of the trade. Pond had been delegated by the commandant at Mackinac to bring spokesmen for the Dakota to that place, and other traders were to bring Chippewa (WHC 18:342).

Pond brought together 11 Dakota spokesmen and others from the Minnesota River to the mouth of that stream. He stated further, in an inimitable style (WHC 18:242–243):

> . . . Hear we found Sum traders who Com from near the Head of the Misseppey with Sum Chippewa Chefes with them. I was Much Surprised to Sea them So Ventersum among the People I had with me for the Blod was scairs Cold—the Wound was yet fresh. . . .

Pond tells us that the Chippewa and Dakota at Mackinac agreed to make peace. The main stipulation was that the Dakota agreed not to hunt east of the Mississippi and that the Chippewa were not to hunt west of it; that the two peoples "Should Live By the Side of Each other as frinds and nighbers" (WHC 18:344–345).

Pond's remark that the Chippewa came down the Mississippi with their traders is significant for two reasons: first, the Chippewa were again recorded as being on the Mississippi north of the Dakota; second, for the first time it was reported that traders were actually in the interior southwest of Lake Superior. These traders had entered the interior for the purpose of marshaling Chippewa for the Mackinac conference, for Pond refers to them in another passage (WHC 18:345) as "People from Lake Supereor," implying that they were still based there, as they had been in Henry's accounts of ten years before.

The Chippewa were strengthening their position in northern Minnesota. The traders, who could only lose through warfare, were trying to stabilize Indian occupancy areas, to promote heavy exploitation of the land for its fur game.

Remarks made by Alexander Henry for 1775 indirectly indicate that the Leech Lake region in northwestern Minnesota, the most important residential center for Chippewa in later years, had not as yet a stable population of Chippewa; this conclusion is reached by putting together a series of statements on his trading ventures west of Lake Superior. Henry found Chippewa villages at various places along the present international boundary as far west as Lake of the Woods (1901: 230ff.). Chippewa at one location, the junction of Rainy River with its southern affluent, the Little Fork, comprised 50 lodges (perhaps 500 persons) and demanded goods from the traders in return for permitting them to proceed further into the interior. Another village located east of Rainy Lake had been virtually destroyed by the Dakota. On Winnipeg River, between Lake of the Woods and Lake Winnipeg, Henry met "several canoes of Indians, who all begged for rum, but, they were known to belong to the band of Pilleurs [Pillagers], also called *rogues*, and were

Bandolier or Shoulder Pouch: From about 1760 onward no self-respecting Chippewa felt he was dressed for ceremonial occasions unless he wore a bandolier. The idea may have originally been adopted in imitation of the bullet pouch carried by British soldiers during the eighteenth century.

In its earlier form the bandolier was largely geometric in design patterns, but gradually floral patterns predominated as it evolved throughout the nineteenth century. Such shoulder pouches seldom were used for utilitarian purposes, and the pocket found in older specimens gradually disappeared to be replaced by a false pocket facade of pure beadwork. In effect, the bandolier was a symbol of social success. Other neighboring tribes utilized the bandolier in comparable fashion, for example, Potawatomi, Menomimi, Winnebago, and Ottawa. (Courtesy Buffalo Museum of Science)

on that   s, was often applied to
the Ch   parently, then, in 1775,
Pillager   t settlements at Leech
Lake, b   nnipeg traverse region,
with R   their focal community.
                                           ssissippi sources region
to hunt   hunting to the east ten
years b   main trade routes north
of the   s that the greatest po-
tentiali

                                           because their statements
concerr   meager in content, were
the last   Chippewa village locales
in nort   r reports which involve
the rec   ippewa *living* at Leech,
Sandy,   8ff.). Before that time,
from t   1760s and 1770s, the
Chippe   es less remote from the
main tr   ile they were advancing
west fr   favorable game regions
for sea

                                           tribal occupancy of the
region of northern Minnesota relevant to this discussion are listed:

1) From 1680 to 1736, Dakota occupied the region west of Lake Superior, but Chippewa, with their residences at Chequamegon and Keweenaw bays, were entering Dakota country peacefully to trade and hunt with the Dakota as middlemen traders for the French.

2) From 1736 to *ca.* 1751, Minnesota was a contested region. The Chippewa, having been bypassed by the French in the trade, broke their alliance with the Dakota. A Chippewa-Cree-Assiniboin coalition, formed as a result of this break in Chippewa-Dakota relations, rendered Dakota occupancy of the Minnesota woodland rice lakes and fur grounds precarious; former wild food resource areas and fur game refuges became war areas.

3) From *ca.* 1751 to *ca.* 1780 Chippewa from the south shore of Lake Superior, mainly Chequamegon, were extending their hunting range into the eastern part of northern Minnesota at the same time that Pillager Chippewa from Rainy River were extending their hunting range south. By 1783, Sandy and Leech lakes had become important centers for Chippewa village residence, after a lengthy period of seasonal hunting and raiding forays from early village locations at Chequamegon and the region of the trade routes to the north, which were out of the range of enemy attack. It was only when the Chippewa had gained a real foothold in northern Minnesota that traders were willing to venture into this region to establish permanent posts and regular trade.

I have noted the difficulty the Chippewa had in establishing, and the Dakota in maintaining, occupation of the Minnesota northern woodlands, as documented in the primary fur trade literature of the second third of the eighteenth century. It is now recalled that Duluth in 1680 had described an area to the east, but still west of Lake Superior, as unoccupied due to warfare, hence a preserve for beaver. Exploitation of this and other regions was carried on only as a result of the Chippewa-Dakota peace and alliance of 1680–1736. From this, a pattern of interrelationship in which territory, warfare and ecology play the major parts can be seen.

Aside from the material on warfare and other factors just presented, there are a few other statements which should be cited, indicating the unwillingness on the part of Indian hunters to venture into contested areas, or "no-man's lands." At this point one must go back to wars of the 1730s between Dakota of central and southern Minnesota and Cree-Assiniboin (who had their villages and trading posts at Rainy Lake and other locations along the international boundary) to find at least two roads of war in northern Minnesota mentioned by the trader-explorer, La Vérendrye (Burpee 1927: 185–186, 233–234, 257–258). One was the present Warroad River which connects the Lake of the Woods by portages and streams to such prominent northern Minnesota sites as Cass and Leech lakes; the other was the Vermilion River, which joins the Rainy River country with that to the south and east around St. Louis River, which leads from the west end of Lake Superior into the Mississippi headwaters region.

A good part of the regions traversed by the war roads must have been unsafe for occupancy, and therefore devoid of human habitation. With Cree frequenting Rainy Lake and Lake of the Woods where La Vérendrye built trading forts, and traveling the routes between and beyond these locations, east and west, the nonoccupied region must have extended south from them and included at least the northern part of the Minnesota lake country.

A statement made in 1751 by the French trader and commandant among Dakota on the Mississippi, Pierre Paul, Sieur de Marin, and a map accompanying the narrative of the travels of the Anglo-American adventurer, Jonathan Carver, who was in the upper Great Lakes-Mississippi River region in 1766–1767, give further support to the inference that a wide tract, including important parts of northern Minnesota, was unoccupied. Marin was ordered by his superior, the Governor-General of Canada (WHC 18:66), to explore the sources of the Mississippi River. Marin wrote that the Dakota had promised to guide him to the Mississippi sources only if they could be assured that the commandant of the Lake Superior-Lake Winnipeg traverse region to the north "had quieted the nations on the Missisipy" (WHC 18:79). These were perhaps Chippewa, but more likely were some of their Cree allies.

Carver, who explored the Mississippi and some of its tributaries as far north as the Falls of St. Anthony (now worn away, but then located within the city limits of the present Minneapolis), provided a map relevant to 1766–1767 to illustrate his discoveries (1779: map facing p. xvi). The region comprising most of northwestern Minnesota is shown to be devoid of tribal occupancy. On the map Carver noted that the sources of the Mississippi were little known and that "Indians seldom travel this way except War Parties." Leech Lake, designated as White Bear Lake on the map, is placed beyond the area designated as the "Road of War" between the Dakota and Assiniboin; this indicates that Leech Lake at

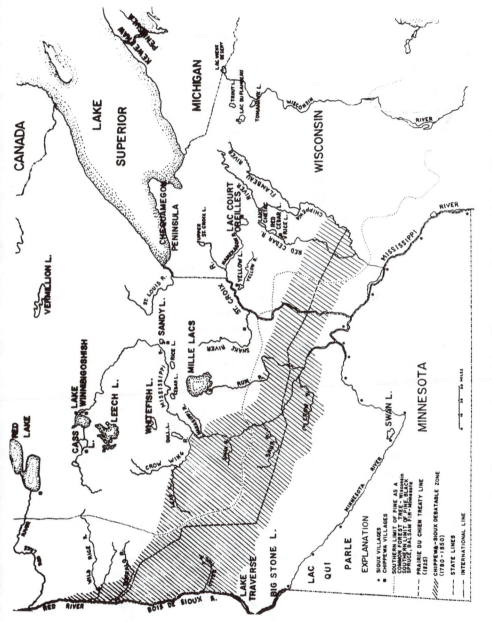

Map 4. Villages, vegetal and debatable zones, and the Prairie du Chien Line.

that time was uninhabited. Carver noted in designating this area that "all Country's not possess'd by any one Nation where War Parties are often passing is called by them the Road of War."

It may be seen, in explicit terms, even though the geography of the area was imperfectly known, that interlocking relationships of trade, exploration, diplomacy and war existed. Resources, especially fur game, and the exploitation of these, were paramount considerations. It may be also seen how war resulted in large areas lying fallow, regions where hunters and warriors dreaded to go. One is also enabled to see, through the examination and analysis of such documents as are at hand, a fairly consistent view of the dynamics of the relationships of the time; how the unoccupied areas shifted in relation to the shifting alignments and changing fortunes among the tribal peoples and Europeans.

In the next section I will show how, once the Chippewa had gained occupancy of woodland fastnesses in Minnesota, and also in neighboring parts of Wisconsin, the "no-man's land"—still contested, at times called "neutral," and always a buffer zone between hostile tribes—became stabilized.

Vegetal Zones and Occupancy

Although the face of much of the countryside of Wisconsin and Minnesota has changed since the first half of the nineteenth century due to such human activities as lumbering, farming, and reforestation, and natural events, especially forest fires, it is possible for botanists to reconstruct what the vegetal areas of over 100 years ago were. They do this on the basis of historical records and accounts, soil analysis, analysis of fossil pollens, a knowledge of the habits of relevant species, and other techniques. One can get a fair picture of the "original" vegetal zones when the Indians were still the chief inhabitants of those areas (for example, for Minnesota, Borchert 1959: 24; for Wisconsin, Curtis 1959). Vegetal cover in turn affected animal populations, and these in turn affected human occupancy and distribution, especially in a region where the population was almost exclusively dependent upon the productions of nature.

In general, the major vegetal zones were more clearly marked in Minnesota than in Wisconsin, as is seen on Map 4 on p. 73. The map shows a heavily forested belt, much of it in conifers, occupying the northern half of both states, while the southern part of Minnesota and sectors in western Wisconsin (especially in the area adjacent to the Mississippi) comprises deciduous forests changing to prairie toward the west. In the central part of Minnesota and contiguous parts of western Wisconsin there is a transitional zone. In Minnesota this takes the form of a mixed deciduous and prairie region, with oak openings and extensive marshes and lakes. This zone, crossing Minnesota from northwest to southeast, varied in width from about 50 to 100 miles.

In Wisconsin the deciduous species were in general more prevalent and the prairie land more limited than in Minnesota. Toward the Mississippi and the lower reaches of such major tributaries as the St. Croix and Chippewa rivers, there were extensive oak savannas and some prairie. The transitional zones, in contrast to the heavily forested areas, whether pine or maple-beech, were excellent country for deer and other game.

Chippewa and Dakota were the principal occupants of Minnesota and contiguous parts of Wisconsin. Their zones of exploitation did not normally interpenetrate, and their occupancy was mutually exclusive. They also, by about 1780, and continuing throughout the pre-reservation period until about 1850, became associated with different vegetal regions, although, as I will show, this applied chiefly to their permanent settlements, and not to their entire range.

By the 1780s Chippewa had settlements at numerous lake and river sites in northern Minnesota and northwestern Wisconsin, all within the heavily forested area. Dakota, after having given up occupancy of the northern wooded areas under Chippewa pressure, located their permanent settlements exclusively along the west bank of the Mississippi, south of the Twin Cities, almost as far as the Iowa border, and along the entire length of the Minnesota River that flows through the prairies of southern Minnesota from its source at the South Dakota border to its junction with the Mississippi not far south of the Twin Cities.

This area, which was rich in game, was entered by men to hunt, and at times to trap, but usually by stealth and in constant dread of being surprised by enemies. In order to understand the apparent paradox of the richest lands of a region lying virtually unoccupied, while the poorer lands (in terms of the specific requirements of the time) were those where the settlements were, inferential evidence from the accounts of eye-witnesses must be consulted, those of traders, expedition leaders and journalists, Indian agents, missionaries, and unofficial travelers, covering the period from the 1780s to almost 1850 when land treaty cessions were made and reservation living began, with consequent restriction of movement.

Integral to the discussion which follows is reference to the findings of naturalists who provide a separate set of data, helping to explain the intricacies of intertribal relations, including the functions of war. But first, more information on sociopolitical organization and demography must be given.

Population

I mentioned Chippewa and Dakota settlements, or *villages*, as they should properly be called, the former on lakes and streams in the woodlands, the latter along the main rivers bisecting prairie lands. The best sources for population of these villages throughout the first half of the nineteenth century are the reports of Indian agents and official travelers, since they carried on government business, which involved making censuses, and did not at that early time, have any reason to falsify records and accounts. Although seldom cited, fur traders were a source of information for agents and more temporary official visitors because of the accounts they kept and their close relationship with the people in whose villages they not only traded, but also married. The following is a list of sources for Chippewa of Wisconsin and Minnesota: explorers Zebulon Montgomery Pike for 1805–1806 (1810: 66), J. D. Doty for 1820 (Williams 1953: 436, 438), J. Allen for 1832 (ASP-MA 5:331, 334, 336), and J. N. Nicollet for 1836 (CDS

1845: 63)); agents and officials H. R. Schoolcraft for 1824, 1831–1832 (1834: 221), and 1847 (1851–1857 1:468), D. P. Bushnell for 1839 (Winchell 1911: 640), and A. Ramsey for 1850 (Winchell 1911: 646–647); traders H. Monk for 1807 (MHB 5:38) and H. M. Rice for 1848 (NA 1848); a missionary, W. T. Boutwell for 1832 (MHS mss.); and an Italian adventurer named Giacomo Constantino Beltrami, after whom a large county in northern Minnesota was named, for 1823 (1828 2:434). Only in the case of Schoolcraft was an attempt made to provide a village-by-village census for the entire region, which lay within his agency at Sault Ste. Marie. In other instances there are figures for one or another village or the region as a whole.

It is the same for the Dakota. Pike (Coues 1895 1:346–347) and Beltrami (1828 2:206–207) gave population figures; also explorers Lewis and Clark (Thwaites 1904–1905 6:82–83, 94) and W. H. Keating for 1823 (1825 1:396, 399–402). The best source on population for eastern Dakota was their agent, Lawrence Taliaferro, who provided census reports in his journals covering the years 1821–1839 (MHS mss.).

Population remained fairly stable over the first half of the century. Disease and warfare counterbalanced natural increase. In all, Dakota and Chippewa each counted about 3000–4000 souls in the region where they contested. These were divided into about 10 major villages for each people, and, in the case of the Chippewa, several smaller settlements, offshoots and to some extent satellites of the larger ones. An "average" village, Chippewa or Dakota, would have about 250–300 members, but there was considerable range, the largest among the Chippewa being Leech Lake with about 800 persons divided in three or four settlements at various places on the lake shore and on Bear Island. One is not, then, dealing with great concentrations of people, but rather village populations generally counted in the low hundreds, and in some cases, less than a hundred.

Polity

There is not enough scope here for a general and detailed description of the polity or the social organization of the village Chippewa or Dakota of the 1780–1850 period. For the Chippewa I would direct the reader to Hickerson (1962a: Chs 2–4). There is no published general account of the eastern Dakota for this period, and this is a great lack in the North American literature. The chief primary source for the Dakota is their agent, Taliaferro, who, although making few explicit remarks on the workings of the culture as such, in the daily entries in his journals over many years, in addition to letters and official reports, provided a modicum of data susceptible to interpretation.

In brief, five of the seven major Dakota divisions (excluding the Assiniboin who, although closely related to the others in language and culture, were in every other way separate) were contesting with the Chippewa. (Aside from Taliaferro, primary sources are Keating 1825 1:401–404; Nicollet 1845: map; Winchell 1911: 552–553; also see Hodge 1907–1910 1:376–378.) These were the *Mdewakanton*, in several villages on the Mississippi and lower Minnesota rivers, and

Wahpeton, Sisseton, Yankton, and *Yanktonai* living in villages and ranging the plains toward the upper reaches of the Minnesota River and also the Red River of the North, and west from there. Yankton and Yanktonai, unlike the majority of their more easterly congeners, had horses, and spent considerable periods of time on the high plains toward the Missouri hunting bison. All the divisions spoke a common language with minor dialect differences, and in their myths and legends portrayed themselves as one people.

The several villages among the five divisions this study is concerned with were, like the Chippewa villages, autonomous. Each was represented by one or more chiefs in matters related to treaties, war and peace, and trade. War was carried on independently by the several villages, and it was not unusual for one village to be fighting while its nearest neighbor was in a state of truce. In treaties with the government, the separate villages usually acted separately. Their territories were demarcated one from another, and presumably each village acted as a separate economic unit. Although there is little data, it is suspected that ceremonies like the Medicine Dance, similar to the Chippewa Midewiwin, was a *village* affair.

In Taliaferro's journal there is expression of village autonomy. In a typical entry (MHS mss. 9: August 30, 1835), he wrote:

> The wars between the Sioux [Dakota] & Chippeways will . . . be a partial one as their feelings of hostility are not by any means national.

Despite the autonomy of villages, there was also a strong tendency for alliances to spring up among neighboring villages, even across divisional lines, for the purpose of waging war. These would break up as soon as a particular objective was achieved or defeated.

Among the Chippewa the separate villages also normally maintained autonomy. Like the Dakota, the Chippewa of Minnesota and Wisconsin spoke a common language, and taking into account minor differences in environment from one local region to another, they gained their livelihood all pretty much in the same way—by hunting, trapping, fishing, and harvesting wild rice, maple sugar, and berries. They had a common store of beliefs, ceremonials and ways of interacting with each other and with outsiders. In addition to common language, culture and outlook, the Chippewa continued to give importance to clan affiliation. Clans in effect were segments cross-cutting villages. Thus, members of the Bear clan could be found in many villages, and could comprise a large or small proportion of the village population; but no village, unless it was so small as to constitute a single family, would normally contain representatives of only a single clan. Certain villages were dominated by certain clans and this would lead, because of the rule of exogamy and an overall proscription of marriage between cousins to the fourth degree, to intervillage marriages.

I cannot say that the Chippewa, any more than the Dakota, were politically unified over this broad region. The separate villages were not related as segments of a single functioning political tribal entity; rather they were potential allies, alliances realized chiefly in war and, at times, in the negotiation of treaties.

The autonomy of the separate villages finds expression in the reports of nineteenth century authors. Schoolcraft (1834: 20) wrote that at one time, before their dispersal in the interior, the Chippewa were a relatively small population that was to some degree unified through the influence of certain chiefs:

> . . . but its increase and spread over the adjacent country, would naturally destroy so feeble a tie of political power, and must soon have left each local band as it now remains, independent and sovereign in its acts.

For both Chippewa and Dakota, examples of the autonomy of separate communities are found in the records of the negotiations of various treaties. (These are available in the National Archives and also in the files of the Lands Division of the United States Department of Justice.) An excellent illustration is the treaty held at Prairie du Chien, Iowa, in August, 1825, among various tribes inhabiting the present states of Illinois, Iowa, Wisconsin, and Minnesota, under the auspices of the government. The ostensible purpose of this treaty was to make boundaries between tribes that, if respected, would contribute to keeping peace among them. The proceedings with regard to the Chippewa and Dakota, recorded in typescript in the William Clark Papers at the Kansas Historical Society (KHS-CP 2–3:170–173) show that spokesmen on both sides, with one or two exceptions, claimed territories on behalf of their separate villages, or, as in the case of the Chippewa, clusters of neighboring settlements, which, in a sociopolitical sense, could be thought of as constituting single "villages." It is not germane at this point in the discussion to record precisely the results of the negotiations, except to remark that there was considerable dispute between the various Dakota and Chippewa spokesmen, but apparently little if any dispute within the delegations. One interesting feature is that tribal lines, or territorial limits, were drawn on birchbark (Schoolcraft 1851–1856: 421–422). However, the main proceedings were conducted by the Indians of the several tribes making their claims verbally, these being translated into appropriate languages, and the English translation of the whole proceedings being recorded by secretaries of Commissioners William Clark and Lewis Cass.

I present here an abbreviated account of the claims made by Dakota and Chippewa spokesmen to illustrate some of the points made.

According to the record of the treaty proceedings, the territorial claims of the Chippewa were heard first. Piajick, or Single Man, from the upper St. Croix River in northwestern Wisconsin, claimed territory from the mouth of Chippewa River, up the east side of Lake Pepin on the Mississippi to the mouth of Sioux [Rush] River, and up the Rush to its source (in southern St. Croix County, Wisconsin). He then claimed from the source of Rush River to the upper end of Lower Lake St. Croix, and from there across to Green Water Lake. (Green Water Lake is not to be found on any modern map, but is probably the present Forest Lake in northwestern Washington County, Minnesota.) From Green Water Lake he claimed to the mouth of Rum River. This area was represented on a strip of birchbark which Piajick presented to the Commissioners for their enlightenment.

Another Chippewa, Nauquanosh, or Forward Man, from Lac du Flambeau in Wisconsin, claimed the Chippewa River from its mouth to its junction with the Eau Claire, and along the Eau Claire to Black River, and beyond to the east. These locations are all in western Wisconsin and are readily found on a road map.

Chiefs from other villages similarly made separate claims covering territories extending as far west as the Red River of the North.

The Dakota also made their claims separately. Wabasha, one of the chiefs of the southernmost village of the Mdewakanton Dakota on the Mississippi, claimed as follows (KHS-CP 2–3:172):

> On the East side of the Mississippi I claim from the mouth of Bout which enters the Mississippi nearly opposite Leak River, the lands at the heads of the Rivers that empty into the Mississippi, to where the Meadow joins the woods.

"Bout" and the place where the "Meadow joins the woods" would be impossible at this time to locate, but at least it is known that the area claimed by Wabasha, with respect to boundary relations with the Chippewa, lay entirely east of the Mississippi in the present state of Wisconsin. And, as in the case of the Chippewa, other Dakota villages and even chiefs from villages within the major tribal divisions, extending west to the Red River, made discrete claims.

Now, there was much conflict in the claims and it took a great deal of negotiating to reach compromises, but finally a "boundary" between the "Chippewa" and "Dakota" was worked out which is shown on Map 4. The exotic references to lakes, rivers, forests, and other locales were worked out on the treaty grounds (unfortunately there is no surviving record of this part of the treaty negotiations), and as far as present research on general conditions of occupancy at that time can tell, the rendering of them by Charles C. Royce (1899) in his reconstruction of treaty cession areas for the entire United States is more than reasonably accurate.

My point has been to show that Chippewa and Dakota each made their claims in severalty, the *village* emerging as the discrete political and territorial unit, thus illustrating and supporting the general remarks I have made on polity.

One now has some knowledge of the size and relationship of communities, among and between the peoples I am discussing. One can also begin to perceive the seriousness of conflict in territoriality exemplified by the negotiations of the Treaty of Prairie du Chien. In the next chapters I further discuss the dynamics of territorial relations among peoples of different tribes in terms of occupancy, competition and war, and biome, and in so doing I hope to explain why the Treaty of Prairie du Chien did not work.

6

Warfare and the Debatable Zone
East of the Mississippi

Early History: 1767–1805

I SET ABOUT HERE to define the debatable zone. To do so I make use of statements by many of the authors I have already cited and others who, for one reason or another, had business in the region. There is a shortcoming in this presentation; that is, I cannot indicate *precisely* in every case the extent of the contested areas. Although the zone in general remained the same over the 70 year period discussed here, there were minor changes. Thus, although a particular lake or creek valley was safely habitable during one decade, during the next it would become unsafe for occupancy, then again it was within safe range of hunters, and so on. If there was a general tendency, it was that Chippewa from various locales in the long run made gains at the expense of particular Dakota adversaries. In no case did these amount to significant accretions of territory or large-scale displacements of population by force. In some limited regions, truces, which in only rare instances lasted for more than a year or two, permitted safe occupancy of normally dangerous zones. Even in the rare cases where truces lasted several years, however, there were bound to be instances of hostility, even if amounting only to the breaking of traps or killing the enemies' dogs, actions that always resulted in a state of alarm.

In 1767, Carver, whom I had occasion to quote earlier, in another passage, described the region of the Chippewa River and its Red Cedar branch (Dunn and Chippewa counties, Wisconsin), as a war road (1777: 102–103):

> The Chipéway River, at its junction with the Mississippi, is about eighty yards wide, but is much wider as you advance into it. Near thirty miles up it separates into two branches, and I took my course through that which lies to the eastward [main branch].

The country adjoining to the river, for about sixty miles, is very level, and on its banks lie fine meadows, where larger droves of buffaloes and elks were feeding, than I had observed in any other part of my travels. The track between the two branches of this river is termed the Road of War between the Chipéway and Naudowessie [Dakota] Indians.

Carver also described Chippewa villages in the upper St. Croix and Chippewa River regions far to the north in the woodland fastness (1779: map facing p. xvi), the first such descriptions: Despite tribulations, and perhaps, at first, evacuation of this or that settlement, the villages survived and even proliferated along branch streams of those rivers, and also along the upper Wisconsin to the east, but these villages were always well within heavily wooded sectors or open areas, usually pine flats, and were separated from Dakota enemies by extensive tracts of woodland, hence were impervious to war parties.

The attempts of British traders to make peace in the upper Mississippi in the 1770s were not successful. By the mid-1780s, warfare had become so disruptive to trade, especially in the St. Croix and Chippewa River regions where several tribes, Winnebago, Sauk and Fox, as well as Chippewa and Dakota, were contesting, that the traders again, in the spring of 1786, appealed to the British government in a memorandum signed by a Committee of Merchants of Montreal. This memorandum asked to hold a peace treaty among the contestants, on the grounds that the traders could not control the warring groups (WHC 11:483–487). Elsewhere the Merchants asserted that although large tracts in the upper Mississippi region were unsurpassed for the abundance of fur-bearing animals, warfare was restricting the amount of peltry brought out by Chippewa and Dakota trappers.

The Merchants attempted to define the territories of the Chippewa and of the Dakota. It is seen how general these attempts at delimitation were. For the Chippewa:

> . . . by far the most numerous and warlike part . . . inhabit the south side of Lake Superior . . . and a very numerous tribe of them occupy the sources of the Mississippi with all the Country on the East side . . . so low as the River of the Chipeways. . . .

As in the 1775 peace arrangements, Chippewa were said to occupy the east side of the Mississippi, but not in safety from Dakota attacks. The Dakota country, according to these same Merchants, lay on the west side of the Mississippi River from the Maquoketa (Manaquanon) River that enters on the west bank in Dubuque County, Iowa, north almost to the sources of the Mississippi. The Merchants stressed that the Mississippi "about the Falls of St Anthony" was an especially prized fur game region, and that the Dakota, who were chiefly bison hunters, were at that time turning their hand to trapping fur.

The Merchants then made a statement indicating the results of occupancy of the area that would result from peace:

> . . . the country too is very extensive that when peace can be brought about, between these two fierce and rival nations, the Manominis, the Picants [Winnebago], the Sakies, and the Foxes go up into that country and make most prodigious

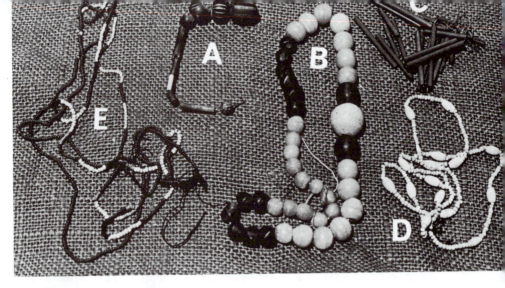

Trade Goods: European trade beads typical of those traded to northeastern wood-land Indians during 250 years of fur trading. A, B, and C were common from 1600–1750 throughout the Great Lakes country. D and E were standard from c. 1750–1850, while type E has continued in use up to the present. (Courtesy Buffalo Museum of Science)

Decorated Shirt: The trade cloth shirt pictured above is from the late nineteenth or early twentieth century. Floral beadwork is heavily embroidered on velveteen as an integral part of the costume, whereas in earlier periods costumes tended to be simpler with colorful accessories providing the decorative element. (Courtesy Buffalo Museum of Science)

Hunts; but whilst they continue at war no Indians nor Trader can shew themselves in that Country with safety.

They then suggested that presents be given to all concerned to bring about peace. The British government took action by holding a council at Mackinac in 1787. The deputy in charge of bringing the Chippewa and Dakota spokesmen, Joseph Ainse, upon arriving in the upper Mississippi country, found the two peoples sending out war parties against each other (WHC 12:85–87). The Chippewa and Dakota actually agreed to peace at Mackinac in 1787 in a treaty, in one article of which they also promised hospitality to the traders (MPHC 11:490; 23:606–608).

One of the results of these negotiations was not, as the traders had hoped, the occupation of the richest fur grounds by members of other tribes not resident in the region, but, with the exception of the Menomini who then and later made use of parts of it, the final expulsion of these tribes from the area, as a result of continuing warfare. After the 1780s there were no longer Winnebago, Sauk, and Fox in the upper portions of the Wisconsin, Chippewa, and St. Croix rivers, the Chippewa, and, to some extent, the Dakota, having driven them away.[1] In the meantime, Dakota and Chippewa kept fighting each other.

The Chippewa-Red Cedar area was a war zone, as I have noted, and continued to be so. The memoirs of a noted trader, Jean Baptiste Perrault, who was active in the entire upper Mississippi area during the years 1783–1799, provides first-hand accounts of war, trade, and other matters (MHPC 37:508–619), only a small part of which can be included here. I will now retreat a year or so before the Dakota-Chippewa peace at Mackinac of 1787. In 1785–1786, Perrault joined a partnership of Lake Superior traders who were supplied by merchants from Mackinac and Montreal. Perrault, at the time a clerk, or junior partner, was assigned to "winter" at the mouth of the Chippewa River with another clerk. Perrault ascended the Mississippi from Prairie du Chien, a major collecting point, to Chippewa River where he remained several days to allow the "savages" he was with to decide where to hunt. Eight lodges (about 80 persons) went with Perrault up to the mouth of Red Cedar River where he built his trading cabin, or "post." Another trader built a second post at the falls of the Chippewa, some distance to the east. These locations were well within the region contested by Chippewa and Dakota.

Perrault does not specifically mention the tribal affiliation of the "savages" who accompanied him up Chippewa River. One can, however, determine this by a close examination of Perrault's reports for other years, and other material. It was the practice of traders during the 1780s and later, on their way to the Mississippi from Green Bay by canoe through the main waterways, to pick up several lodges of Menomini at Butte des Morts, near Lake Winnebago, in eastern Wisconsin, and have them hunt in the upper Mississippi on contested lands. Perrault in 1786–1787 mentioned specifically that Menomini (called *Fols Avoines*, French for the Algonquian eponym, *Menomini*, or *wild rice people*) were trapping for trading

---

[1] This represented a complicated series of events in itself and cannot be discussed here. (For references, see WHC 11:102–105, 111–112, 383; Warren 1885: 242–248; Schoolcraft 1851–1857 2:149–150; 5:524–527.)

posts in the Chippewa River vicinity, and at Crow River, which enters the Mississippi on the west bank in Wright County, Minnesota, within the contested area (MPHC 37:536–539, 541–547). The only other "savages" Perrault negotiated with during those years were Dakota from Minnesota River, but they had their own traders on that stream where they also had their villages, and Perrault indicated that he did not care to trade with them (MPHC 37:538, 547–548). In 1788–1789 Perrault mentioned that traders were wintering with Menomini at Sauk River (Le Grande Rapide), not far north of the Crow, and still, as will be seen, within the contested zone (MPHC 37:551).

The next year Perrault gave a stronger indication of hostilities. As mentioned, he and other traders met Menomini in eastern Wisconsin, and from there journeyed to the Mississippi. According to the trader,

> When they arrived, they said they would be glad to have us winter on the river a la Corneille [Crow River], because they wished to winter on the river a L'au de vie [Rum River, which enters the Mississippi on the east bank in Sherburne County, Minnesota] and on the river aux marais [St. Francis River, just south of the Rum] as that would be more advantageous for them.

Perrault built his post at the Crow, and mentioned incidentally that a Dakota war party ascended the St. Croix River to attack a group of Chippewa on that stream. This was taking place at precisely the time that emissaries were making peace at Mackinac.

In 1788–1789, Perrault gave an eyewitness account of the warfare. He and another trader established their post on the Red Cedar branch of the Chippewa where, again, they were trading with neutral Menomini. During the winter, Perrault was visited by a band of Mdewakanton Dakota from a village on Minnesota River. These Dakota, 28 strong, led by Little Crow, had taken trading credits at another post and were temporarily hunting on the upper part of a branch of the Red Cedar. Their visit to Perrault's post occurred very shortly after six Chippewa from Lac Courte Oreilles, far up Chippewa River, had arrived at the post to trade. The Chippewa had been hunting beaver at Lake Chetac, not far north in Sawyer County, Wisconsin, but still within the heavily wooded area.

Although Perrault feared that there would be difficulty, the Chippewa and Dakota exchanged greetings, and Little Crow presented the Chippewa with a "gift." (Documents do not indicate what this gift was.) Little Crow told the Chippewa that the Dakota had "taken the liberty of approaching your lands for awhile" to hunt deer in the thick woods. Little Crow asked permission to remain on the "upper waters of that branch of your river," and said they would leave the country as soon as they had gotten provisions, that is, deer meat, for the spring. The Chippewa agreed, but ordered the Dakota to move away in March, lest they frighten the Chippewa families.

Next day, as the Chippewa were leaving, they were ambushed by the Dakota, and two of them were killed. The Dakota then left the region and were seen no more by Perrault, who thereafter traded only with Menomini. Later a large number of Chippewa from Lac Courte Oreilles came to Perrault's post, and demanded and received reparation for the slain. These Chippewa later gratuitously supplied Perrault with meat (MPHC 37:547–553).

Later that spring Perrault traveled up the Mississippi past the Crow River, where there was a trading post, to the present Sauk Rapids. At that place a post had been in operation during the winter. He collected payment from the Menomini who had wintered in the vicinity.

During the 1780s, then, a definite picture begins to form of the contested region lying between the Dakota and Chippewa, lying east of the Mississippi, extending from Chippewa River northward past the St. Croix to the region of the Rum and St. Francis rivers, and the Crow and Sauk rivers in Minnesota. Occupancy by the Menomini constituted a buffer between the Dakota and Chippewa and permitted the traders to harvest at least part of the valuable fur available in the region. It is not known, but one may guess, that Chippewa and Dakota received some payoff from this trapping, which would undoubtedly have been trade supplies. At least, they often got permission from Dakota and Chippewa to trap in those areas (cf. Taliaferro MHS mss: *passim*; Hickerson 1962a: 17–19).

Although a Dakota detachment of 28 men had entered the Red Cedar River, there is no indication from sources of the time that this was an habitual seasonal movement on their part. Their meeting with Chippewa was fortuitous, and a feeble attempt at negotiations quickly broke down.

The Chippewa who had come to the Red Cedar post had been trapping beaver a good distance upstream, although to the south of their village at Lac Courte Oreilles. Occupancy south of there was not feasible due to the hostility of the Dakota, who, though willing to venture into the region in force, left it hastily in fear of retaliation after they had killed Chippewa.

In summary, one sees again the relationship of war, hunting, and trade emerging concretely. It becomes more obvious that the contested, or debatable, zone was a rich game area, and a buffer zone between hostile villages.

There exist detailed journal accounts covering 1803–1805, by fur traders trading in northern Wisconsin and adjacent parts of Minnesota in the upper valleys of major streams and along such prominent tributaries of the St. Croix as the Yellow, Snake, Kettle and Clam rivers. Two of these, by F. V. Malhiot and M. Curot, are translated and annotated in the Collections of the State Historical Society of Wisconsin (19:163–233; 20:396–471). Another, by T. Connor, is found in Gates (1933), a collection of five journals of traders active in the Northwest at the turn of the nineteenth century. These accounts show various separate Chippewa bands, each associated with a trading post, hunting and trapping along the lakes and streams of the country. Often when they ventured south and west of heavily wooded areas, they were alarmed by the suspected or actual presence of Dakota.

According to Curot, Clam Lake, in Burnett County, Wisconsin, was apparently considered safe from Dakota raids (WHC 20:425–426), even though, as Curot notes elsewhere, Yellow Lake to the north (also Burnett County) was not. Snake River, in contiguous Pine County, Minnesota, was the southern limit of Chippewa occupancy in the St. Croix River region, but Chippewa and their traders felt insecure there, and fortified themselves against a possible attack. However, extensive activity on the Snake would indicate that they felt safe enough to risk hunting throughout the fall and spring seasons, and no alarm was sufficient to drive them away for long (see WHC 20:403–404; *passim*).

All in all, from the journals cited and other materials, it is apparent that Chippewa were occupying extensive tracts in the St. Croix valley, and in the upper Chippewa and Wisconsin rivers. Their main subsistence pursuits were fishing and wild rice and maple sugar production, carried on close to their permanent lake and riverside villages; hunting carried on a distance from the settlements; and trapping done on a number of tributary streams of the major rivers. Warfare with Dakota placed a limitation on the areas of hunting and trapping, but did not interfere with pursuits carried on in the vicinity of the villages.

The Journal of Zebulon Montgomery Pike

An excellent source on the war areas of the upper Mississippi was Lieutenant Pike (the same who blundered on Pike's Peak) who led a small military expedition to the sources of the Mississippi to study the topography of the region, the state of the British controlled fur trade, and Indian relations, and also to assert American authority over territory which had come to the United States by the Louisiana Purchase two years before. One of Pike's major accomplishments was shooting down the Union Jack at Leech Lake. Pike left a detailed journal of his activities. By consulting a large-scale geological survey map where topographic features such as rapids and small creeks are represented, it is possible to pinpoint his progress. One is helped in this by his editor, Elliot Coues (1895), who himself traveled the exact route followed by Pike. One of Pike's missions was to make peace between the Dakota and Chippewa.[2]

Pike found Dakota and Chippewa at war and mentioned several incidents which seem typical of the kind of warfare they were waging. When he arrived at the mouth of the Minnesota River, Little Crow (Petit Corbeau), the leading chief of the Dakota village then located on the west bank of the Mississippi, nine miles downstream from its junction with the Minnesota, had just returned with 150 men from a war expedition, probably against Chippewa of the St. Croix River, their nearest foes. The large size of the party indicates that several Mdewakanton villages were jointly involved. They had abandoned their excursion when they heard that Pike was in the area. A few days later Pike saw a small party of Dakota painted for war at the Falls of St. Anthony, and suspected that they were on their way to fight the Chippewa, despite the fact that he had recently urged them in council to remain at peace.[3]

Pike found signs of warfare at places along the Mississippi. Opposite the mouth of Crow River he found the remains of eight Dakota canoes and several broken Chippewa arrows. There were signs marked on the canoe paddles indicating

---

[2] Rather than give page citations for each statement from Pike, I simply refer the reader to Coues (1895: *passim*). Coues provides a very adequate index. I give page references for quoted passages.

[3] It is feasible in some instances to take the appearance of such war parties with a grain of salt. There is no hard evidence, but a show of war *would* invite a council which meant the distribution of trade goods and food in the form of presents, and also the opportunity for the Indians to present a case for particular interests. Hence, these Dakotas may only have looked as if they were about to go to war.

several Dakota had been killed. These were undoubtedly pictographs, widely used among woodland peoples to transfer information, and they could have been drawn by either Chippewa or surviving Dakota, but probably the former. Above Crow River, in the region between the present Otsego and Monticello, in Wright County, Minnesota, Pike found old fortified Dakota camps and stated that a battle had been fought in that vicinity five years before. At an abandoned Chippewa summer encampment of 15 lodges at Pine River, above the junction of the Crow Wing with the Mississippi, Pike found records, again probably pictographs, drawn this time on birchbark, indicating that a war party of 50 Chippewa had attacked and killed eight Dakota; these people had dug emplacements for the protection of the women and children in case of a return attack.

Pike indicated that warfare was affecting the land occupancy of the two peoples in the region. The most northerly sign of Dakota occupation was the fortified camps just north of Crow River. The first signs of Chippewa encampments (and these were not villages or permanent settlements) were just above the present Fort Ripley, Crow Wing County. These must have been on the east side of the Mississippi, for Pike stated that the expedition."had not entirely left the Sioux [Dakota] country on the western shore" (Coues 1895 1:127). Between a point slightly north of Crow River, and a point slightly south of Crow Wing River (a straight line distance of over 75 miles), there were no traces of Dakota or Chippewa occupancy. The first actual Chippewa that Pike met were several miles above the entrance of Pine River, well to the northeast of the Crow Wing on the Mississippi.

Pike passed the winter of 1805–1806 in a blockhouse he built at the mouth of Swan River near Little Falls, Minnesota, and therefore had time to observe relations in the surrounding countryside. Concerning the contested zone, he wrote (exaggerating the time span, however), (Coues 1895 1:350–351):

> The country E. of the Mississippi, from Rum river to the Riviere De Corbeau [in this case the Crow Wing], is . . . in dispute between them [Dakota] and the Chipeways, and has been the scene of many a sharp encounter for near 150 years past.

He did not specifically mention conflicting interests on the west bank. However, Pike did mention that the hunting grounds of the Sisseton division of Dakota, with their villages along the middle course of the Minnesota, were "eastward to the Mississippi, and up that river as far as the Riviere De Corbeau" (Coues 1895 1:343).

As in Perrault's time, one learns from Pike, in frequent references, that Menomini were hunting and trapping in the precise region contested by the Dakota and Chippewa. One Menomini, Chien Blanche, told Pike that he had wintered in the area for ten years past and even had a maple sugar camp nearby (Coues 1895 1:121). Pike wrote of the Menomini (Coues 1895 1:341):

> . . . owing to the very high estimation in which they are held both by Sioux and Chipeways, they are frequently permitted to hunt near Raven [Crow] river on the Mississippi, which may be termed the battle-ground between those two great nations.

Pike's material, then, detailed war zones and the activities taking place within them; also, he recorded the abundance of game of all kinds. The presence of Menomini, who were never in the region in great force, could not have had a pronounced effect on the supply of game, except in this or that local area, but the absence of Chippewa and Dakota, who were in much greater numbers, must have had the effect of preserving game, as neither could hunt or trap without being disturbed.

Late History: 1809–1838

A statement by a trader, John Johnston, made in 1809, succinctly expressed the relationship of war and game supply. Of the Chippewa and Dakota he wrote (Masson 1889–1890 2:170):

> The tract of country lying between the two nations for near one hundred and fifty leagues in length and from thirty to fourty in breadth, is now visited by stealth, and if peaceably hunted would be more productive than the richest mine of Peru.

There is, in this statement, the suggestion of a tract of uninhabited land far greater in extent than has so far been described. The country to the west of the Mississippi was as bitterly contested as that to the east. I will consider this below. First, however, reports by explorers, agents, and traders right through to the late 1830s, when much of the land east of the Mississippi was ceded to the United States by Chippewa and Dakota (cf. Royce 1899, Minnesota 1, Wisconsin 1; United States Statutes at Large 7:536, 538), indicate continuing warfare. Examples, in brief, are:

1820: Lewis Cass, who led an expedition to the sources of the Mississippi from Lake Superior, and later descended the river, wrote about the country south of the Crow Wing (Williams 1953: 327):

> The title to this land is in dispute between the Chippewa and Sioux, and their long hostilities have prevented either party from destroying the game in a manner as improvident as is customary among the Indians.

Another expedition member, J. D. Doty, wrote about this contested area as follows (Williams 1953: 452):

> Both parties seem to entertain the most sovereign fear and dread of each other, so their dividing line may be considered at least 200 miles wide, for this tract of country lies untraversed by them. It is consequently well stocked with game, for to this tract all animals have fled as a place of refuge. If a hunting party of Sioux should venture upon this land, the report of a Chippewa's being within its borders would frighten them off.

1824: Schoolcraft, then agent at Sault Ste. Marie, in a report to his superior, Cass, then Governor of Michigan Territory (William L. Clements Library mss., Michigan Papers), described extensive Chippewa settlement and fur trade activities in the St. Croix region, the headwaters of Chippewa River, including Lac Courte Oreilles and Lac du Flambeau. The main theater of war was the Chippewa River:

> This is the old war road of the Chippeways against the Sioux, and all their expeditions from time immemorial, have descended this fine navigable river. The most thickly settled part of the Chippeway territories is about the sources of this stream; and that part of the country being a flat table land, of considerable elevation both above the Mississippi & Lake Superior, is admirably calculated for the theater of a predatory war. A large Indian force can be corcentrated upon this stream in a few days, and after making a rapid incursion into the enemies country, can reascend this stream at the driest season, and in a few days return to their villages. This has been the policy long pursued.

1831: Schoolcraft noted similar conditions upon his visit to the Chippewa River region in 1831 (1834: 268–269, 278). He described the Red Cedar River country south of Rice Lake, in Barron County, Wisconsin, as follows (1834: 268–269):

> At the latter place [Rice Lake], at the distance of perhaps sixty miles from its head, I found the last fixed village of Chippewas on this stream, although the hunting camps, and other signs of temporary occupation, were more numerous below than on any other part of the stream. This may be attributed to the abundance of Virginia deer in that vicinity, many of which we saw, and of the elk and moose, whose tracks were fresh and numerous in the sands of the shore. Wild rice is found in all the lakes. Game, of every species common to the latitude, is plentiful. The prairie country extends itself into the vicinity of Rice Lake. . . . A country more valuable to a population having the habits of our North-Western Indians, could hardly be conceived of; and it is therefore cause of less surprise that its possession should have been so long an object of contention between the Chippewas and Sioux.

I have presented data, mainly direct testimony, selected from a greater wealth of material, on the contested, debatable, area east of the Mississippi. Indeed, war did not occur every year, nor was it constant in any given year. It was, however, the main preoccupation of Indians in the region and the Euro-Americans with whom they dealt. The total number of persons killed from villages on both sides, (and these were by no means only men of martial age) was usually not great, in terms of expectations inherent in advanced technological warfare. One or two killed in a given battle, from a community of 100–200 does not appear to be a great number, but if projected to 100–200 killed in a community of 10,000, the number takes on greater significance. Even so, a quote by an agent, Thomas Forsyth, stationed at Prairie du Chien, who met the Dakota chief, Little Crow, on an official trip up the Mississippi in 1819, indicated the difficulty of making peace and the risks the Indians were willing to take to maintain *some* hold over hunting grounds (WHC 6:213).

> I mentioned to LITTLE CROW, one of the principal chiefs of the Sioux Indians, the barbarous war that existed between them and the Chippewas, and if there was not a possibility of bringing about a peace between the two nations.

He observed that a peace could easily be made, but said it is better for us to carry on the war in the way we do, than to make peace, because, he added, we lose a man or two in the course of a year, and we kill as many of the enemy during the same time; and if we were to make peace, the Chippewas would over-run all the country lying between the Mississippi and Lake Superior, and have their villages on the banks of the Mississippi itself. In this case we, the Sioux, would lose all our hunting grounds on the north-east side of the river; why then, said he, should we give up such an extensive country to another nation to save the lives of a man or two annually. I know, said he, it is not good to go to, or make war too much, or against too many people. But this is a war for land which must always exist if the Sioux Indians remain in the same opinion that now guides them. I found the Indian's reason so good, that I said no more on the subject to him.

In fact, the Treaty of Prairie du Chien, held six years later, represented an attempt to establish the kind of boundaries which would isolate warring factions within recognized territories, thus preventing the type of conquest envisioned by the astute Little Crow.

Warfare was, however, more drastic at times. There were incidents in which as many as eight persons lost their lives, and then the older accounts in which scores were killed. On one occasion, in 1839, after a long series of hostilities in the St. Croix River region, the very area discussed by Little Crow in his talk with Forsyth in 1819, a Dakota party ambushed Chippewa returning to their villages on St. Croix River and at Mille Lacs Lake and Rum River, from the Indian agency at Fort Snelling; the Dakota killed, in a few hours, more than 100 Chippewa men, women and children (Taliaferro MHS mss. 13: July 2–3, 21, August 7, 1839). This was most unusual, but it serves to show the intensity to which conflict could grow under conditions of deprivation and frequent starvation. The Mille Lacs Lake village population was all but destroyed by this attack.

There were also periods of peace, especially in the years following the Treaty of Prairie du Chien, but only in the immediate vicinity of the Indian agency at the Mississippi-Minnesota junction, where the agent, cooperating with peacefully inclined civil chiefs, could act as a one-man board of arbitration. From 1825 to 1838, the Chippewa of the St. Croix and adjacent places, and Mdewakanton Dakota from two or three villages near the agency maintained a troubled truce, at times even hunting together, playing lacrosse, and exchanging gifts (for example, Taliaferro MHS mss. 5: July 13, 15, 26–27, 1829; August 8, 13, 17, 1830). It should be kept in mind, however, that the agency also acted as a distribution center for food and other goods during hard times. With intensified hunting in the former neutral grounds, game soon gave out (cf. Hickerson 1965b: 53; for primary references, Taliaferro MHS mss. journals for 1825–1831), and by 1831, hostilities, initiated by the Dakota war chief, Medicine Bottle, had begun again. Although these were soon resolved, and another period of truce followed, the resumption of warfare at that time was nothing more or less than a reaction to a shortage of game, and its effect was to return the country of the lower St. Croix for a while to its former status as a debatable no-man's land.

7

Warfare and the Debatable Zone West of the Mississippi

The Bean Survey of 1835

For the area west of the Mississippi, I will present a few statements from an abundancy of material. These, as in the last chapter, are published and unpublished accounts of explorers, traders, missionaries, and agents. So intensive has this search been that again, despite minor discrepancies here and there, the picture that emerges is a very consistent one over a long period of time. Author after author found the same general areas untenable, and again there are constant references to subsistence and trade as the controlling variables for warfare.

It was seen in Chapter 5 that Dakota and Chippewa claims on the Treaty of Prairie du Chien grounds were in conflict west as well as east of the Mississippi, and that a boundary line was established to split the difference. I will initiate this section of the discussion by stating that the boundary, no more respected west of the Mississippi than east, was finally surveyed ten years after the Treaty, in 1835. The survey started from the southeastern end at Chippewa River in Wisconsin, and terminated prematurely at Otter Tail Lake, in Otter Tail County, west-central Minnesota. There, the survey, which was to be carried to the terminus of the putative Prairie du Chien boundary line, at the mouth of Sheyenne River on the west bank of the Red River of the North, was interrupted by the desertion of the military escort and the interpreters for the Indian guides, as a result of signs of hostility on the part of the Indians. Taliaferro stated in his journal (MHS mss. 9: August 6, 10, 1835), that mounted Dakota had stabbed a mule and a horse belonging to the survey party. These, of course, were symbolic acts denoting the possibility of something more serious. He also reported that a Minnesota River Mdewakanton chief, ironically named Annongenasiah, or Good Road, complained that the Chippewa were throwing down the boundary markers set up by the surveyors, and also that the markers allowed the Chippewa too much territory.

The survey leader, Major Jonathan S. Bean, in his official report to William Clark, then Superintendent of Indian Affairs at St. Louis, commented on the attitude of the Chippewa and Dakota whose boundary he was marking (NA/GLO):

> . . . abandoned by the escort and left without interpreters through whom I might be able to make known to the different tribes of Indians the object of my labors. The two contending nations too, embittered against each other from their long contention for the very land now about to be divided according to what they might choose to consider an arbitrary power, and this coupled with their habitual aversion to recognize any but natural boundaries, which causes them to bear equal animosity against any person attempting to erect artificial ones, rendered any attempt on my part further to progress not only dangerous but rash in the extreme—inasmuch as one of the great objects of the expedition (the settling the line in presence of and by mutual consent and knowledge of each of the disputing nations) was placed out of the question. Under these circumstances I felt myself constrained to abandon the work and make my returns to you of what has been executed. . . .

The survey had been attempted at a time of bitter hostilities involving Chippewa from Sandy Lake and Leech Lake and Sisseton and Wahpeton Dakota enemies. There are detailed descriptions of fighting and deaths on both sides in the manuscript journals of missionaries Edmund F. Ely (for example, MHS mss. 8:20) and Boutwell (MHS mss:117–118), and more especially, the agent, Taliaferro (MHS mss. 9:June 1–2, 4, 1835). The boundary survey, which was conceived as a measure to settle territorial differences and to contribute toward peace and understanding, actually had the effect of intensifying differences, since the line, as marked, was unsatisfactory to the Dakota and the Chippewa.

Early History: 1793–1807

One of the first explicit statements of extensive unoccupied, or neutral, tracts west of the Mississippi was made by a trader, Robert Dickson, in 1793. In a letter to a British-Canadian official, he stated that the region between the Minnesota River and Red River of the North contained the best beaver grounds, "but the Indians seldom hunt there as it is the War Road of the Sioux and Sauteux" (Cruikshank 1923–1925 1:388–390). Dickson was actually referring to the Otter Tail River, which drains Otter Tail Lake into the stream today known as Red River near Breckenridge, Wilkin County, Minnesota. Because it is the main branch, the Otter Tail was considered as the Red River proper in Dickson's time. Dickson's statement carries the implication that debatable grounds between the Dakota and Chippewa were not confined to the Mississippi valley itself; they extended continuously as far west as Red River.

There are other statements about the region over the period 1797–1849, which I present in this and following sections in summary in an attempt to explicate significant features.

1797–1799: In 1797, a party of Dakota attacked and killed at least 40 and possibly as many as 65 Chippewa from Sandy Lake (perhaps near the Lake itself) in Aitkin County, just east of the Mississippi. The Dakota lost only five men (MPHC 20:523; Tyrrell 1916: 263–264). Sandy Lakers, however, were in the habit of hunting west of the Mississippi, as far south of the Crow Wing junction as they dared venture. In 1799 the explorer-trader David Thompson, who visited a Northwest Company trading post at Sandy Lake on his way down the Mississippi, stated that Chippewa from there were hunting "in the plains on the west side of the Mississippe to make half dried meat, and procure skins for leather of the Bison. . . ." The women who had remained at Sandy Lake were apprehensive, since their men "were hunting on what is called the War Grounds, that is, the debatable lands between them and the Sioux Indians" (Tyrrell 1916: 281). These "plains" west of the Mississippi were south of the Crow Wing, the land north being heavily wooded or burned out.

1799: Our old friend, the trader Perrault, in 1799 traveled from Cass Lake in Cass-Beltrami counties, northern Minnesota, to Clearwater River in Clearwater County to the west in the transition forest region (MPHC 37:574–575). He found the route

> . . . was dangerous . . . on account of the hostiles. It was absolutely necessary to traverse the war trails which lay between the country of the Sauteux from that of the Scioux. We were in constant dread until we reached the riviere a L'eau Claire [Clearwater].

1806–1807: George Henry Monk, a trader for the Northwest Company stationed at Leech Lake, in a report to his superior Roderic McKenzie, a partner of the Company (MHB 5:35–36), described Sandy Lake and the countryside around. The lake

> . . . empties itself into the Mississippi by a River four miles long, in the vicinity of which lakes and small rivers are numerous. . . .
> Beaver formerly abounded here, but is now very scarce, and dangerous to hunt; being in the neighborhood of the Sioux, the implacable enemy of the Sauteux. Deer abound on the frontiers, say about white fish lake [northwestern Crow Wing County] . . . thence downward the deer is a constant inhabitant of the banks of the Mississippi.

Hence again, the notion of finding fur and large game in "frontier" sectors dangerous to exploit is expressed.

The Henry-Tanner Data

1806–1808: Indications of "frontier" warfare and the risks that Indians were taking to hunt in contested areas were graphically portrayed by the fur trader, Alexander Henry, the younger, the nephew of the man cited previously whose name he bore. Henry had a post at the present town of Pembina, on Red River, in extreme northeastern North Dakota, where he traded with Chippewa from a number of locales to the east and the north. In a journal that he kept daily over the eight years he was at Pembina (1800–1808), edited and annotated by

Coues (1897), Henry recorded numerous battles and alarms experienced by the Chippewa in the area up the Red (south) toward Turtle, Goose, and more particularly, Sheyenne River, all in North Dakota, and Red Lake and other rivers on the Minnesota side (cf. Hickerson 1956). This region, along the middle courses of the Red, and to some extent, the open prairies to the west as far as the Turtle Mountains of northern North Dakota, was the western limit of the contested area, parts of it lying neutral and usually unoccupied, between the Wahpeton, Yanktonai, and Yankton Dakota on one side and Pillager and Red Lake Chippewa on the other.

Supplementing descriptions by Henry were those of the famed Indian captive, John Tanner (1840). Tanner was an interesting character. Captured as a young boy by Indians in Kentucky opposite Cincinnati, Ohio, in the 1780s, he was taken to the Detroit area, where he was adopted by an Ottawa family, to replace a youth who had been killed by the Whites. He later moved with them to the Red River country in about 1790. Tanner forgot English, and, to all intents and purposes, became an Indian, spending most of his life among the Ottawa and Chippewa. Tanner, who lived briefly at Sault Ste. Marie in the 1830s as official interpreter, where he only poorly relearned English, narrated the account of his life through an interpreter to a literary army surgeon, Edwin James, who published the account. Tanner, to whom I cannot possibly do justice in the brief compass of these pages, is an excellent source, not only on Indian-trader relations, but also on the ethnology of the Ottawa and Chippewa of Minnesota and Manitoba at the turn of the nineteenth century.

Henry wrote that in the early part of 1806, an Ottawa chief, Pishawbey, living in proximity to Chippewa in the Red River district, passed through Pembina "on his way to Otter Tail Lake" (Coues 1897 1:274). Three months later he returned from Pelican River, a small stream that enters the Otter Tail from the north near Fergus Falls, Otter Tail County, Minnesota. According to Henry, this Ottawa brought with him "300 beavers and 40 prime otters. They had seen Sioux repeatedly, but always avoided them" (Coues 1897 1:275). Tanner commented independently about the same hunt (1840 2:112–114):

> I went with a large party of Indians to some of the upper branches of the Red River [the Otter Tail River] to hunt beaver. I know not whether it was that we were emboldened by the promise of the prophet,[1] that we should be invisible to the Sioux, but we went much nearer than we had formerly ventured to their country. It was here, in a border region, where both they and ourselves had been afraid to hunt, that we now found beaver in the greatest abundance. . . .

Tanner recorded that the Chippewa built a fortified camp in the area. He himself took refuge in the camp when he found Dakota tracks near his own hunting camp.

In the fall of 1806, Henry built an outpost on Sandhill River in southern

---

[1] The Shawnee Prophet at that time was sending emissaries throughout the Northwest to rally Indians to his "nativistic" banner. Part of the message was that with the use of proper medicines the people would be impervious to the weapons of adversaries. Although the area occupied by Tanner's people was too remote from the center of the activities of the Prophet and his military brother, Tecumseh, to be greatly affected, some of the preachments took hold.

Polk County, just north of Wild Rice River, where "most of the Indians" established a winter camp. In the spring of 1807, 50 Dakota attacked the Chippewa hunting there, killing one Chippewa, and also one Canadian who was a trading post *engagé* (Coues 1897 1:422–423).

In the fall of 1807, a large Dakota party attacked the

> principle body of Saulteurs in camp at Grosse Isle, near Folle Avoine [Wild Rice] river, killed a leading chief, Tabashaw, and members of his family. The Chippewa fought off the Attack (Coues 1897 1:427).

According to Tanner, the Chippewa who fought this battle had recently arrived from Leech Lake to hunt at Wild Rice River (1840 2:120–123):

> . . . there was a very general movement among the Ojibbeways of the Red River toward the Sioux country; but the design was not, at least avowedly, to fall upon or molest the Sioux, but to hunt. . . . A part of this band stopped at the Wild Rice River, and went into the fort. . . . Here they began to hunt and trap, and were heedlessly dispersed about, when a large party of Sioux came into their neighborhood. . . .

Then Tanner recorded that two Chippewa were killed. The contested region east of Red River was not the only battleground. Henry recorded a battle (Coues 1897 1:427–428)

> fought by the Saulteurs of Leech and Red Lakes against 30 tents of Sioux, near Riviere de L'Aile du Corbeau, wherein 20 tents were destroyed; the Saulteurs lost but seven men, and brought away many of the enemy's horses.

The Chippewa party at the Crow Wing consisted of about 200 men, and must have represented almost all the available manpower of the two lakes. Tanner remarked (James 1940 2:123) that this battle was fought against 40 Dakota lodges at the "long prairie" [Long Prairie River in Todd County, Central Minnesota] in the contested zone.

The movement described by Tanner was apparently not successful. Henry, in the spring of 1808 (Coues 1897 1:428, 431), wrote of the Red River Indians as being

> . . . in such a state of consternation from the Sioux having fallen upon them that they have given over hunting this season, and are collecting about the houses [trading posts] to go northward out of danger. This affair had seriously injured my department; I shall lose two-thirds of the debts I gave out last fall. . . .

He then recorded that the Leech Lakers were attempting to organize a large war party to go against the Sioux in the fall to retaliate. Tanner did not mention this party going out, and Henry did not return to the region the next season, or ever after, so the outcome, if any, is not known. It is apparent from the preceding material that the Red River country and adjacent areas were rich in fur and other game, but not available to the Leech Lake and other Chippewa for safe hunting. So much can also be said for the Dakota who contested for that region.

The Debatable Zone: 1823–1831

1823: Major Stephen H. Long of the United States Topographical Engineers led a scientific and military expedition to explore the Minnesota River and the Red River of the North during the summer of 1823, and to establish the location of the boundary (49th parallel) between the United States and the "British Possessions." William H. Keating, a professor of natural science at the University of Pennsylvania and the geologist of the expedition, wrote the narrative of explorations and also described extensively the ethnography, hunting territories and the population of the Indians in the general region explored by the expedition (1825). When Long's expedition reached a point on Red River (Sioux River) about ten miles north of Lake Traverse (Bois des Sioux), the sources of Red River in Traverse County, Minnesota, they had reached, according to Keating, "the northernmost limit of the undisputed property of the Sioux on Red River." Keating wrote (1825 2:9):

> Beyond this they never hunt without being prepared for war, as the prairies between this place and the Wild Rice River to the east, and Turtle River to the west of Red River, form a sort of debatable land, which both Chippewas and Dacotas claim, and upon which both frequently hunt, but always in a state of preparation for hostilities.

Thus, again, a section of the country which formed the "debatable" zone is depicted in specific terms, a zone that hunters entered only when "prepared for war." Again, the implication is that the area was rich in game and it was for this reason that the hunters were willing to risk their necks. It is also evident that hunting of such areas could not be so intensive as to destroy the game. For one thing, women could not enter such areas to process and store meat; for this reason alone hunting could not be carried out on as orderly and systematic a basis as elsewhere, where conditions were secure.

1829–1831: I have recited a series of incidents involving Chippewa and Dakota, along a large extent of their frontier, as recorded by the agent, Taliaferro, who, at the time, was trying to use the Treaty of Prairie du Chien as an instrument to promote mutual respect of territory and peace. At that time, although nominally within Schoolcraft's agency at Sault Ste. Marie, Chippewa regularly visited Taliaferro's agency, which was much closer to their villages, to hold councils, including negotiations with various contingents of Dakota on war and peace. Here, then, is a brief summary of affairs, again merely a sample of transactions occurring over many years. (The remainder of this section is taken from volumes 5 and 6 of the Taliaferro journals [MHS mss.] and volume 6 of the Clark Papers [KHS-CP].) In May, 1829, Dakota who lived near the agency danced before the lodges of Chippewa encamped there, and the Chippewa and Dakota held a formal council in the agency house (Taliaferro MHS mss. 5:8–10),

> to form a *Truce* for *one year* to enable both Tribes to hunt immediately on their *Boundary* line above *Sauk River*. . . . After agreeing to hunt in peace the Chippeways finally left for their homes. . . .

These Chippewa were mainly from Sandy Lake. The truce was of short duration. Taliaferro wrote in his journal in June that the American Fur Company trader, William Aitkin, had offered ammunition to the Chippewa if they would send 100 men against the Wahpeton Dakota at Lac Qui Parle on the Minnesota River, an attack directed against a trading post there (it will be seen later that traders in the back country entertained vitriolic rivalries, but seldom made war on each other). On the same day, June 4, 1829, he noted that a Dakota chief had assembled 20 men to attack Sandy Lake Chippewa returning home from the agency along the east bank of the Mississippi.

In another entry, Taliaferro stated that the Dakota near his agency were starving. At the same time, however, they were trading with Chippewa from Mille Lacs Lake for birchbark canoes to help them in their wild rice gathering. Several days later a speech was made by a Dakota chief at the agency; it was recorded by Taliaferro as interpreted by his official interpreter (MHS mss. 5:16–17):

> We made peace with the Chippeway and gave them much of our Lands—but it appears that they are not satisfied with this but continue to trespass on our Lands which are bad enough & take everything clean from the Earth as they go. . . .
> We suffer much in consequence of this and we must blame you some for it—for if we had been left as we were—we could have hunted our game, & disposed of our Enemies—whenever they came in our way—but you caused us to be at peace and we are now in the Situation you see poor and badly off. . . .
> . . . we want to Know whether we are to occupy our Lands.

Taliaferro chided the Dakota, saying that they had not hunted those lands for years before he became agent, and that they should go to their hunting grounds on Sauk River and send the Chippewa away, or else they, the Chippewa, would never leave them. He then remarked that the Chippewa visiting the agency could not deplete the game, for they hunted only along the Mississippi itself, and that the Dakota had land enough if they would hunt it.

Less than a month later, in July, 1829, Taliaferro recorded that a Wahpeton had killed a member of a Chippewa war party from Leech Lake at the head of Crow River, and that many of the Dakota who had been hunting in the "upper Country above the Falls" [of St. Anthony] were returning "unexpectedly" to their villages on the Minnesota. At the same time Taliaferro recorded a battle between Pillagers of Leech Lake under their chief, Flat Mouth, and Yankton Dakota near Lake Traverse, a battle in which ten Dakota and six Chippewa were killed. An interesting feature of this material is that war resulted in withdrawal from the hunting grounds. Also, it is quite plain in the narratives of Taliaferro that warfare was, as he stated elsewhere, "partial" and not "national." It broke out here or there, but when it did, no matter where, it affected all alike.

There was more war in the fall of 1830. In a letter to Clark, Taliaferro wrote that Pillagers from Leech Lake had killed a Dakota youth 20 miles south of Crow River, and that the attack was in retaliation for an attack the Wahpeton Dakota from Lac Qui Parle had made on the Pillagers, since during that battle they killed the son of a chief, in the neighborhood of Otter Tail Lake. The Dakota in turn were determined to re-retaliate.

The difficulties in the western sectors of the Dakota-Chippewa front were recognized by Taliaferro as an outcome of the competition in territory and trade, as the following letter he wrote to Clark would indicate (KHS-CP 6:133):

> I must call your attention to the Post at *Leaf Lake* established for the Chippeways which is immediately on the Sioux line—the Chippeways are pushed by the traders to hunt on the line from Otter tail Lake down towards the Mississippi—which has caused the war with those more remote bands—the Sioux complain heavily and with just cause too that the Chippeways are often found hunting a days march or more upon their lands—& this Sir is one of the fruits of the Indian trade in the north.[2]

In late January, 1831, however, Taliaferro noted that Dakota and Chippewa had been hunting in proximity between the Crow and Sauk rivers, and peace was maintained along the 340-mile stretch of their frontier, from the Chippewa River of Wisconsin to Otter Tail Lake and Red River of western Minnesota. In late February, however, it is reported that some Dakota returning to the agency reported that a Leech Lake Chippewa had been killed by Dakota, at a location not given. Another round of warlike incidents followed, and so it went.

The relations of war and peace involved insoluble contradictions. When at peace, the *lands* were despoiled, when at war, the *people*. Although the causes for war were always expressed in terms of grievance and retaliation, one sees that the land could not, given the conditions of trade and technology of the time, support in comfort as many Chippewa and Dakota as were in the region. The agent was begging recognition of a fiction, a boundary, respect for which would have resulted in starvation, the abandonment of the country by large sections of its population, and the end of the trade (cf. Hickerson 1965b: 52–53).

The Schoolcraft-Allen Expedition

1832: In 1832 Schoolcraft led an expedition to discover the main source of the Mississippi, which turned out to be Lake Itasca, generally accepted as the main source today. The expedition, on its return, stopped at Leech Lake, descended Crow Wing River past its junction with the Leaf, and on to the Mississippi, where a council was held with Chippewa of Sandy Lake, and from there downstream to Fort Snelling, and beyond. Three accounts of the expedition and related matters are extant, one the official version by Schoolcraft, published by a commercial press in 1834 along with an account of his 1831 trip to Chippewa River, which I cited above; another was by Reverend Boutwell, who accompanied the explorers

---

[2] Dakota complaints of Chippewa encroachments had their counterpart in complaints lodged by the Chippewa to Schoolcraft, their agent, of Dakota encroachments (Schoolcraft 1834: 86, 115–116), always with reference to the Prairie du Chien treaty line. As the Dakota complained to Taliaferro that the fur traders, by pushing their posts close to the treaty line, were causing Chippewa to encroach (see also Taliaferro MHS mss. 7:June 25, 1832), so did the Chippewa of Leech Lake in 1832 complain to Schoolcraft that Dakota traders would "induce the Sioux to extend their hunting grounds across the boundary line." The concept of the boundary line itself was a crude one, except for Indian agents. I will comment further on the role of traders in warfare and other relations below.

to search out a good place for an American Board (Presbyterian) mission station, on file in the St. Louis County, Minnesota, Historical Society, with a copy in the Minnesota State Historical Society in St. Paul; and an official account was published by Lieutenant J. Allen (ASP-MA 5), who commanded a small military detachment assigned to the expedition. Allen was an astute observer who, like expedition predecessors and followers, commented lengthily on natural resources, topography, population, intertribal relations, trade, and other topics.

These remarks of Allen indicate the richness of game in the Crow Wing River country (ASP-MA 5:336):

> The Crow Wing river country, and that of all its tributaries—Prairie [Long Prairie], Shell, and Leaf rivers, and two or three little streams coming in from the east—is rich in furs and game, such as beaver, marten, rats, bears, &c., and deer; but much of it is not hunted, because of its border character to the Sioux territory.

Woven Yarn Bags: A traditional Chippewa craft originally employing buffalo hair wool, basswood fibers, and natural dyes, the yarn began to change in composition during contact in the seventeenth century. Wool from old trade blankets was used along with wool yarn produced in Europe and the colonial settlements. The craft has continued into the present as a tourist trade commodity, although the production is no longer very intensive. (Courtesy Buffalo Museum of Science and A. and S. Einhorn Collection)

Of the territory betweeen Long Lake, in Hubbard County, and Crow Wing River, he remarked (ASP-MA 5:335),

> The country passed through today has no other novelty than that of its total destitution of Indian habitations; being too near the borders of their respective territories to be used by either the Sioux or Chippewa, excepting as a route for their war parties and as an occasional hunting ground for some of the daring young men of the Leech Lake band. . . .

He mentioned that game, which was scarce in their own hunting grounds, that is, in the vicinity of Leech Lake itself, was abundant there, as I have shown, due to its not being hunted. It was there, Allen noted, that many Leech Lakers lost their lives, providing the basis for Chippewa complaints about the Dakota, it being "Chippewa country." He noted that members of his party (guides and interpreters from the region) were apprehensive when they reached the mouth of Leaf River that they would meet a Dakota war party.

Schoolcraft, who preceded Allen through the country by a day or so, noted "signs of temporary occupancy, in the standing camp-poles and meat racks which frequently met the eye in our descent" (1834: 243). This was north of the junction of the Leaf, as Schoolcraft indicated further on, the Leaf being the Prairie du Chien treaty line in that region, and one does not learn from Schoolcraft whether such encampments were visible elsewhere. No living Chippewa or Dakota were mentioned by Schoolcraft or the others along the entire extent of the Crow Wing until near its junction with the Mississippi.

Schoolcraft also described the Long Prairie River, which enters the Crow Wing from the south at Motley, Minnesota, as a Leech Lake war road against the Dakota, probably those with their villages on the middle reaches of the Minnesota River directly to the south (1834: 108, 111). Thus, the entire country from Long Lake to the Crow Wing-Mississippi junction, as well as Long Prairie River flowing in from the south, was a contested region, a no-man's land unsafe for occupancy of any kind, but occasionally exploited for game by Chippewa at the risk of life and limb; as in other instances of the kind, this country was described as being rich in game and valuable for trade and subsistence.

The Role of the Trading Companies

1836–1837: Accounts of events of 1836–1837 add another dimension to intertribal relations and Indian-trader relations, the latter of which has by now been recognized to have been of extreme importance. In this section one also gets a glimpse of the role, direct and indirect, played by the large trading companies, in Indian warfare and diplomacy. One sees how far-flung the ramifications of these forest-prairie relationships were; how each Indian ambuscade in Minnesota had its reverberation in the great fur sales of London, Leipzig (where there was a great annual sale and the furs of the east met the furs of the west), and even Moscow. First, after the abortive survey of the Prairie du Chien treaty line of 1835, cited above, the American Fur Company trader in charge of the entire northern Minnesota region (Fond du Lac Department), the aforementioned William Aitkin, petitioned the agent, Taliaferro, to issue a license to establish a trading post for the Chippewa at Otter Tail Lake, which was squarely on the Prairie du Chien boundary.[3] It was at Otter Tail that Major Bean, it is recalled, had decided to abandon his survey due to Indian hostility. Taliaferro refused to license the post (MHS mss. 10:July 19–21, 1836) on the grounds that

This position if taken up for such a purpose, would at once be the signal for continuing the war between the Sioux and Chippeways. . . .

Taliaferro ordered Aitkin to stop construction of the trading house already under way.

Apparently the chief American Fur Company trader among the Dakota of southern Minnesota, Henry Hastings Sibley, had opposed Aitkin's post at Otter Tail, for Aitkin complained in a letter to Ramsey Crooks (AFCP: Letter 2,049), President of the American Fur Company whose office was in New York:

The outfit from Otter Tail Lake was withdrawn from the place some time ago, but it is not exactly as Mr. Sibly says with the interference of his post of Lac Traverse it would have been a barrier to the Scious coming to war in the chippeway country and it is in that section of the country that a good part of our Indians go and make their hunts and another thing he is not correct for he has been trading with our Indians below and making advances [credits] but people are always right when their own interest is at issue. . . .

A letter from Crooks to his counterpart in a London firm exporting trade goods to the American Fur Company[4] reflecting news he had received from the back country posts, shows how the traders felt about the effect of war on trade (AFCP:Letter 2,226):

We have letters from the Fond du Lac country to the middle of October [1836], but it was then too early to form any thing like a correct opinion of what the fall hunts would produce. . . . The issue will of course depend upon the nature of the Winter, and the preservation of peace among the Indians—at one time last summer there was cause to apprehend hostilities between some important bands of Chippewas, and the Sioux of the Upper Mississippi, the effect of which would have produced so general an alarm, and insecurity in a considerable extent of valuable territory as much have diminished our next years returns materially—The differences between these wild peoples have however been fortunately allayed for at least the hunting season by common consent of the belligerents through the persevering exertions of our traders, and we hope to be able in the Spring to persuade both parties that peace is far preferable to war.

---

[3] Because no trading post could be legally established without a license issued by the Indian agent, agents' reports are a valuable source for the location of such posts in this and other areas.

[4] The American Fur Company, the largest business concern in the United States at that time, imported most of its woolen and metal wares, including weaponry, from British firms, and its trade beads from Venice; there was no great American manufacturing then.

The reference to there having been "cause to apprehend hostilities" may be interpreted as a reflection of Crooks' notification by Sibley of Aitkin's intention of building at Otter Tail!

The policy, as stated by Crooks, was one of peace to preserve tranquility in the best hunting territories, which, because of a long history of strife between Dakota and Chippewa, and consequently periods of nonuse, tended to lie along tribal frontiers. Crooks, however, expressed policies which would ensure returns from all the tribal regions; it mattered little to the home office whether it was a Dakota or Chippewa who hunted the fur. This was not the case with the back country traders, in whose interest it was that "their people" would exploit the largest possible territory. The argument between Aitkin and Sibley developed out of their long-standing rivalry over fur returns.

One cannot, then, look upon the Indian conflicts as a development of indigenous systems of exploitation. It was in the interest of traders, themselves competing to push their outposts as far as possible into the frontier sectors, especially as it was in those areas that fur was most abundant. This had been as true in the time of Duluth in the seventeenth century and of the elder Alexander Henry in the eighteenth as among the traders of the American Fur Company in the nineteenth century. The American Fur Company, which held a virtual monopoly over the trade of the entire West, attempted to mediate differences among their traders in the field, as the traders did among the Indians. It would seem evident, then, that much of the competition between Chippewa and Dakota developed out of the necessity to over-exploit, for the demands of the trade were exorbitant, the appetite of the traders and the Company insatiable. This was heightened during the 1830s as land cession treaties were made, reflecting the advance of the Euro-American frontier. As that frontier moved westward, fur trapping lost its primary importance (land speculation was its first major replacement), and it was in the interest of the barons and the agents of trade to seize as much fur as the traffic could bear for immediate sale in the great commercial fairs of Europe, such as the famed Leipzig Fair, or for storage. Rampant spoliation meant immediate enrichment of major traders and Company, but exhaustive impoverishment for the Indians and the minor figures of trade, the canoemen and interpreters, most of them halfbreeds, or Métis, who depended on a continuing trade for their meager livelihood.

Later I will show, however, that other causes underlay intertribal rivalry—indeed, it was conceivable that differences among the tribal villages and trapping bands across frontiers respecting fur areas could have been and were often resolved for a season or a year, but that warfare in general was not. One must keep in mind, with respect to this, that competition among villages within tribal groups, that is, among Chippewa on one hand, and among Dakota on the other, was minimal, even though the villages were independent. In other words, they did not compete among themselves for the fur game areas, but were able through tacit respect for each other's trapping areas, to remain at peace.

A Nineteenth-Century Chippewa: Okee-Makee-Quid, a Chippewa chief c. 1825, painted in full regalia by Charles Bird King and published in History of the Indian Tribes of North America, 1848, *by Thomas L. McKenney and James Hall. Note the European cut of his clothing uniquely blended with typically Indian accoutrements, such as beaded legbands, animal head (wolf) breast plate or sash, ballhead war club, and peace pipe. The animal head sash shown in this print has been matched with an identical specimen acquired among the Chippewa during the nineteenth century and presently in the collections of the United States National Museum, Washington, D.C. (Courtesy United States National Museum)*

Late History: The 1840s

Conditions of war, subsistence, and trade generally worsened in the western part of our area through the 1840s. Indeed, starting in the late 1830s, Pillager Chippewa from Leech Lake brought Otter Tail Lake on the frontier more and more under their control. This was one of the minor advances on the part of the Chippewa over the 70-year period mentioned in Chapter 5. By 1847 the Pillagers, according to Schoolcraft (1851–1857 1:468), had a permanent village at Otter Tail Lake. This was confirmed in a report by the Superintendent of Indian Affairs in Minnesota Territory, Alexander Ramsey, who wrote of the Pillagers in 1850 (Winchell 1911: 647):

> Within a few years past, a fragment of the band have moved gradually to the western outskirts of their country, and established themselves at Ottertail Lake. They hunt altogether on Sioux land, as recognized by the lines established by the treaty of Prairie du Chien in 1825.

By "Sioux land," then, Ramsey was referring to the time-honored treaty. But general conditions in the area had not changed, as is learned, from the reports of two scientific-military expedition leaders, David Dale Owen and Major Samuel Wood, both of whom were in the Otter Tail Lake country.

1848–1849: Owen in 1848 ascended the Crow Wing and Leaf rivers, arriving then by portages at Otter Tail Lake, and descended Otter Tail River (which he, according to the fashion of the time, termed Red River) to the true Red River, thence down Red River to Pembina (1852: xxv). Wood, in 1849, took a more southerly route, from Sauk Rapids to Otter Tail River, passing to the south of Otter Tail Lake, thence to Pembina overland (CDS 577:10, 14). Both these expeditions, then, passed through areas traditionally contested.

Owen remarked, upon arriving at the mouth of Otter Tail Lake, that a guide he had hired at Crow Island [mouth of Crow Wing River] deserted him because he feared entering the Chippewa-Dakota war zone. The expedition met a small party of Pillagers on the "upper watters of Red River [Otter Tail River] in search of fish . . . who sought to deter us from proceeding, by accounts of war-parties of Sioux roaming about lower down the stream. . . ." Actually, Owen met no more Indians all the way to Red River and down that stream to Pembina (1852: xxvii–xxviii).

At Elbow Lake in northcentral Grant County, about halfway between Otter Tail Lake and Lake Traverse, Wood's expedition of 1849 met 25 Pillagers from Otter Tail Lake on a war party, although *they* stated they were a hunting group. According to Wood, they were seeking out the Dakota to avenge the slaying of a Chippewa woman. Wood commented that the Chippewa at Otter Tail Lake had an abundance of game, fish, wild rice, wild potatoes, and that they made maple sugar (CDS 577:14, 23).

Hence, even though Chippewa had solidified their hold on Otter Tail Lake, the area of alarm and war had not substantially changed. Land cession treaties in the mid-1850s made by Dakota and Chippewa involving almost the entire western

Minnesota area, those peoples by then in severely straitened circumstances, dropped the curtain on the drama of war. The new era, ushered in by the expanding Euro-American frontier, brought a whole range of new difficulties, but these fit more the modern scene and are therefore out of the compass of this present study. Schoolcraft wrote in 1855 (1851–1857 5:187) that the "last considerable fight" between Chippewa and Dakota occurred in the winter of 1847. Fifty Dakota attacked 26 Pillagers who were hunting bison on the prairie west of Red River. One man on each side was killed, and several wounded. In 1849, however, six Pillagers, evidently from Leech Lake, joined 80 Chippewa from Red Lake in an attack upon Dakota, but the location is not given (Schoolcraft 1851–1857 5:187). That was it.

Warfare, Boundaries, and Biome

I have given a general idea of the extent of the debatable zone on Map 4. I show how the Prairie du Chien treaty line bisected this zone from its southeastern to its northwestern terminus. I have shown in the foregoing that the zone, with its favorable vegetation and topography, was rich in game; so much so that Menomini Indians from eastern Wisconsin at various times came into it to hunt and trap, and even Dakota and Chippewa, mortal enemies, made as much use of the area as they could. Menomini acted as a kind of buffer between the combatants, and, indeed, in the next chapter I show, through the employment of a new set of data, how the area itself was a "buffer zone," not only a contested sector, but a preserve for game of certain kinds.

Ethnohistorical sources have given a very general picture. I continue to use such sources for the following, but turn also, as I have said, to the natural historians for further enlightenment. As a last word for this chapter, it is now evident that the Chippewa and Dakota were not "natural" enemies. As mentioned in Chapter 3, they were at one time friends and allies.

8

Biome and Warfare: Discussion Concluded

Chippewa and Dakota Subsistence

ALTHOUGH THE CHIPPEWA AND DAKOTA RELIED on many kinds of food in different seasons, game animals always played a critical role. Eastern Dakota also farmed maize at their villages, and Chippewa placed great reliance on wild rice, for which they had developed a specialized technology, but, unlike agriculturalists to the south and east, and in some of the western river valleys, neither Chippewa nor Dakota harvested enough of either crop to be able to store a substantial surplus for consumption over more than the few months of fall and early winter. Indeed, for the Chippewa, the wild rice crop was only successful about one year in three, damage frequently resulting from flood, wind, drought, or hail. The Chippewa did a considerable amount of fishing, especially in summer and early fall, the Dakota less so; but fish, important as it was in the diet of many lake and riverine peoples, was at best a seasonal staple. Also, once the fur trade became important, those Chippewa who did not actually live on the Great Lakes where the most abundant and reliable fisheries were, were in their trapping grounds by the time the great November whitefish runs took place [see Hickerson 1965a: 13–14, where Boutwell (MHS mss:396–397) is quoted].

The relative importance of fishing in the interior Minnesota economy was indicated in an exchange between the Leech Lake chief, Flat Mouth, and the Commissioner of Indian Affairs, Thomas A. Manypenny, with whom the Chippewa were negotiating a treaty (NA 1855: 137). It was the custom at such cession treaties to clear up old "debts" owed by the Indians to traders who petitioned for recovery through regular channels. These were invariably discussed with the treaty makers, because such payments, which at times were in the thousands of dollars, were subtracted in effect from the monies paid for the lands. The Commissioner asked Flat Mouth if a certain George Bondee were entitled to the recovery of 500 dollars (brackets in text):

> Flat Mouth. If any man is entitled to money from the Indians, this man is. He is poor, and has always been the friend of the Indians. If he was not, how would his house smell so fishy? [The interpreter explained that this meant, that he was so poor, he was compelled to rely upon fish for support.]

The ethnohistorian finds such raw statements illuminating in assessing the relative value of different kinds of subsistence. Maple sugar, berries and various but limited amounts of wild plants made up part of the diet, as did fur game animals, including beaver and muskrat (the latter sold, by the way, in certain fashionable nineteenth century hostelries in Milwaukee and Chicago as "marsh rabbit"), but these were not major items, except for very brief periods when other food was not available. As has been indicated so often in the above, the most important food was large wild game.

There were many varieties of the larger animals in the Wisconsin-Minnesota area during the period I am discussing, animals including bear, moose, the woodland variety of caribou, elk (wapiti), and the white-tailed, or Virginia deer. The bear was never common enough or accessible enough to be more than an occasional source of food; in fact, the bear was considered more in the class of fur game. Moose and caribou, never abundant in Wisconsin, and only relatively so in Minnesota, were confined to the northern heavily forested parts of those states, and chiefly in low-lying areas where conifers provided cover. The woodland caribou, unlike his tundra cousin, but like the moose, tends to be a solitary critter, and also, like moose, is not usually susceptible to intensive group hunting of the kind that would provide a steady supply of meat at given seasons (Schorger 1956: 2–3; Dahlberg and Guettinger 1956: 27). Also, the range of the moose and caribou was in general far to the north of the trapping grounds and villages of the Chippewa who confronted the Dakota, and completely out of the area where Dakota could go.

The bison, of course, as noted in several citations, was hunted by Dakota, who continued to find herds on the prairies south and west of their villages until about the early 1830s, when they became extinct in Wisconsin and Minnesota (Hornaday 1887: map p. 485); bison were also occasionally hunted by Chippewa who in going to prairie areas far to the south and west of their villages, were risking their lives. But the bison were erratic in their migration paths and general distribution, and, unless thickly clustered where they could be driven and surrounded by large numbers of hunters, they were extremely difficult to hunt on foot. Even when bison were still occasionally in the area of the Mdewakanton and other Dakota, that is, before the 1830s, there are numerous references in Taliaferro's journals to Indians going hungry. Except for a few limited areas in the great river valleys and draws of the high plains far to the west, bison became staple food only for peoples who wholeheartedly adopted the horse; even for them the hunts, especially in winter, were not always successful. So, although bison during the early part of the 70-year period did provide some food, especially for Dakota, and much less for Chippewa, reliance could not be placed on there being an adequate supply at any given time.[1]

This leaves elk and Virginia deer, both of which were mentioned frequently in the early literature, as I have already shown. It is very difficult to discover, through a search of early sources, the relative importance of elk in the subsistence of Chippewa and Dakota. Elk are grazing animals and occupied the same general habitat as the prairie bison, that is, the open grasslands of the prairies and high plains. The biologist A. W. Schorger, who did extensive historical research, including the study of seventeenth century authors like Radisson and the Jesuits, as well as more recent, but still historical, county-by-county surveys (1954: 5, 7), on the distribution of elk in Wisconsin, shows the animal to have occupied, in great numbers, only the southern and extreme western parts of the state, precisely the prairie and oak-opening areas. The greatest incidence of elk reported by travelers in Wisconsin and mapped by Schorger (1954: 9) were in the western counties along the lower Wisconsin, Chippewa, and St. Croix river valleys. These were of course exactly the sectors contested by the Chippewa and Dakota. No elk were recorded in the woodland region of northern Wisconsin.

It is assumed that the conditions of elk distribution in Minnesota were relatively the same. The elk was an inhabitant of the prairie and open areas of the transition forest lying between Chippewa and Dakota village and hunting areas. It is known from Pike's accounts, for example (Coues 1895 1), that elk were in herds in the region along the Mississippi contested by Chippewa and Dakota. He and the Menomini who visited his blockhouse in that area hunted elk. One of the more important eastern tributaries of the Mississippi in that region, in Sherburne County, and so called in Pike's time, is Elk River.

Schorger states (1954: 7) that the elk, a "large, unwary animal, was extirpated quite early on the prairies." Chances are that elk, where they could be hunted in safety by Indians and traders with firearms, were hunted out early, surviving in scattered droves only in regions unsafe to hunt. This fits a picture in which elk are not often mentioned as a primary source of food.

My guess is, based on the frequency of mention in the literature, hence weight of testimony, that Virginia deer were much more important as game animals to both Dakota and Chippewa. I have already shown in the numerous references to the distribution of deer above, deer hunting, and even fighting over deer, as in the incident narrated by Perrault for 1788–1789, p. 84 above. Taliaferro, throughout his journal, mentions the importance of deer, usually in terms of their lack causing hunger and distress. I will study one or two of these statements later. In comments by Monk, Schoolcraft and others, it is mentioned that deer were a focus of attention for hunters. The journals of Curot, Connor and Malhiot, cited

---

[1] This is quite clear in a statement made by a Minnesota River Mdewakanton chief to Taliaferro asking that traders not be withdrawn from their country during an "uprising" by neighboring Winnebago in 1827 (Taliaferro MHS mss. 4:August 29, 1827): "My Father You know that the Medawarkantongs cannot be without the Traders if they are stopped we must Starve to death—the Sioux of the plains say they can jump on their horses & with their bows and arrows can kill what they want and do not want your assistance. We my Father cannot do this."

above, contain numerous references to bands of hunters going toward, or already in, frontier regions to hunt deer for food to support themselves and the traders during the winter's trapping. For example, Connor, who was in the St. Croix River region in 1804–1805 (Gates 1933: 258–259), mentioned that the Chippewa with whom he was trading could find no deer, "which determines [them] to go a considerable distance in search of Beaver," that is, they could not live on beaver without deer.

As early as 1798, David Thompson, on several occasions, described the Chippewa who lived in northern Minnesota and Wisconsin as being in great distress because they had no access to deer (Tyrrell 1916: 281, 286, 297–298). Of the Chippewa living in a village at the west end of Lake Superior:

> The Natives that trade at this House are about thirty Men of family, and are about 210 souls. In Winter, from the poverty of the country they can barely live, and a small stock of [maple] sugar is part of their support. Deer are almost unknown and they are supplied with leather, as with other necessaries [by the traders].[2]

There are other statements to indicate reliance on deer, or suffering from a lack of deer. Thomas G. Anderson, a British trader among the Dakota on Minnesota River, gave good indication in 1812 of the reliance of the Mdewakanton on the Virginia deer (WHC 9:91). During the summer of that year Anderson accompanied a band of Dakota hunters up the Mississippi above the Falls of St. Anthony. The first day out they hunted on the west side and encamped at Crow River. On succeeding days they hunted on both banks, staying within gunshot sound of the river. When they approached the "borders of their Chippewa enemies"—and Anderson does not say exactly where this was—they had frequent alarms. They formed a war party which ascended the river farther, but not meeting any Chippewa, they returned south of the Falls. The whole expedition, including the war party, took about a month. It is not stated how many deer were taken, but it is assumed a good supply of meat was consumed or put in storage.

Two quotes from the early 1830s by Schoolcraft and a trader, William Johnston, are of interest. The first (Schoolcraft 1834: 268–269) has already been cited on p. 89, the one referring to Chippewa hunting camps on the Chippewa River, "attributed to the abundance of Virginia deer in that vicinity. . . ." Johnston, an independent trader in "opposition" to the American Fur Company at Leech Lake in 1833–1834, in one of a series of letters written to his sister-in-law, who was also Schoolcraft's wife, described Sandy Lake, a major Chippewa village (MPHC 37:173–174):

> Sandy Lake is considered as the central trading post, of the Fond du Lac department, from which clerks separate for the Upper and lower Mississippi; and occupied by the principle trader. It is only for the above cause that it is occupied, and the clerks having always to rendezvous at this place before proceeding to

---

[2] This was in the days before the traders supplied foods to the Indians, except meat, wild rice, corn and other foods they had traded from the Indians in the first place. In those days traders were chiefly dependent upon the Indians for their own food supply, although they did grow vegetables and did some fishing near the post.

[Leech] Lake. As for the Indian population, which was numerous, they say; formerly; it has lately dwindled away to only a few lodges; which was caused by the encrease of the red [Virginia] Deer, at places south of this.

As early as 1820, Schoolcraft had written of the Chippewa of Sandy Lake (Williams 1953: 152):

They have neither the deer, buffaloe, or elk. In the fall they gather large quantities of the wild rice, which is the only bread stuff of the region. No corn is ever raised. . . .

And it will be remembered that the trader, Monk, had said in 1807 that deer were to be found only toward the frontiers to the southwest of Sandy Lake.

The importance of deer to both Chippewa and Dakota is indicated by the large communal parties organized to hunt them. Those of Little Crow and other Dakota described by Perrault and Anderson have their counterparts in references to deer hunting bands among the Chippewa. From Curot, who was on an upper branch of the St. Croix in 1803–1804, three brief references, selected from several, referring to communal deer hunting are given (WHC 20:436–437, 442, 448). In January, 1804:

This Morning all the savages left to be gone on a deer Hunt for several days.

On February 14:

The Two Bands have United to go and make sugar together, and also for the Spring hunt.

On March 2:

Mr. Sayer's Men arrived after Dinner today with 20 pieces of dried meat, the remains of 41 Deer that the savages of the river au serpent had killed.

At Leech Lake in 1833 the missionary, Boutwell, reported in December (MHS mss:December 2, 1833 [Mr. D. refers to the American Fur Company trader, William Davenport]):

Mr D's men inform us that the band of Chippewas, 24 lodges, whom they found together, were about to visit a Sioux encampment, one day's march from the [hunting grounds to the west of Leech Lake], for the purpose of smoking and making a truce. . . . They tell us that there was a light fall of snow when they reached the lodges, which is almost indespensable in killing deer, 36 of these beautiful animals were brought into us as the fruit of one days chase.

Earlier, in October, William Johnston had mentioned that the Indians were anticipating the hunting of the red deer. Then, in reference to an old war chief, Great Cloud, he stated (MPHC 37:190; emphasis mine) "his age and inclination would not allow him . . . of going out with the *Band* to hunt the Deer."

I believe the material presented is sufficient to indicate the overriding importance of deer to the subsistence of Dakota and Chippewa, but I am not saying, of course, as I have indeed emphasized, that a sufficiency of deer would have meant a rich subsistence. A deer gives very little besides its meat and skin. On the contrary, Virginia deer and other food, both plant and animal, but mainly deer, supported an economy based on a variety of production, the most important in terms of survival being the fur trade and trapping, introduced by Europeans. Without deer, however, subsistence would have been impossible in the long run. It is evident that competition over trapping areas was a significant feature of frontier relations among various Dakota and Chippewa. What I am saying, in effect, is that the shape of the neutral, or buffer, zone was determined more by competition over deer, and to some extent perhaps, although it is not known how much, over elk as well.

In general, as mentioned before, the Chippewa villages were located in woodland strongholds, especially on lakes and streams in the coniferous cover of northern Wisconsin and Minnesota, while the Dakota villages were in open prairie country in major river valleys in southern Minnesota. Between these lay open or partially open areas where game was abundant and where hunters from both sides were normally loathe to go, except in large parties that could not remain for long for fear of attack. Certain early authors, as has been seen, attributed the abundancy of game in these neutral areas to the lack of hunting because of war. But some hunting *was* carried on, not only by bands of Dakota and Chippewa, but also at various times by Menomini who held a position of neutrality between them, and were given permission to exploit the contested sectors by the belligerents. Menomini exploitation, although involving some hunting, and even the harvesting of maple sugar, was chiefly trapping for the fur trade—they were always in direct association with a trading post established for the purpose of dealing with them alone! The assumption here is that Dakota and Chippewa did not care especially that Menomini *trapped* these contested areas, that is, took fur game, since they did not have access to it themselves. There is also abundant reason to infer that even with the state of war, which so often characterized the frontier, enough fur game was available until almost the end of the period being discussed, even with heavy exploitation, to afford Dakota and Chippewa access to the introduced technology—guns, hatchets, knives, cloth, awls, mirrors—passed in the trade. True, at times, rich proceeds came from trapping in "border" areas (for fur game could also accumulate in relatively unused sectors), and traders, as I have shown, were prone to urge those trapping for their posts to go into these areas. But fur game existed throughout the wooded and prairie areas—beaver, otter, and muskrat on streams in wood and prairie, and marten, always important, in the pine itself. Muskrat in particular inhabited low-lying areas in the prairie, and beaver were to be found in the smaller stream valleys where there were ample aspen and willow for their food.

Let me, then, at this point, suggest: 1) fur game was available to Dakota and Chippewa in areas safe for trapping, although never in as great supply as they or the traders would have wished; 2) large game, although present in many varieties, was either scarce through habit, as moose and caribou, through vulnerability, as bison and elk, or through the demands of habitat, as in the case of the Virginia deer. With respect to the last, I ask the question: were the contested sectors rich in game because they were not hunted, or were they not hunted because they were rich in game? The answer to this gives significant clues into the dynamics of intertribal relations.

The Virginia Deer: Habit and Habitat

First let me turn once again to the biologists to see what they say about the habits and the habitat of the Virginia deer. There is at hand a greater amount of data for Wisconsin than for Minnesota, but it can be readily seen, supplemented by selected sources, how the Wisconsin material applies also to Minnesota.

The deer is a creature of open forests, where there is a lot of "edge" and brush providing a great amount of browse. The deer is not a grazer, and therefore shuns open grasslands where there is no cover. Also, the deer avoids mature forests where there is little understory due to the heavy high canopy. The deer is not a resident of monotypic forests, that is, forests consisting of a single species, and hence without a variety of browse.

One habit of deer in northern areas, resulting from their need for cover and food during the coldest months, is "yarding." Wisconsin biologists (Swift 1946: 8, 57; also Dahlberg and Guettinger 1956: 57–58) have estimated that the winter range of a deer herd is approximately 10 percent of the summer range, and also that deer tend to return to the same yards winter after winter. The main yarding months are December–January to March–April, depending on latitude, and the favorite type of winter cover is white cedar among other of the smaller conifers growing in low-lying swampy areas. Then in summer the deer spread out. An effect of yarding, of course, is the deer's vulnerability to wolves and other predators, especially men. Also, returning to the same yards, their trails become known, and hunters can station themselves at the appropriate places to kill in large numbers (Stenlund 1956: 34; Christensen 1959: 232–233; Dahlberg and Guettinger 1956: 56, 62). According to Wisconsin biologists, Dahlberg and Guettinger (1956: 145–146):

> The principal characteristic of a yarding area is its topographic location and cover; lowland or swamp areas are particularly favored, especially if the cover is coniferous. These areas provide shelter from winter winds and to some extent they limit snow depth, depending on the character of the cover present. Adequate food supplies may or may not be present. Deer tend to choose areas where the requirements of cover are most adequately met regardless of the status of food supplies.

Hence, in the northern areas where Indians could hunt undisturbed, the deer population could be swiftly reduced. That this occurred in Wisconsin and Minnesota in the heavily wooded areas is amply demonstrated in many of the citations I presented above. In the contested areas this would have been more difficult, because not only did the deer not yard as much, but killing, processing and transporting the carcasses in areas well known would have been hazardous.

But aside from the greater vulnerability of deer to hunters in northern forested areas, their incidence in those areas was not great to begin with. First, it may be assumed that past distribution may be inferred from knowledge of the habits of the animals in combination with a knowledge of the original vegetal cover. In the words of Dahlberg and Guettinger (1956: 13–14):

> The biologist can reconstruct with a fair degree of accuracy the original distribution of game based on a knowledge of habitat requirements and an account of the original vegetation for certain areas.

Then:

> The original distribution and density of the white-tailed deer . . . in Wisconsin was likewise related directly to its original habitat. The extensive virgin forest that covered the major portion of the state was composed for the most part of big timber. The forest floor under these tall trees was relatively bare of vegetation because the heavy canopy of leaves prevented much sunlight from reaching the ground. Thus northern habitat was considerably smaller than it is today, being limited to the edges of swamps, marshes and scattered areas where natural catastrophes such as wind or fire had opened up the forest.
> Original deer numbers cannot be estimated except in relative degrees of density based on present-day knowledge of maximum and minimum density for similar habitat.

> The general dividing line between the northern deer range in the hardwood-evergreen forest and the southern deer range in the oak-maple forest interspersed with prairie openings is based on the distribution of native vegetation determined by the Wisconsin Geological and Natural History Survey. . . .

The Minnesota biologist M. H. Stenlund, who made a study of the distribution and habits of the timber wolf in Superior National Forest, in the Arrowhead district of northeastern Minnesota north of Lake Superior (1955: 41), notes:

> Deer populations are low in the uncut wilderness area of the Border Study Area despite the facts that they are not hunted and wolf populations are lower than in neighboring cutover areas. . . . Rocks, jack pine, and mature hardwoods which make up the habitat in these wilderness areas are not conducive to large deer production.

With specific reference to Wisconsin, Swift (1946: 8) writes:

> Southern Wisconsin had a tremendous amount of "edge;" therefore, conditions were highly ideal for deer.
> In the north, vast areas with little or no marsh or forested swamps and with a mature stand of pine, hemlock, and northern hardwoods, were not conducive to sustaining many deer. Other areas, broken up with forest swamp, open marsh, lakes which produced "edge," or creeks and small rivers which encourage deer food such as dogwood and mountain maple along their borders, carried greater populations. These factors of cover type are, therefore, basic in sustaining a deer population.

Again, with respect to the northern forest (1946: 17):

The territory covered with solid stands of mature timber was tremendously large and, except along creek bottoms and in cedar swamps or blowdowns, there was little for a deer to eat.

Further, "Deer are not a creature of the virgin forests" (1946: 23).

Dahlberg and Guettinger present a map of Wisconsin (1956: 15) in which they divide the state into three parts, in conformation with what they conceive deer distribution to have been before 1800. However, their map would hold as well for the period up to the 1840s, when logging began to change the face of the countryside and interfered with old density ratios. They write (1956: 15–16):

> The eastern portion of the northern area contained more favorable habitat for deer than the western portion of the north. A considerably higher acreage of swamp type interspersed with ridges of timber provided a greater area of "edge" that was suitable habitat for deer. However, this northeastern area was far less desirable range than the southern area. A probable density of 10 to 15 deer per square mile is indicated.
>
> The northwestern portion of the state probably had the fewest deer per square mile. A minimum of "edge" in the original habitat leads us to conclude that here the density of deer was probably less than 10 per square mile.
>
> The southern portion of the state with its prairie openings and hardwood islands provided deer with adequate habitat. The edge of the prairie openings provided a suitable environment for low-growing woody vegetation. The hardwood islands provided both cover and food. Oak ridges produced mast for fall fattening and winter food. Sizeable deer populations existed.

The Prairie du Chien treaty line bisects the most favorable deer areas, leaving about as much of it in Wisconsin to the Dakota as to the Chippewa.

These statements indicate relatively high deer density in the contested area in contrast to low deer densities in areas safe for occupancy, not only because of warfare in the contested zone, but also because of habitat requirements. The question I posed at the end of Section I: were the contested sectors rich in game because they were not hunted, or were they not hunted because they were rich in game?— seems to be at least partially answered. This, although important, is not the whole story, as is seen in the remaining paragraphs of this chapter.

There are corroboratory statements from other game biologists of Wisconsin and Minnesota, some of which I give because they provide varying perspectives on the problem. E. M. Christensen (1959: 231) wrote that, "Historical records indicate that large areas in Northern Wisconsin were essentially monotypes of vegetation. . . ," hence poor deer habitat. Schorger, in his detailed study of the history of the distribution of Virginia deer in Wisconsin (1953: 216ff.), points to statements by David Thompson, Schoolcraft, and Lieutenant Allen among others I have cited above on the scarcity of deer in the Lake Superior region and its relative abundance elsewhere. In his county-by-county survey, although it relates chiefly to deer distribution in the 1880s after extensive logging, it is clear that deer were plentiful in the western counties and scarce in the northern counties like Vilas (1953: 241) where the Chippewa had a heavy village population. Schorger cites the trader, Malhiot (1953: 199–200) who had his post at Lac du Flambeau high up on a branch of Chippewa River in Vilas County in 1804–1805:

On October 5 he recorded that he had traded for 528 deer skins. It is impossible to determine how many of them represented deer taken in the immediate vicinity. Allen stated in 1832 that the Indians of this lake, in fall and winter, kill large numbers of deer which are very plentiful along the Chippewa River. This stream lies about 40 miles west of Lac du Flambeau. It is possible that the Indians, to obtain deer in quantity, descended the Flambeau River to its junction with the Chippewa in extreme southern Rusk County.

Rusk County is far downstream and begins to verge on the Dakota-Chippewa frontier, although it is still within the wooded area. From Schoolcraft's descriptions for 1831 that I have cited above, however, it is known that Flambeau Chippewa were descending the Chippewa farther than that for their hunts. Although Malhiot himself did not state *where* the Chippewa were hunting deer (WHC 19:225 and *passim*), it is significant that a biologist of the eminence of Schorger should have assumed it was at a great distance south of their village and trading post. It has been clearly seen from sources I have cited that the lower Chippewa River had a great deal of hunting activity; in fact, it was often described as the best hunting region in that part of the upper Mississippi valley (cf. Schorger 1954); it also was a major theater of war and a contested zone.

Let me turn now briefly to statements by Minnesota biologists, again giving corroboration to the findings of their Wisconsin colleagues. Stenlund, writing on wolf-deer relations in northeastern Minnesota (1955: 16–17), attributes the frequency of deer in once heavily timbered areas to logging that occurred, of course, long after Chippewa and Dakota had been confined to reservations, hence long after their wars. Of one region in St. Louis and Lake counties:

It is especially significant to note that concentration of wolf activities and deer populations occur concurrently in the cutover area. This area comprises some ten townships and lies north and northeast of Ely to the Canadian Border. The area was logged in the early days (1896–1920) and the resultant second growth timber supports a deer population which is considerably larger than that found in the uncut areas lying to the west and east. Since jack pine, balsam, and spruce were not taken to any extent in early logging days, this area was not clear cut and still supports a good coniferous stand of trees. Only choice red and white pine were removed. Cedar, alder, spruce, and tamarack swamps remained untouched as did some virgin stands of aspen and birch.

The two uncut areas to the east and west of the cutover area were not logged during the heyday of Paul Bunyan's ax for a variety of reasons. These areas are rockier and the topography is rougher making for more difficult logging. There was less red and white pine and more jack pine. Finally, the Superior National Forest established in 1909 in the midst of the falling timber, included these two uncut areas where the accompanying cutting regulations prevented the former large-scale operations.

Travelers in these uncut regions during both winter and summer often remark as to the scarcity of game life of any kind.

Again,

It is evident that although populations of both deer and wolves exist in the virgin areas, they are both found in greater numbers in the cutover area north

of Ely because of more abundant deer browse plant species on the logged and
burned over lands.

It is assumed that deer (and their predators) were scarce, then, not only
in Superior National Forest, but elsewhere in the virgin timber, especially the
great white and Norway pine forests which covered most of northern Minnesota
during pre-logging times.

That logging had a profound effect on changing game ratios, especially
deer, is indicated in another statement, by biologists A. B. Erickson and D. W.
Burcalow (1954: 8), who studied game conditions in St. Croix Park, in the
vicinity of Kettle River in Pine County, Minnesota, an area in which Chippewa
of the upper St. Croix River region did considerable trapping in early days:

> Lumberjacks began the work of turning the future St. Croix Park area into deer
> country about 1870. Constantly recurring fires, the great Hinckley fire of 1894
> among them, continued their work in maintaining the brushy cover in which
> deer thrive.

Here, then, it is explicitly stated that deer did not occupy the St. Croix-Kettle
River region under the tall timber that existed there before the 1870s.

Finally, there is a general statement for Minnesota as a whole, which confirms what I have been concluding on the basis of studies of particular areas.
According to the naturalist, G. Fredine (1940: 41):

> The white-tailed deer was originally restricted in range to the hardwood forests
> and prairie lands of the southern portion of the state. . . . Up to about the
> year 1860 deer were not common in the coniferous forests of the north central
> and northeastern portions of Minnesota. Under the big timber that existed in this
> area, there was very little undergrowth to serve as food and cover for deer.

In both Wisconsin and Minnesota, then, the deer's best habitat was exactly
the transition forest area where the prairie met the woodland, where there was
brush browse and forest edge in plenty. This area was in turn precisely the neutral
zone contested by Dakota and Chippewa over the 70 years during which they
confronted each other without being disturbed by Euro-American settlement, that
is, before logging, mining, and farming changed the face of the country. Although
deer were also potentially present in smaller numbers in prairie and virgin forest,
lack of cover in the former and the need to yard during the winter in the latter
resulted in their depletion. Indians who relied on deer as their primary source
of animal food were forced to find and hunt them in the only area in which they
were able to survive, the transition area. As I have written elsewhere (1965b: 62):

> Warfare was a function of competition over game and was waged chiefly in the
> areas where prime game was most abundant. Throughout the period of the
> existence of such contested, or buffer, areas . . . the Virginia deer, of all game
> animals the most important for the Chippewa and Sioux, because of its habitat
> requirements and its habit of yarding in the winter was scarce in regions open
> to undisturbed hunting. The effect of warfare, then, was the regulation and
> preservation of a supply of deer in and near the buffer zone for the use of Indians

hunting in bands, often at great risk of their lives. Such warfare, except in the one local region in which the Indian agency was a disturbing factor in the regulation of Indian relations, was chronic, and even during times of temporary truce was endemic.

The contested areas took their character and shape from the distribution and habits of the Virginia deer. Subtract any species besides the deer, including even the beaver, from such areas, and the war zone—warfare itself—would hardly have been altered. Subtract the deer, leaving the other fauna, and the configuration would have been entirely different.

Remarks and Conclusions

A few concluding ideas: there is further ethnohistoric evidence alluded to in the above passage for the importance of deer from the journals of Taliaferro. As I said earlier, Taliaferro and peacefully inclined civil chiefs were able to keep the peace, or at least a state of uneasy truce, among Chippewa and Dakota in the St. Croix River region for several years following the Treaty of Prairie du Chien (MHS mss. journal entries for 1825–1839). Taliaferro frequently reported Chippewa and Dakota hunting in each other's neighborhood, exchanging gifts and dances, and in other ways behaving in a congenial way. In other words, in that one region (only the briefest truces occurred in other areas) hunting was for a few years carried on undisturbed. This gives a test case for the theory. Reports of famine affecting those at peace began coming in in 1828, three years after the Treaty. Complaints of trespass and even minor outbreaks of hostility, such as breaking traps, began occurring on a large scale in 1831, but no real warfare yet took place. In 1835, Taliaferro wrote about Chippewa visiting his agency (MHS mss. 9: July 6, 1835):

> It would move the feelings of a Deist or the Devil himself much less a Christian Man to look on the garb & conditions of most of the Chippeways of the St. Croix—Snake, and Rum Rivers.

The Dakota of that region were starving throughout the 1830s. In 1838, a Dakota chief complained to Taliaferro that the Chippewa (MHS mss. 12: July 9, 1838)

> have swept off all our game on the Mississippi & the small streams—coming & going from this Post—once they never were to be found below Crow Island [mouth of Crow Wing River] when we were at War—but since your Fort was established here & peace was started our lands have suffered to such an extent that we cannot see a Deer or a Bear—in all our days journey.

Where there was peace there was starvation. But ironically, success in war must also have meant starvation, for that would have involved Dakota or Chippewa, whichever was successful, overrunning the country at the expense of the other, hence having free use of the once-contested area, and, because of resulting excessive demands on game, namely deer, exploiting it to depletion. There was, then, a selective advantage in not winning, but only through steady attrition maintaining

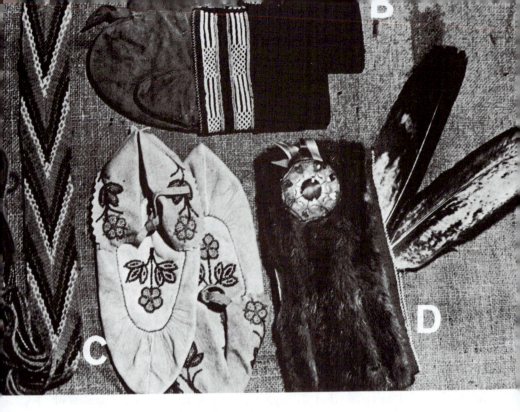

Clothing Accessories: Colorful and fancy clothing was common among woodland Indians from 1750 through the twentieth century. This assemblage of Chippewa accessories is illustrative of the common vogue. A. finger woven wool yarn sash, B. leather mittens with trade cloth binding and lacelike beadwork, C. puckered soft sole woodland moccasins with floral beadwork decoration, D. men's fur turban with eagle feathers and German-silver brooch. (Courtesy A. and S. Einhorn Collection)

a precarious balance through which the neutral zone could be maintained as a deer reserve to be tapped vicariously on either side, but not exhausted. This is essentially what Little Crow had told Forsyth in 1819. Better a steady little than nothing.

Finally, why could the Indians not have worked out a system by which the game reservoir would be maintained through systematic peaceful husbandry of game? This indeed has happened in fur game areas of Canada, where trapping territories have been apportioned and demarcated among family bands, and game "farmed," some beaver areas alternately being allowed to lie fallow, while others are exploited. Among Chippewa and Dakota truces *were* made to permit peaceful hunting and trapping, but these were local. No political organization was in existence among either Chippewa or Dakota to permit general negotiation by, say, representative councils of the whole. These were villages, not cohesive tribal aggregates. Needs in different locales were different—famine in one area was not necessarily duplicated in another; there was in general no economic basis for overall political solidarity over a very large region.

As important, perhaps, were the demands of the fur trade, which entailed much larger Chippewa and Dakota populations than the land could adequately support once the trade technology and the constant need to replenish it had been introduced. These peoples were necessarily thrown into competition. After all, the traders were operating within the framework of a profit system, and even in times when a single company held a virtual monopoly over the trade of the entire region occupied by both peoples, the traders at the several posts, who in effect worked on commission only, were in competition with each other. Although they complained repeatedly in their official correspondence about warfare interrupting the trapping, it may be abundantly seen in their journals and in some of their correspondence how avid they were in pushing *their* Indians to the limits of their territory. In the long run, the Indians were pawns in the trade, exploited, despoiled, and finally extinguished. Their warfare, based ultimately on traders' competition over fur, but reflecting and taking its specific character from the need for deer for subsistence, was only an episode in that process.

Epilogue

I HAVE PRESENTED THREE PHASES of Chippewa life, extending over 200 years, beginning with the earliest European contacts and ending at the point when one major branch of that diversified people, the Southwestern branch (cf. Hickerson 1962a) terminated as congeries of viable social groups and ceded their lands to the United States. I also looked at their relations with neighbors, other Central Algonquians and the Siouan Dakota. No view of Chippewa history and culture can be complete without reference to their extensive contacts with outsiders, Indian and European.

My aim was not to present a rounded picture of Chippewa "culture" in the traditional anthropological sense. In fact, there is no "Chippewa culture" that can be described at this point. To what time period and local area would it relate? At one time, before the coming of the Whites, there *was* a Chippewa culture founded in the relations among clan villages that formed the ancestry of the present people. Or, there were the cultures, slightly varying, of the several clans. Today there are Chippewa communities dispersed over a great extent of country in the United States and Canada, all of which lend themselves, as communities invariably do, to description. Many have been and are being described. But to attempt such descriptions, or to put in meaningful terms the old tribal Chippewa culture and that of the modern reservation Chippewa, historical devices, including as one of the most important, research into documents, is essential. Without having attempted a description or analysis of an integrated functioning Chippewa culture in this, I hope I have at least made that point.

But another important facet of this study emerges from the nature of the material I have presented: without a grounding in the anthropological discipline, much of the documentary material on intertribal relations, and on internal organization of communities—villages, bands, clan groups, and so on—is meaningless. In the third chapter, for example, the catalogue of peoples by the Jesuits and others, many of them bearing names suggestive of animals, in addition to the mention by Perrot of the animal ancestry of certain villages, along with other statements, would, to the uninitiated, suggest the occult or the strange. Anthropologists or students of anthropology know, however, that the *unilineal clan*, of which these are indicators, is a widespread feature of tribal, or primitive, life; therefore these institutions are entirely consistent with human history. It is also known, from the tracing of changes in the social organization, that the peoples catalogued by the Jesuits did not "disappear" simply because they no longer appear to exist; only that their social organization changed. It then becomes fascinating to document and explain changes in the light of such historical events as the impact of trade and the development of the techniques of warfare and diplomacy.

There is no mystery about the use of historical documents. Once research on a given problem or a people is under way, documents lead to documents, and common sense judgments may be made as to their validity in this or that instance, on the basis of general and accumulating specific knowledge. The bias of reporters, it is true, appear in their writings, as those of missionaries who cannot objectively report a "pagan" ceremony, or those of traders who cannot understand how a community can exert itself to accumulate wealth only to give it all away on the occasion of a ceremony such as the Feast of the Dead. Such bias must be appraised, and this falls under the general heading of textual criticism, in some branches of history a science in itself. Anthropologists are often happy to find, however, that many authors of the past—missionaries, traders, officials—were very astute, and presented their data quite intelligently and with a conscious attempt at objectivity. The success of appraisal of sources and the discrimination with which textual material is used, I believe, reflects the skill of the investigator in seeing consistency and his ability to comprehend problems as unified wholes. In fieldwork, anthropologists are confronted with similar problems. They must appraise informant testimony in the light of an accumulating sense of consistency and unity in the cultural entity they study. That is why, if at all possible, field studies involve the use of multiple informants, in addition to personal observation. In documentary as well as field research the question always arises, "does this make sense?"

I went to great lengths in Chapters 5–8 to put together a great mass of ethnohistorical and biohistorical references (rather more than were actually necessary to make my point) to show the causes and effects of warfare, and the nature of war with respect to political organization, biome, and so on, in the Chippewa-Dakota frontier. I think consistency was found in this purview of ecologic-economic relations—trapping, hunting, technology, vegetal and game distribution, trade, politics, and profit. I did not describe warpath customs, even though, by looking in Tanner and other sources I could have done so. This is, of course, a proper subject for anthropologists. Nor did I attempt to assess the impact of war and trade, for example, on the group personality structure (assuming that such a thing might exist), which may also be a fit subject for anthropological research. This book was simply not about such questions. But questions of custom and of "personality and culture," the persistence of certain traits and attitudes, and the interruption and extinction of others, cannot, no matter how skillful the scholar is, be viewed except in the perspective of history, or ethnohistory as the term is applied in anthropology.

Finally, documents are not readily available for all, or even most, peoples, not only in North America, but elsewhere in the world where tribal and unlettered peasant cultures have but recently given way under the impact of western and other civilizations. Other historical techniques, many of which I briefly surveyed in the introductory chapters—archeological, structural, linguistic—may be employed, and have at times been successfully employed by anthropologists to get at past cultural organization and to explain, or at least identify, stages at which change has taken place, in kinship and other social patterns, styles of technology, migrations, and so on.

On the other hand, documentary history has not been exploited by working anthropologists to any great degree. Anthropologists appear to find work in archives distasteful and tend to base their reconstructions on informants' statements and their own logical deductions of what must have happened in the past. They have often been wrong. Such great repositories as the various Indian affairs sections of the National Archives and the Archives of the Hudson's Bay Company in London and Ottawa await exhaustive research. So do archives of state historical societies, of Seville, Mexico, Moscow and a host of other places. It would literally take an army of researchers to go through domestic and foreign archives on North American Indians alone to get solid representative ethnohistorical work started. Museums are also good places for technological-historical research to abet field work. Certain coastal New England museums and historical societies, as the ethnohistorian, Ernest Dodge, has recently pointed out (1968), contain rich material, not just on American Indians, as one would guess, but on Polynesian and other peoples and cultures of the Pacific that had multifarious contacts with New England whalers and traders—material in old ships' logs and other documents.

Indeed, if one takes the view, and I believe this is widely held, that *tribal* culture as such is to all intents and purposes extinct, documents must be consulted. Anthropologists must, in other words, turn more and more to history as the primary means to salvage ancient culture, not for nostalgic reasons, but in order to explain evolution, the foundation upon which all cultural activity is built. Studies of contemporary cultures, whether marginal to the mainstream of economic and political life or not—poverty cultures, like most reservation Indian communities, peasant communities in Latin America and elsewhere, and ghettos in the great cities, and the introduction of the solutions to problems, political, economic, and social-psychological, are vastly important. The relaxation of world crisis rests in part on such solutions. Much of anthropology and sister disciplines is concerned with this, and many social scientists have succeeded in avoiding commitment to reactionary governments and private interests by pursuing research and suggesting solutions free of prejudice. (How much they are listened to is, of course, another question.)

But whole provinces of anthropology remain, notably those involving the theory of culture change and the history of social relations; these questions, with their broad implications for evolution, which is past *and* future, are basic to an understanding of contemporary relations. Anthropologists are fortunate, as tribal culture, from which all known culture stems, everywhere had great amounts of material in common, if only because the sociopolitical systems of tribes were universally founded in kinship. Exploiting cultures also had, and continue to have, common goals, the chief of which are profits derived from the spoliation of natural wealth by labor recruited in impoverished areas. Exploiters everywhere exploited much in the same way, although specific conditions varied from continental area to area, and tribesmen everywhere exhibited similar reactions involving at first apathy and distress, later revival, and finally resurgence. Case studies of the history of such relations, and new relations involving, as a primary feature of the contemporary political scene, the upsurge of nationalism following the extinguishment of tribalism, inevitably requires exhaustive work in documents. If one can no longer watch the corpse die, one can read its epitaph. An accumulation of such studies, samples of the process, so to speak, will give laws of the decay of tribes and the growth of nations. It remains for the future to apprise and comprehend the decay of nations.

It is here, then, that the prosaic research into dusty documents finds its place. Anthropology has not yet begun seriously to comprehend the evolution of man and of his society. There have been queen-pawn-four openings. The game is yet really to begin.

Recommended Reading

Chapter 1

There are several general texts on North American Indians that place Northern and Central Algonquians in the perspective of surrounding areas and contain extensive ethnographic material. First, the two volumes of the *Handbook of American Indians North of Mexico* edited by Hodge (1907–1910)[1] is still a very useful reference for data on the location of peoples, tribal synonymies, and customs. Also, it is a good guide to primary published sources on virtually all areas in the United States and Canada. Wissler's general study (1917) still remains interesting and informative. Of more recent works, there are: Jenness (1958), Driver (1961), Spencer and Jennings (1965), Oswalt (1966), Owen and others (1967), and most recently, Farb (1968).

Among recent studies on various aspects of Chippewa life under reservation conditions, most advancing a variety of points of view and some argumentation, the reader is directed to Landes (1937), Hilger (1939), Barnouw (1950), Friedl (1956), and James (1961). On the Chippewa of northern Ontario there are two excellent studies, Dunning (1959) and Rogers (1962). Hallowell (1955) presents a collection of essays written over many years and based not only on extensive fieldwork in the Lake Winnipeg region, but also to a considerable degree on research into early source material. My own work, well represented in *References Cited*, is based almost entirely on documentary research.

Among the many general works on the history of the fur trade, I would suggest two that have many references to the impact of the trade on Indian life: Innis (1956) and Phillips (1961). For specific ethnohistorical perspective on the trade and its impact on Algonquians, Leacock (1954) and Hickerson (1967a) are recommended. For opposing points of view see Cooper (1939) and Speck and Eiseley (1939).

---

[1] Full bibliographical data of these and *Recommended Reading* sections appended to chapters following appear in *References*.

Chapter 2

For documentary ethnohistory, articles by Sturtevant, Hudson and Fenton that appear in a single issue of *Ethnohistory* (1966) present varying approaches. The journal itself carries articles, annotated primary documents published for the first time, and reviews by anthropologists and historians, representing many ways in which documentary and other historical material has been used as evidence to illustrate culture change, and as an aid in reconstructing pre- and protocontact cultures, and relationships among peoples.

There are numerous works discussing age and area method. Among the most important are Wissler (1923; 1926), Sapir (1916), Kroeber (1931), and for a general critique, Bennett (1944). Thompson, throughout his book, *The Folktale* (1946), makes critical remarks pertaining to historical and geographical relations in folklore. Excellent examples of the application of age and area method are the works of Lowie (1916) and Spier (1921).

To supplement discussion of space-time equivalence in evolution, I suggest, as outstanding examples, Morgan (1963) and Service (1962; 1963).

For the application of space-time equivalence in history, in addition to passages quoted in the text, I would suggest G. D. Spindler (1955) and L. Spindler (1962). For a critique of this method see Hickerson (1967a:326–327).

On historical linguistics, in addition to Sapir (1916), I recommend Hoijer (1956), Hockett (1964), on glottochronology, Lees (1953), Swadesh (1952), and for a general review and criticisms, Hymes and others (1960).

Murdock has been most instrumental in stimulating the use of statistics, especially in his application of them to the evolution of social structure (1949). Driver has employed statistics in both empirical and theoretical studies (1956; Driver and Massey 1957). Naroll and his critics have given clarity to the problem of ethnic unit classification (1964). I recommend most highly articles by Ember (1963) on unit classification, and the same author and also Carneiro (1968) for formulations of gradients of cultural complexity to provide leads for evolutionary reconstruction.

For an authoritative discussion of the value of oral tradition in historical reconstruction by an anthropologist-historian, the reader is directed to Vansina (1961 [especially 183–186]).

An excellent example of the use of maps to illustrate the chronology of exploration, discovery, and contact in the Great Lakes-Mississippi region is the compilation by Tucker (1942) of maps from the Jesuit Relations map of 1670 right up to survey and other maps of 1835. Tucker verifies each of the 54 plates and annotates each one. The National Archives in Washington has an excellent cartographic department, and United States topographical survey maps, often with Indian settlements included, are scattered among the files of several government agencies.

Chapter 3

This chapter is based primarily on Hickerson (1960a; 1962a; 1966). The reader is directed to the bibliographies in these works for references to primary sources. In addition to Innis and Phillips, already cited, Hunt (1940) is an excellent secondary source on early fur trade relations in the Great Lakes area. I would also recommend the general work on Indians of the Great Lakes by Kinietz (1940), based on documentary research.

Chapter 4

In addition to sources given in the text, an authoritative general work on revivalist, or nativistic, cults is Wallace (1956). An earlier study of the Plains Ghost Dance by Mooney (1896) shows the nature and spread of the cult from tribe to tribe in the 1870s–1890s. Aberle (1966) recently has published a comprehensive study on peyotism in the Southwest.

This chapter is based primarily on Hickerson (1962b; 1963; 1965a). A recent work by Landes (1968) gives psychological insights based on fieldwork done in the 1930s into the Midewiwin and its practitioners.

Chapters 5–8

There is a vast literature in anthropology on warfare. I would select, for reading, the sections on war in Evans-Pritchard's book on a Nilotic people, the Nuer (1960) and an article by Newcomb (1950) on Plains Indian warfare. Also recommended are Sahlins (1961) and Vayda (1961).

Also, an article by Murphy (1957) on warfare among the Mundurucú, a South American tribe, a critique of the article by Wilson (1958), and Murphy's answer to the critique (1958) are interesting.

These chapters are based primarily on Hickerson (1957; 1962a; 1965b). The main primary sources are given in the text and in the bibliographies to my articles, especially 1962a and 1965b.

References

ABERLE, D. F. AND OTHERS, 1966, *The Peyote Religion among the Navaho.* Viking Fund Publications in Anthropology, No. 42.

AFCP, 1831–1849, *American Fur Company Papers.* New York Historical Society mss. (see also, 1945, G. L. Nute, ed., Calendar of the American Fur Company's Papers. 2 parts. In *Annual Report of the American Historical Association for the Year 1944.* 3 vols. Washington).

ASP-MA, 1832–1861, American State Papers, Military Affairs. 7 vols. Washington.

BARNOUW, V., 1950, *Acculturation and Personality among the Wisconsin Chippewa.* American Anthropological Association Memoir 72.

BELTRAMI, G. C., 1828, *A Pilgrimage in Europe and America, Leading to the Discovery of the Sources of the Mississippi and Bloody Rivers. . . .* 2 vols. London.

BENNETT, J., 1944, The Development of Ethnological Theory as Illustrated by Studies of the Plains Sun Dance. *American Anthropologist* 46:162–181.

BLAIR, E. H., trans. and ed., 1911, *The Indian Tribes of the Upper Mississippi Valley and the Region of the Great Lakes as Described by Nicolas Perrot, French Commandant in the Northwest; Bacqueville de la Potherie, French Royal Commissioner to Canada; Morrell Marston, American Army Officer; and Thomas Forsyth, United States Agent at Fort Armstrong.* 2 vols. Cleveland: Arthur H. Clark Co.

BLASINGHAM, E., 1956, The Depopulation of the Illinois Indians. *Ethnohistory* 3:193–224, 361–412.

BLOCH, M., 1961, *The Historian's Craft.* New York: Alfred A. Knopf.

BORCHERT, J. R., 1959, *Minnesota's Changing Geography.* Minneapolis: University of Minnesota Press.

BOUTWELL, W. T., 1832–1837, *Journals.* Mss. Department, Minnesota Historical Society. St. Paul.

BURPEE, L. J., ed., 1927, *Journals and Letters of Pierre Gaultier De Varennes De La Vérendrye and His Sons.* Toronto: The Champlain Society.

CAMERON, D., 1890, The Nipigon Country. In L. R. Masson, ed. *Les Bourgeois de la Compagnie du Nord-Ouest . . .* 2:231–265. Quebec.

CARNEIRO, R. L., 1968, Ascertaining, Testing, and Interpreting Sequences of Cultural Development. *Southwestern Journal of Anthropology* 24:354–374.

CARR, E. H., 1962, *What Is History?* New York: Alfred A. Knopf.

CARVER, J., 1779, *Travels through the Interior Parts of North America in the Years 1766, 1767, and 1768.* London.

128 · REFERENCES

CDS, Congressional Documents Series. Washington.
CHRISTENSEN, E. M., 1959, A Historical View of the Ranges of the White-tailed Deer in Northern Wisconsin Forests. *American Midland Naturalist* 61:230–238.
CLIFTON, J. A., ed., 1968, *Introduction to Cultural Anthropology.* Boston: Houghton Mifflin Company.
COLLINGWOOD, R. G., 1946, *The Idea of History.* Oxford: The Clarendon Press.
CONNOR, T., 1933, The Diary of Thomas Connor. In *Five Fur Traders of the Northwest* . . . C. M. Gates, ed. Minneapolis: University of Minnesota Press.
COOPER, J. M., 1939, Is the Algonquian Family Hunting Ground System Pre-Columbian? *American Anthropologist* 41:66–90.
COUES, E., ed., 1895, *The Expeditions of Zebulon Montgomery Pike, to Headwaters of the Mississippi River, through Louisiana Territory, and in New Spain, during the Years 1805–1806–1807.* 3 vols. New York.
———, 1897, *New Light on the Early History of the Greater Northwest. The Manuscript Journals of Alexander Henry, Fur Trader of the Northwest Company, and of David Thompson, Official Geographer and Explorer of the same Company, 1799–1814. Exploration and Adventure among the Indians on the Red, Saskatchewan, Missouri and Columbia Rivers.* 3 vols. New York.
CRUIKSHANK, E. A., ed., 1923–1925, *The Correspondence of Lieut. Governor John Graves Simcoe, with Allied Documents Relating to His Administration of the Government of Upper Canada.* 3 vols. Toronto: Ontario Historical Society.
CUROT, M., 1911, A Wisconsin Fur-Trader's Journal, 1803–1804. Collections of the State Historical Society of Wisconsin 20:396–471.
CURTIS, J. T., 1959, *The Vegetation of Wisconsin: An Ordination of Plant Communities.* Madison: University of Wisconsin Press.
DAHLBERG, B. L. AND R. C. GUETTINGER, 1956, The White-Tailed Deer in Wisconsin. Pittman-Robertson Project W-4-R. *Technical Wildlife Bulletin* 14. Game Management Division, Wisconsin Conservation Department. Madison, Wisconsin.
DODGE, E. S., 1968, The American Sources for Pacific Ethnohistory. *Ethnohistory* 15:1–10.
DRAY, W. H., 1964, *Philosophy of History.* Englewood Cliffs, New Jersey: Prentice-Hall.
DRIVER, H. E., 1956, An Integration of Functional, Evolutionary and Historical Theory by Means of Correlations. *Indiana University Publications in Anthropology. and Linguistics,* Memoir 12. Bloomington, Indiana.
———, 1961, *Indians of North America.* Chicago: The University of Chicago Press.
DRIVER, H. E. AND W. C. MASSEY, 1957, Comparative Studies of North American Indians. *Transactions of the American Philosophical Society,* 47. Philadelphia.
DUNNING, R. W., 1959, *Social and Economic Change among the Northern Ojibwa.* Toronto: University of Toronto Press.
EGGAN, F., 1955, *Social Anthropology of North American Tribes.* Chicago: University of Chicago Press.
———, 1966, *The American Indian.* Chicago: Aldine Publishing Company.
ELTON, G. R., 1967, *The Practice of History.* New York: Thomas Y. Crowell Company.
ELY, E. F., 1833–1854, *Journals.* Mss. Department, Minnesota Historical Society. St. Paul.
EMBER, M., 1963, The Relationship between Economic and Political Development in Nonindustrialized Societies. *Ethnology* 2:228–248.
ERICKSON, A. B. AND D. W. BURCALOW, 1954, The St. Croix Park Deer Herd. *Conservation Volunteer* 17:6–17.
EVANS-PRITCHARD, E. E., 1940, *The Nuer.* Oxford: The Clarendon Press.
FARB, P., 1968, *Man's Rise to Civilization as Shown by the Indians of North America from Primeval Times to the Coming of the Industrial State.* New York: E. P. Dutton & Co., Inc.

FENTON, W. N., 1940, *Problems Arising from the Historic Northeastern Position of the Iroquois.* Smithsonian Miscellaneous Collections, vol. 100, pp. 159–251. Washington.

————, 1966, Field work, Museum Studies, and Ethnohistorical Research. *Ethnohistory* 13–14:71–85.

FREDINE, G., 1940, Deer Inventory Studies in Minnesota. *Proceedings of the Minnesota Academy of Science* 8:41–49.

FRIEDL, E., 1956, Persistence in Chippewa Culture and Personality. *American Anthropologist* 58:814–825.

GATES, C. M., ed., 1933, *Five Fur Traders of the Northwest, Being the Narrative of Peter Pond and the Diaries of John Macdonell, Archibald N. McLeod, Hugh Faries, and Thomas Connor.* Minneapolis: University of Minnesota Press.

GRANT, P., 1890, The Sauteux Indians. In L. R. Masson, ed. *Les Bourgeois de la Compagnie du Nord-Ouest* . . . 2:307–366. Quebec.

HALLOWELL, A. I., 1955, *Culture and Experience.* Philadelphia: University of Pennsylvania Press.

HENRY, A., 1901, *Travels and Adventures in Canada and the Indian Territories between the Years 1760 and 1776.* Boston.

HICKERSON, H., 1956, The Genesis of a Trading Post Band: The Pembina Chippewa. *Ethnohistory* 3:289–345.

————, 1957, *Anthropological Report before the Indian Claims Commission.* Treaty of February 22, 1855. (Mimeo.) United States Department of Justice. Washington.

————, 1960a, The Feast of the Dead among the Seventeenth Century Algonkians of the Upper Great Lakes. *American Anthropologist* 62:81–107.

————, 1960b, *Anthropological Report before the Indian Claims Commission.* Treaty of July 23 and August 5, 1851. (Mimeo.) United States Department of Justice. Washington.

————, 1962a, *The Southwestern Chippewa: An Ethnohistorical Study.* American Anthropological Association Memoir 92.

————, 1962b, Notes on the Post-Contact Origin of the Midewiwin. *Ethnohistory* 9:404–423.

————, 1963, The Sociohistorical Significance of Two Chippewa Ceremonials. *American Anthropologist* 65:67–85.

————, 1965a, William T. Boutwell of the American Board and the Pillager Chippewa: The History of a Failure. *Ethnohistory* 12:1–29.

————, 1965b, The Virginia Deer and Intertribal Buffer Zones in the Upper Mississippi Valley. In A. Leeds and A. P. Vayda, eds., *Man, Culture and Animals, the Role of Animals in Human Ecological Adjustments.* Publication 78, American Association for the Advancement of Science, pp. 43–65. Washington.

————, 1966, The Genesis of Bilaterality among Two Divisions of Chippewa. *American Anthropologist* 68:1–26.

————, 1967a, Some Implications of the Theory of the Particularity, or "Atomism," of Northern Algonkians. *Current Anthropology* 8:313–343.

————, 1967b, A Note of Inquiry on Hockett's Reconstruction of PCA. *American Anthropologist* 69:362–363.

————, 1967c, *Land Tenure of the Rainy Lake Chippewa at the Beginning of the Nineteenth Century.* Smithsonian Contributions to Anthropology, vol 2, no. 4. Washington.

HILGER, M. I., 1939, *A Social Study of One Hundred Fifty Chippewa Indian Families of the White Earth Reservation of Minnesota.* Washington: The Catholic University Press.

HOCKETT, C. F., 1964, The Proto Central Algonquian Kinship System. In W. H. Goodenough, ed., *Explorations in Cultural Anthropology*, pp. 239–258. New York: McGraw-Hill Co.

HODGE, F. W., ed., 1907–1910, *Handbook of the American Indians North of Mexico.* 2 parts. Bureau of American Ethnology Bulletin 30. Washington.

HOFFMAN, W. J., 1885–1886, The Mide'wiwin or "Grand Medicine Society" of the Ojibwa. Bureau of American Ethnology, 7th Annual Report, pp. 143–300. Washington.

HOIJER, H., 1956, Athapaskan Kinship Systems. *American Anthropologist* 58:309–333.

HORNADAY, W. T., 1887, The Extermination of the American Bison. Reports of the United States National Museum 2:369–548. Washington.

HUDSON, C., 1966, Folk History and Ethnohistory. *Ethnohistory* 13–14:52–70.

HUNT, G. T., 1940, *The Wars of the Iroquois: A Study in Inter-Tribal Trade Relations.* Madison: University of Wisconsin Press.

HYMES, D. H., 1960, Lexicostatistics So Far. *Current Anthropology* 1:3–44.

INNIS, H. A., 1956, *The Fur-Trade of Canada.* (Revised edition.) Toronto: University of Toronto Press.

JAMES, B., 1961, Social-Psychological Dimensions of Ojibwa Acculturation. *American Anthropologist* 63:721–746.

JAMES, E., ed., 1940, *Narrative of His {John Tanner's} Captivity among the Ottawa and Ojibwa Indians.* Occasional Papers, Reprint Series no. 20, parts 1–2, Sutro Branch, California State Library. San Francisco.

JENNESS, D., 1958, *The Indians of Canada* (4th edition.). National Museum of Canada Bulletin 65. Ottawa.

JR, 1896–1901, *The Jesuit Relations and Allied Documents: Travels and Explorations of the Jesuit Missionaries in New France, 1610–1791.* R. G. Thwaites, ed. 73 vols. Cleveland: The Burrows Brothers Company.

KEATING, W. H., 1825, *Narrative of an Expedition to the Source of St. Peter's River, Lake Winepeek, Lake of the Woods, &c. Performed in the Year 1823, by Order of the Hon. J. C. Calhoun, Secretary of War, under the Command of S. H. Long, U. S. T. E.* 2 vols. London.

KEESING, F. M., 1939, *The Menomini Indians of Wisconsin. A Study of Three Centuries of Cultural Contact and Change.* Memoirs of the American Philosophical Society, vol. 10. Philadelphia.

KHS-CP, n. d., Kansas Historical Society mss. William Clark papers. Vols. 2–3, 6. Topeka.

KINIETZ, W. V., 1940, *The Indians of the Western Great Lakes, 1615–1760.* Occasional Contributions from the Museum of Anthropology of the University of Michigan, no. 10. Ann Arbor: University of Michigan Press.

KROEBER, A. L., 1925, *Handbook of the Indians of California.* Bureau of Ethnology Bulletin 78. Washington.

————, 1931, The Culture-Area and Age-Area Concepts of Clark Wissler. In S. A. Rice, ed., *Methods in Social Science.* Chicago: University of Chicago Press.

LANDES, R., 1937, *Ojibwa Sociology.* Columbia University Contributions to Anthropology, vol. 29. New York: Columbia University Press.

————, 1968, *Ojibwa Religion and the Midéwiwin.* Madison: The University of Wisconsin Press.

LA POTHERIE, B. DE, 1911, History of the Savage Peoples Who Are Allies of New France. In E. H. Blair, trans. and ed., *The Indian Tribes of the Upper Mississippi Valley and the Region of the Great Lakes . . .* 1:273–372; 2:13–136. Cleveland: Arthur H. Clark Co.

LEACOCK, E. B., 1954, *The Montagnais "Hunting Territory" and the Fur Trade.* American Anthropological Association Memoir 78.

LEES, R. B., 1953, The Basis of Glottochronology. *Language* 29:113–127.

LIND, M., n. d., Unpublished Translations of the Manuscripts of J. N. Nicollet.

LOWIE, R. H., 1916, Plains Indian Age-Societies: Historical and Comparative Summary. In C. Wissler, ed., *Societies of the Plains Indians.* Anthropological Papers of the American Museum of Natural History 11:877–984. New York.

McLOUGHLIN, J., 1822–1823, Reports from J. McLoughlin to the Hudson Bay Company Concerning the Indians of the Rainy Lake-Lake-of-the-Woods Area near the Canadian-Minnesota Border Containing a Brief Description of the Area, the Natives, and the Wild Life. State Historical Society of Wisconsin mss. Madison, Wisconsin.

MALHIOT, F. V., 1910, A Wisconsin Fur Trader's Journal, 1804–1805. Collections of the State Historical Society of Wisconsin 19:163–233.

MARGRY, P., 1886, Découvertes et Établissements des Français dans l'Ouest et dans le Sud de l'Amérique Septentrionale (1614–1754): Mémoires et Documents Originaux (6 vols), vol 6. Paris.

MASSON, L. R., ed., 1889–1890, Les Bourgeois de la Compagnie du Nord-Ouest, Récits de Voyages, Lettres et Rapports Inédits Relatifs au Nord-Ouest Canadien. 2 vols. Quebec.

MHB, 1915-, Minnesota History Bulletin. 38 vols. Minnesota Historical Society. St. Paul, Minnesota.

MHC, 1860–1920, Collections of the Minnesota Historical Society. 17 vols. St. Paul, Minnesota.

MHS, n. d., Minnesota Historical Society mss. St. Paul, Minnesota.

MOONEY, J., 1896, The Ghost-Dance Religion. Annual Reports of the Bureau of American Ethnology, no. 14, pt. 2, pp. 640–1136.

MORGAN, L. H., 1963, Ancient Society. E. B. Leacock, ed. and annot. Cleveland: The World Publishing Company.

MPHC, 1877–1929, Historical Collections of the Michigan Pioneer and Historical Society. 40 vols. Lansing, Michigan.

MURDOCK, G. P., 1949, Social Structure. New York: The Macmillan Company.

MURPHY, R., 1957, Intergroup Hostility and Social Cohesion. American Anthropologist 59:1018–1035.

————, 1958, Reply to Wilson. American Anthropologist 60:1196–1197.

NA (NATIONAL ARCHIVES), 1824, Historical Table Showing the Number and Location of the Different Bands of Indians Comprised within the Agency of Sault Ste. Marie, Michigan Territory. Field Records, Letters Sent at Michigan Superintendency, vol. A. Records of the Bureau of Indian Affairs. Record Group 75. Washington.

————, 1848, H. M. Rice to William Medill, February 12. La Pointe Sub-Agency File. Record Group 75. Washington.

————, 1855, Journal of the Proceedings of the Treaty of February 22, 1855. Record Group 75. Washington.

NA-GLO, 1835, J. S. Bean to W. Clark, November 11. General Land Office Files. Record Group 49. Washington.

NAROLL, R., 1964, On Ethnic Unit Classification. Current Anthropology 5:283–312.

NEWCOMB, W. W., 1950, A Re-examination of the Causes of Plains Warfare. American Anthropologist 52:317–330.

NICOLLET, J. N., 1845, Report Intended to Illustrate a Map of the Hydrographical Basin of the Upper Mississippi River. Congressional Documents Series 464. Washington.

NYCD, 1853–1887, Documents Relating to the Colonial History of the State of New York. 15 vols. Albany.

OSWALT, W. H., 1966, This Land Was Theirs. New York: John Wiley & Sons, Inc.

OWEN, D. D., 1852, Report of a Geological Survey of Wisconsin, Iowa, and Minnesota; and Incidentally of a Portion of Nebraska Territory. Made under Instructions from the United States Treasury Department. Philadelphia.

OWEN, R. C., J. J. DEETZ, AND A. D. FISHER, eds., 1967, The North American Indians. New York: Macmillan.

PERROT, N., 1911, Memoir on the Manners, Customs, and Religion of the Savages of North America. In E. H. Blair, trans. and ed., The Indian Tribes of the Upper

Mississippi Valley and the Region of the Great Lakes . . . 1:31–272. Cleveland: Arthur H. Clark Co.

PHILLIPS, P. C., 1961, *The Fur Trade*. 2 vols. Norman: University of Oklahoma Press.

PIKE, Z. B., 1810, *An Account of Expeditions to the Sources of the Mississippi . . . during the Years 1805, 1806, and 1807*. Philadelphia.

PLEKHANOV, G., 1940, *Essays in Historical Materialism*. New York: International Publishers.

QUIMBY, G. I., 1966, *Indian Cultures and European Trade Goods*. Madison: The University of Wisconsin Press.

RADISSON, P. E., 1943, *Voyages of Peter Esprit Radisson, Being an Account of His Travels and Experiences among the North American Indians, from 1652 to 1684*. G. D. Scull, ed. New York: Peter Smith.

REDFIELD, R., 1965, *The Folk Culture of Yucatan*. Chicago: University of Chicago Press.

REPORT OF THE COMMITTEE ON HISTORIOGRAPHY, 1946, *Theory and Practice in Historical Study*. Social Science Research Council Bulletin 54.

————, 1954, *The Social Sciences in Historical Study*. Social Science Research Council Bulletin 64.

ROGERS, E. S., 1962, *The Round Lake Ojibwa*. Royal Ontario Museum, Art and Archaeological Division. Occasional Papers, no. 5. Toronto.

ROYCE, C. C., 1899, *Indian Land Cessions in the United States*. Bureau of American Ethnology, 18th Annual Report, part 2. Washington.

SAHLINS, M. D., 1961, The Segmentary Lineage: an Organization of Predatory Expansion. *American Anthropologist* 63:322–345.

SAPIR, E., 1916, *Time Perspective in Aboriginal American Culture*. Memoirs of the Canada Department of Mines, Geological Survey 90:1–87.

SCHOOLCRAFT, H. R., 1834, *Discovery of the Sources of the Mississippi, or Narrative of an Expedition through the Upper Mississippi to Itasca Lake, the Actual Source of this River; Embracing an Exploratory Trip through the St. Croix and Burntwood (or Broule) Rivers; in 1832*. New York: Harper & Brothers.

————, 1851–1857, *Information, Respecting the History, Condition and Prospects of the Indian Tribes of the United States; Collected and Prepared under the Direction of the Bureau of Indian Affairs. . . .* Philadelphia: J. B. Lippincott & Co.

SCHORGER, A. W., 1953, The White-Tailed Deer in Early Wisconsin. *Transactions of the Wisconsin Academy of Sciences, Arts and Letters* 42:197–247. Madison.

————, 1954, The Elk in Early Wisconsin. *Wisconsin Academy of Sciences, Arts and Letters*, vol. 43. Madison.

————, 1956, The Moose in Early Wisconsin. *Wisconsin Academy of Sciences, Arts and Letters*, vol. 45. Madison.

SERVICE, E. R., 1962, *Primitive Social Organization, an Evolutionary Perspective*. New York: Random House.

————, 1963, *Profiles in Ethnology* (revised). New York: Harper & Row.

SCHUSKY, E. L., 1965, *Manual for Kinship Analysis*. New York: Holt, Rinehart and Winston, Inc.

SPECK, F. G. AND L. C. EISELEY, 1939, Significance of Hunting Territory Systems of the Algonkian in Social Theory. *American Anthropologist* 41:269–280.

SPENCER, R. F. AND J. D. JENNINGS, eds., 1965, *The Native Americans*. New York: Harper & Row.

SPIER, L., 1921, The Sun Dance of the Plains Indians. *Anthropological Papers of the American Museum of Natural History*, vol. 16, pp. 451–527.

SPINDLER, G. D., 1955, *Sociological and Psychological Processes in Menomini Acculturation*. University of California Publications in Culture and Society, vol. 5. Berkeley: University of California Press.

SPINDLER, L., 1962, *Menomini Women and Culture Change*. American Anthropological Association Memoir 91.

STENLUND, M. H., 1955, *A Field Study of the Timber Wolf (Canis lupus) on the Superior National Forest, Minnesota.* Minnesota Department of Conservation, Bureau of Wildlife Development, Technical Bulletin 4. St. Paul, Minnesota.
————, 1956, How To Produce Deer. *The Conservation Volunteer* 19:33–36.
STEWARD, J. H., 1938, *Basin-Plateau Aboriginal Socio-Political Groups.* Bureau of American Ethnology, Bulletin 120, pp. 1–346. Washington.
————, 1955, *Theory of Culture Change.* Urbana: University of Illinois Press.
STURTEVANT, W. C., 1966, Anthropology, History, and Ethnohistory. *Ethnohistory* 13–14:1–51. (Reprinted from J. A. Clifton, ed., *Introduction to Cultural Anthropology,* pp. 450–475.)
SWADESH, M., 1952, Lexicostatistic Dating of Prehistoric Ethnic Contacts. *Proceedings of the American Philosophical Society* 96:452–463.
SWANTON, J. R., 1946, *The Indians of the Southeastern United States.* Bureau of American Ethnology, Bulletin 137. Washington.
SWIFT, E., 1946, *A History of Wisconsin Deer.* Wisconsin Conservation Department, Publication 323. Madison, Wisconsin.
TALIAFERRO, L., 1821–1839, *Journals.* 13 vols., 2 letterbooks. Mss. Department, Minnesota Historical Society. St. Paul, Minnesota.
TEGGART, F. J., 1960, *Theory and Processes of History.* Berkeley and Los Angeles: University of California Press.
THOMPSON, S., 1946, *The Folktale.* New York: Holt, Rinehart and Winston, Inc.
THWAITES, R. G., ed., 1904–1905, *Original Journals of the Lewis and Clark Expedition, 1804–1806.* 8 vols. New York: Dodd, Mead and Company.
TUCKER, S. J., 1942, *Indian Villages of the Illinois Country.* Illinois State Museum, Scientific Papers, vol. II, pt. I, Atlas. Springfield, Illinois.
TYLOR, E. B., 1889, On a Method of Investigating the Development of Institutions; Applied to Laws of Marriage and Descent. *Journal of the Royal Anthropological Institute of Great Britain and Ireland* 18:245–269.
TYRRELL, J. B., ed., 1916, *David Thompson's Narrative of His Explorations in Western America 1784–1812.* Toronto: The Champlain Society.
VANSINA, J., 1961, *Oral Tradition: A Study in Historical Methodology.* H. M. Wright, trans. Chicago: Aldine Publishing Company.
VAYDA, A. P., 1961, Expansion and Warfare among Swidden Agriculturalists. *American Anthropologist* 63:346–358.
WALLACE, A. F. C., 1956, Revitalization Movements: Some Theoretical Considerations for Their Comparative Study. *American Anthropologist* 58:264–281.
WARREN, W. W., 1885, History of the Ojibwa Nation, Based upon Traditions and Oral Statements. *MHC* 5:21–394.
WHC, 1855–1931, *Collections of the State Historical Society of Wisconsin.* 31 vols. Madison, Wisconsin.
WHS, n. d., *State Historical Society of Wisconsin Mss.* Madison, Wisconsin.
WILSON, H. C., 1958, Regarding the Causes of Mundurucú Warfare. *American Anthropologist* 60:1193–1196.
WINCHELL, N. H., 1911, *The Aborigines of Minnesota, a Report Based on the Collections of Jacob V. Brower, and on the Field Surveys and Notes of Alfred J. Hill and Theodore H. Lewis.* St. Paul: Minnesota Historical Society.
WISSLER, C., 1917, *The American Indian.* New York: Oxford University Press.
————, 1926, *The Relation of Nature to Man in Aboriginal America.* New York: Oxford University Press.

The Chippewa and
Their Neighbors:
A Critical Review

by Jennifer S.H. Brown and Laura L. Peers

The Chippewa and Their Neighbors was by no means a comprehensive ethnohistory of the Chippewa in the mode of, say, Bruce Trigger's studies of the Huron (1969, 1976); nor did Hickerson intend it as such. His focus was on methodology. He explored how documentary sources could be used to study evolving relationships among social structure, resources, trade, and warfare. But the limited space available to him in this slim volume did not allow full discussions of those topics, and necessitated a highly selective presentation of his Chippewa data. Further, as he freely admitted in his epilogue, his documentary research was not exhaustive; much remained to be done. Nor did he incorporate field or oral-history data, an omission for which he offered justification in chapter 2, but one which has brought him some strong criticism.

The book has other limitations for which its author was not responsible. The last twenty years have seen a florescence not simply of further Algonquian studies, but also of entire new subfields of ethnohistorical research pertaining, for example, to fur trade social and economic history, to women and their roles, and to the Métis (people of mixed Indian-European descent) who were an active presence in Chippewa country by the mid-1700s. The newer data and publications not only test Hickerson's conclusions about Ojibwa ethnohistory; they also offer a variety of perspectives on the utility and limitations of his interpretive frameworks. This review essay seeks to open doors for further study, placing the book in the context of recent data and topics of discussion.

The Chippewa and Their Neighbors

Both "the Chippewa" (Ojibwa) and "their neighbors" may appropriately be construed more broadly than this volume suggests. In the nineteenth century, "Chippewa" became the term used in the United States for those Northern Algonquians who in other regions have most commonly been known as Ojibwa(y) or Mississauga (Ontario), or Saulteaux (the term mainly used in Western Canada), or among the people themselves, Anishinabe (aniššina·pe·, 'human being'). To trace the historical roots and movements of all these closely related Chippewa/Ojibwa groups in recent scholarship, some of the best places to start are volumes 6 and 15 of the new *Handbook of North American Indians:* vol. 6, *Subarctic* (Helm, ed., 1981), and vol. 15, *Northeast* (Trigger, ed., 1978); the general and specific subject articles in each volume afford basic overviews and reference materials. Each also includes linguistic explanations of these and other group and tribal names, tracing their history and etymology and listing synonyms. It should be noted that the "Chippewa" as portrayed by Hickerson are really only the Southwestern Ojibwa of Wisconsin and Minnesota, and his data cannot be assumed to apply to all the regional groups of Ojibwa.

Note too that Hickerson's Map 1, showing the Ojibwas' maximum range in the early 1800s, does not fully represent that range as it is now understood. The Ojibwa still occupied much of southern Ontario in that period (Rogers 1973: 85). They also extended farther into Saskatchewan and Alberta than older writers recognized. Fur trade documents show that Ojibwa were then residing, at least in small numbers, along the North Saskatchewan River as far as Edmonton and Lesser Slave Lake; they later withdrew from these areas as trading conditions deteriorated (Peers 1987).

For Hickerson, the Chippewas' "neighbors" were essentially the Dakota Sioux beyond the "debatable zone" to their west and south. Chippewa interactions with the Menominee, Fox, Ottawa, Cree, and other native peoples, not to mention the growing numbers of white settlers and Métis, lay largely beyond the scope of this volume. These historical relationships are increasingly well documented, however (see, for example, Trigger, ed., 1978; Tanner 1987), and have a bearing particularly on Hickerson's portrayal of Chippewa-Dakota relations and the "debatable zone," as we shall see.

Baselines Revisited: Archaeology and Linguistics

As Charles Bishop notes in his foreword, Hickerson was interested in establishing the "aboriginal baseline conditions" of Chippewa social structure and culture, before postcontact developments brought about (in his view) their destruction. The methods of study that Hickerson helped to develop have themselves led ethnohistorians to question the concept of an aboriginal baseline, with its corollary assumptions of a precontact society evolving slowly in undisturbed conditions and a postcontact society hurtling toward defeat and disintegration. The rapid growth of archaeological knowledge in the last years has facilitated the tracing of sometimes very considerable changes in aboriginal communities — changes involving settlement patterns, migration, warfare, technological and dietary modifications, etc. Bruce Trigger in *Natives and Newcomers: Canada's "Heroic*

Age" Reconsidered (1985) strongly affirms the need to integrate both pre- and postcontact archaeological data into ethnohistorical interpretation. His point is relevant to Hickerson's work; some specific archaeological researchers are now revising earlier ideas about the origin of the Midewiwin and about Chippewa resource use (for some examples, see Conway 1987, Arthurs 1986, Cleland 1982).

Ojibwa prehistory has also drawn increasing attention from linguists. Hickerson called attention to the uses of glottochronology and to the work of Charles Hockett (1964) and Fred Eggan (1966) in reconstructing Algonquian and other kinship systems and social structure through the study of linguistic categories, and the literature continues to grow (see, for example, articles and references cited in the two Handbook volumes mentioned above). One topic which has drawn linguistics and archaeology together is that of locating the oldest homeland or *urheimat* of Algonquian-speaking peoples; Frank Siebert's effort at its reconstruction through the study of plant and animal names (1967) and the discussions that it provoked (e.g., Snow 1976) suggest ways in which both linguists and archaeologists can deepen our time perspectives and our understandings of precontact changes.

Recently, Bruce Trigger has vigorously advocated the usefulness of another domain of linguistics, that of ethnosemantics. Too often, ethnohistorians have little or no knowledge of the languages of the peoples they study and hence, no grasp of "the categories in terms of which native people perceived and interacted with the world" (Trigger 1986: 262). The study of the various meanings of words to native speakers, and in turn, to Europeans trying to understand or translate them, is an immensely important area. As Trigger observes, "Even when assessing European documents in which no native words appear, a knowledge of the native usages that were involved in transmitting information may clarify meanings in a manner that outstrips in importance any contextual analysis of the documents" (ibid.).

To date, few studies have incorporated this approach. But two exceptions, Bruce White's analysis of the rhetoric of Ojibwa trading and diplomacy (1982) and Mary Black-Rogers' essay on the semantics of the term "starving" in fur trade documents (1986), demonstrate how native discourses, even after translation, reveal added layers of meaning, once native categories, their connotations, their figurative meanings, and the etiquette governing their usage are examined. In Ojibwa speech, expressions such as "pity us" or "we are starving," as uttered to a European fur trader, commonly betokened the speakers' caution, respect, or efforts to manipulate the trader rather than standing as statements to be taken literally, at face value (Black-Rogers 1986: 353-354, 373). The analysis of the intercultural rhetoric embedded in the historical documents throws new light on many of the statements quoted by Hickerson, suggesting alternative or multiple interpretations of their contents.

Fur Trade History and Cultural Persistence

Just as recent developments in linguistics and archaeology have implications for doing ethnohistory, so too do changing assessments of fur trade history and of the issue of native North American cultural persistence and survival. In chapters 1 and 2, in the conclusion to chapter 8 and in his epilogue, and in the general tenor of his analysis, Hickerson's descriptions of modern Chippewa evoked strong discontinuity and the old image of the Vanishing Indian (Berkhofer 1979: 29-31). He did not mince words: "In terms of the aboriginal past, Chippewa culture is a shambles, so much have the people everywhere had to accommodate to the new conditions imposed by their relations with Euro-Americans" (p. 17). As for the fur trade, "in the long run, the Indians were pawns... exploited, despoiled, and finally extinguished" (p. 119). From this perspective, the "extinguishment of tribalism" by exploiting cultures meant that exhaustive documentary research was the only way back to the native North American past: "if one can no longer watch the corpse die, one can read its epitaph" (p. 123).

On both the death of Indian cultures and the impact of the fur trade, there are strongly opposing views. No one would deny that drastic changes have occurred; the effects of epidemics of European origin on native peoples during the protocontact and fur trade eras are now seen to have been more serious, in fact, than Hickerson realized when he was writing (Dobyns 1976, 1983, 1984, with qualifications by Snow and Lanphear [1988]). But Hickerson's denial of Chippewa cultural persistence has not stood up well. In his review ot *The Chippewa and Their Neighbors* (1973), Edward S. Rogers pointed out that if Hickerson had gotten to know the twentieth-century Chippewa he would not have described their culture as a shambles. He observed that Hickerson in his section on memory ethnography (chapter 2) was far too dismissive of the extent to which oral traditions and distinctive thought patterns and points of view persist among Ojibwa people generally. In later writings, Rogers and Mary Black-Rogers have both emphasized how strongly Ojibwa culture has persisted, "not only in explicit knowledge but also in patterned ways of thinking and reacting" (Rogers and Rogers 1982: 168-169; see also Black-Rogers 1988 for her essay on a Minnesota Chippewa elder intent on "keeping our Indian way"). Scholars have been learning to treat native oral histories with increasing seriousness, both in response to articulate native spokespeople, and because they are finding that oral materials greatly enrich the limited documentary record by furnishing thematic content and insiders' perspectives and by supplying many factual details (among numerous examples citing their value, see Morantz 1984, Helm and Gillespie 1981). The uses of oral history (complemented by archaeological and other data) are richly illustrated in a new book-length history of the Yukon Indians, *Part of the Land, Part of the Water* (McClellan 1987).

Studies of the fur trade have proliferated in the last two decades. Most diverge from Hickerson's views of its effects as expressed in this volume and in a subsequent article (1973), although a more measured analysis by Patricia McCormack (1984) of the Athapaskan Indians in the trade takes a similar theoretical perspective. A major development has been the greatly increased usage by scholars of the Hudson's Bay Company Archives, available in Winnipeg since 1974. This collection documents the company's trade across northern North America from its 1670 founding into the twentieth century. Hickerson drew upon it for some of his work (1967c), but its intensive usage to generate new data and approaches came after the end of his professional career. Peterson and Anfinson (1984) have surveyed this newer literature extensively. In brief, the main thrust of most recent work is that Indians were not simply "pawns in the trade"; at least until its late period, they were active in setting its terms and conditions, in making demands as sophisticated consumers, and in responding to the economic and cultural changes that it brought in creative and innovative ways (Francis and Morantz 1983, Ray and Freeman 1978, Ray 1980, Hamell 1982, Thistle 1987).

Among recent ethnohistorians, Calvin Martin (1978) perhaps most closely parallels Hickerson in seeing the fur trade era as the crucial period of native cultural and economic destruction, although his arguments for a breakdown of Indian-animal spiritual relationships and a consequent "war" of hunters and trappers against their former game allies follow a very different tack (see Krech, ed., 1981 for critiques of this thesis). A considerable body of literature takes issue with both Hickerson's and Martin's views that twentieth-century Northern Algonquians can be assumed to have lost their old religious and cultural values and practices pertaining to hunting and trapping (see, for example, Tanner 1979, Feit 1987).

Another subfield of fur trade studies has closely analyzed the dynamics of the multifaceted social and domestic relationships that grew up over two or more centuries between individual traders of European origin and their Indian partners. Indians seeking reliable trading ties cast those ties in the idiom of alliance and kinship, often seeking to assimilate the newcomers into their communities by adoption or intermarriage. The Europeans, in turn, had varied and sometimes very limited understandings of the meanings of these tactics, but arriving as they did without women or families from home, many hundreds of traders ultimately took native wives, "according to the custom of the country," as such unions were often described. The characteristics of these alliances and their considerable social, demographic, and other consequences have been examined for several periods and regions: for the Great Lakes of the 1600s to 1800s see Peterson 1978; for the Dakota Sioux of Hickerson's region, see Anderson 1984; and for the British-origin traders of the Hudson's Bay Company and North West Company and their native families in the 1700s and 1800s, see Brown 1980, Van Kirk 1980.

These ties led to the rise of a substantial population of mixed origin around the Great Lakes and farther to the north and west by the early 1800s. In Canada, the political visibility of the Métis (as they are most commonly called) from the late 1800s into the present has given them historical visibility as well. American scholars have been slower to recognize the historical roles and influences of the Métis in the Great Lakes and prairie regions. Métis history is a rapidly growing field, however, on both sides of the border; for samplings of numerous authors' work, see Peterson and Brown 1985, Brown 1987.

The Uses of Biography

A further ethnohistorical field, that of biography, has made growing contributions to understandings of native people as individuals. Going beyond the old focus on great men and heroes, researchers have increasingly found that remarkable amounts of information may be teased out of documentary and oral sources about persons who themselves left few or no written records. Some large-scale publication projects such as the multi-volume *Dictionary of Canadian Biography* (University of Toronto Press), whose editors have encouraged the inclusion of native biographies, have fostered this enterprise. Several individual scholars such as David Edmunds in his study of Tecumseh (1984), James A. Clifton (1978), Anderson (1986), and Donald B. Smith (1987) have demonstrated that the native names mentioned in documents can often be brought alive to a striking degree with detective work and the magnifying glass of biography (see also the dozen new biographic essays in Clifton, ed., 1988, and for biographic materials on native women, Green 1983 and Broker 1983). As this work advances, some writers are also examining the issues involved in bringing the study of native North Americans into a Western literary-historical mode, that of the personal, chronological life history, which diverges from native conceptualizations of the past and of individuals and their significance (e.g., Krupat 1983).

The Chippewa and Their Neighbors mentions numerous names of both Indians and whites whose lives intersected in the documentary record. Although Hickerson's identifications of most of them were minimal, the activities and personalities of many can be retrieved and examined to improve our understanding of the on-the-ground relationships of these "natives and newcomers." The enterprise is worthwhile and can lead to new interpretations of the broader historical scene.

Clans, Resources, and the Question of "Atomism"

Hickerson's views on early Chippewa social structure and its resource base (see chapter 3) have proved no less provocative than his ideas about the fur trade and native cultural collapse. One manifestation of the Chippewas' disintegration, he believed, was the decay of a strong corporate communal life, originally embedded in a system of unilineal, totemic, exogamous clans. When twentieth-century observers described the Chippewa as atomistic and fragmented (Landes 1937, James 1961), it was because they were seeing the end results of the fur trade and other destructive forces. Hickerson made these points briefly in chapter 3, but his most intensive discussion of the issue appeared in his essay, "Some Implications of the Theory of the Particularity, or 'Atomism,' of Northern Algonkians" (1967a), which spelled out, as well, the Marxian evolutionary framework in which his data were cast.

This portrayal of Chippewa social evolution found both approval and rejection; the reactions of more than a dozen scholars, which were printed with the 1967 essay, exhibit the range of responses. Some later work on twentieth-century Chippewa social organization has fueled criticism of Hickerson's picture of contemporary communities. In the 1970s, James G.E. Smith concluded from his fieldwork that Minnesota Chippewa are not atomized but have a political and social organization that serves their values and priorities well — "an adaptive social structure that places great importance on the preservation of egalitarian values, and negatively evaluates aggressive individualism" (1973: 33). Drawing upon Sol Tax's description of many North American Indian groups as "polycephalic," exhibiting "great flexibility through highly diffuse systems of leadership," Smith has viewed modern Chippewa as preserving basic continuities in their political and social structure, from the earliest recorded periods into the present (1979: 305).

The question of whether the precontact and early historic Chippewa had a social structure based on clans and clan villages has equally stirred debates. That they had named social groups, often with animal names, is accepted, but so did other Northern Algonquian groups that showed no trace of clan organization. Further, the derivation of the Chippewa term dodem (totem) from ode.na (village), an etymology which Hickerson used to postulate the early existence of clan villages (p. 47), is not substantiated linguistically (Rogers 1973: 84; Mary Black-Rogers, James G.E. Smith, personal communications).

The argument for corporate clan villages raises, in turn, the issue of what the resource base of such relatively large units would have been. In this volume and elsewhere, Hickerson argued that the Chippewa at contact were not scattered hunters and gatherers, but "maintained abundant fisheries at various river mouths, bays, and inlets" along the shores of Lakes Superior and Huron in the Sault Ste. Marie region; these served as village bases for a good part of the year (p. 40; see also Hickerson 1967a: 324) The fur trade, however, turned many Chippewa from a communal, seasonally sedentary life toward an increasingly dispersed and individualistic social pattern oriented to hunting and trapping.

The significance of Ojibwa fisheries, and their growth or decline compared to other means of subsistence, are subjects that have drawn increasing attention. E.S. Rogers, commenting on Hickerson's 1967 essay, noted grounds for doubt about whether the early Chippewa fisheries were as plentiful as Hickerson assumed (1967: 333-334); later, writing of the Northern Ojibwa, he described fish as "a dependable source of food when other resources failed" (1983: 94). For the upper Great Lakes and northwestern Ontario, on the other hand, archaeologists are increasingly emphasizing the importance of aboriginal fisheries (Cleland 1982, Arthurs 1986). Most recently, a study of the Ojibwa sturgeon fishery on the Rainy River, Ontario, has shown that it was immensely productive from prehistoric times through the fur trade era until the intrusion of the commercial fishing industry in the late 1800s (Holzkamm, Lytwyn, and Waisberg 1988). The authors do not address Hickerson's clan-village thesis. But they document the persistence and continuity of this fishery as a cooperative, large-scale, seasonal enterprise, involving considerable processing of the various sturgeon products (pemmican, isinglass, etc.) as well as the fishing itself. The sturgeon resource could have facilitated substantial seasonal village life, although there seems no functional necessity for it to have been clan-based. What perhaps is most interesting in the light of Hickerson's arguments is the extent to which the fishery thrived throughout the fur trade period — in contrast to his portrait of the social and economic degradation of that era.

Our revised perspectives on the sturgeon fisheries are reminders that assumptions about native social organization and resource use, and the interpretations built on those assumptions, are often based on incomplete knowledge of the past and a lack of attention to questions that later emerge as important. Native claims arising from the terms of Treaty 3 in northwestern Ontario have generated the new ethnohistorical research on sturgeon, which in turn requires a reexamination of older interpretations of Chippewa community life and resources before and during the fur trade era. The evolving roles of wild rice, maple sugar, and agriculture similarly need reassessment. D. Wayne Moodie (1988) has argued, for example, that during the fur trade the Ojibwa were effectively managing and extending the ranges of their wild rice crops. In turn, this new attention to fish and plant foods and their processing raises a matter quite outside the scope of *The Chippewa and Their Neighbors* — the economic productivity of women (for one sampling of the growing literature on this subject, see Dahlberg, ed., 1981). Priscilla Buffalohead (1983), looking at the social and political roles of women, also offers some revised perspectives on Ojibwa social organization that do not enter into Hickerson's analysis. Juxtaposing her findings with those of James G.E. Smith on Ojibwa leadership as polycephalic and "highly diffuse," we find that Ojibwa communities offered considerable scope for women to exercise power and influence in a variety of spheres.

Clearly, some key questions have only begun to be asked. Among recent writers, James G.E. Smith has addressed the issue of clans most systematically, particularly in an as yet unpublished manuscript on early Ojibwa social organization (1988) which extensively reviews relevant documentary evidence. Ethnohistorical work such as his, along with further archaeological and linguistic studies and analyses of both men's and women's work and resource use, serves to place Hickerson's writings in a far broader perspective than was possible when *The Chippewa and Their Neighbors* appeared.

The Origins of the Midewiwin

In chapter 4, Hickerson presented his views on the much debated origins of the Ojibwa ceremonial known as the Midewiwin or Grand Medicine Society. He postulated that the Midewiwin developed after 1680 as a nativistic movement responding to changes accompanying European contact. His interpretation has been widely accepted (for example, Dewdney 1975: 167, Vecsey 1983: 174), although Dewdney believed that what he termed "proto-Mide rites" could be identified among some groups somewhat earlier (1975: 168).

Ojibwa oral tradition, in contrast, holds that the Midewiwin was aboriginal (Deleary 1986, Benton-Banai 1979), and a seemingly Midewiwin birchbark scroll has recently been radiocarbon-dated to the protohistoric period (Kidd 1981). Excavations at Whitefish Island near Sault Ste. Marie, Ontario show evidence of fully developed elements of Midewiwin ceremonialism (articulated bear paws that may have been Mide bags and dog feasts involving multiple sacrifices) dating to the late 1600s (Conway 1987: 8, 25). The "negative evidence" argument used by Hickerson (p. 51) to argue for the postcontact origin of the ceremonial is thus challenged, and so, by extension, are his ideas about the relationships among the Feast of the Dead, the establishment of multiclan villages, and the development of the Midewiwin (p. 53). Negative evidence, of course, is always subject to revision by new data. And as E.S. Rogers mentioned in his review of *Chippewa*, written records may omit much (1973:85).

Aside from the seeming failure of the earliest documents to mention this ceremonial institution, Hickerson's other main basis for denying its antiquity was its use of European symbols and goods. Hickerson maintained that the cross seen by French explorers in an Algonquian village in 1673 was not a precontact Midewiwin symbol as some had argued, but had been introduced by visiting Roman Catholic priests. The ceremony's use of European trade goods as payments for initiation also demonstrated its post-contact origin, he believed.

Incorporation and syncretism are commonplace occurrences, however, in situations of contact between different religious systems. The cross may well have been borrowed by Midewiwin specialists after contact. Or we may be dealing with independent invention; several pictographs in northern Ontario depict crosses which may be aboriginal (Conway, personal communication; Rogers 1973: 85, citing Dewdney and Kidd 1962). On the question of trade goods, George Hamell's work on the spiritual associations that certain European goods (metal artifacts, red cloth, glass beads) acquired among northeastern native peoples suggests how such goods were integrated into aboriginal systems, replacing or supplementing other items as functional equivalents in meaning and use (Hamell 1982). John S. Long's (1987) exploration of the creative recombination of religious ideas and artifacts by the

James Bay Cree affords another example of such syncretism at work among Algonquians.

Hickerson's discussion of the Midewiwin was based mostly on nineteenth-century sources (Boutwell, Warren, Schoolcraft), which may or may not have accurately reflected the ceremony's functions during the earlier period he considers. Nor do these sources aid in examining the shift of leadership from clan elders to Midewiwin priests which, Hickerson claimed, occurred earlier with the establishment of multiclan villages. These developments, the decline of the seventeenth-century Feast of the Dead, and the role of the Midewiwin as an integrating force in Chippewa society (Benton-Banai 1979, Vecsey 1984) are all topics deserving of more attention.

As a final general point, it is necessary to bear in mind that for the purposes of his analysis, Hickerson isolated the Midewiwin from the context of Ojibwa religion as a whole. Readers may wish to consult other works on Northern Algonquian religion (for example, Vecsey 1983, Kohl 1985, Brown and Brightman 1988, and relevant essays in Hallowell 1955) to place the Midewiwin in a broader perspective.

Warfare and the Debatable Zone

In chapters 5-8, Hickerson traced the expansion of the Chippewa into the upper Mississippi River area and sought to explain the Chippewa-Dakota warfare that occurred during this expansion. He contended that the Chippewa dispersed from their Lake Superior villages because of "the meager game resources afforded by the barren boreal forest region" around the western shores of the lake (p. 66). Further, their 1679 truce with the Dakota, which had enabled them to use Dakota lands, broke down in 1736. The subsequent warfare, Hickerson believed, was related to competition over game, and the development of a zone of intermittent and potential conflict between the two peoples (the "debatable zone") had the ecological function of conserving the population of Virginia deer, an important staple for both groups.

Hickerson's concept of a kind of "no-man's-land" functioning to keep hostilities in equilibrium and to preserve a game resource required by both warring parties is a classic, elegant formulation that brings order and pattern to the complex and often confusing documentary data. His descriptions of Chippewa warfare and his definition of the debatable zone have held up well. Further documentary and other research, however, has called into question some of the sequences of events he described, and has also added to the complexity of explaining those events.

As noted earlier, the Chippewa who settled to the south and west of Lake Superior had a rather more diversified resource base than Hickerson allowed for; both he and his documentary sources tended to overlook fish, wild rice, corn, and other foods that were less conspicuous to outside observers than deer or other large game. The western Lake Superior forests and waterways from which the Chippewa dispersed, and for which Helen Tanner has described wild rice as "the economic mainstay" (1987: 19) were less barren than Hickerson believed, making his explanation of their motives for moving to the west and south less convincing.

According to Hickerson, the breakdown of peace with the Dakota in 1736 was a major factor influencing the Chippewas' movements and causing them to take action to drive the Dakota beyond the western Great Lakes woodlands. Gary Anderson has noted, however, that a considerable mythology has grown up around the idea of "Chippewa imperialism," particularly through the influence of Chippewa historian William W. Warren (1885, new ed. 1984) whose work "is not supported by French documents, has many inaccuracies, and runs counter to Sioux oral tradition" (1984: 47). Hickerson's chronology of Chippewa/Dakota peace and war has also been challenged by Tim Holzkamm (1983). Hickerson's source describing peaceful relations between the parties before 1736 was the French fur trader and explorer, Nicolas Perrot. But Perrot had his own political reasons for not mentioning French failures to secure lasting peace between the Chippewa and the Dakota (Holzkamm 1983: 227). Other sources suggest to Holzkamm that "the entire period of Ojibway-Dakota relations from 1679 to the early nineteenth century can be described as a situation of omnipresent potential for violence" (1983: 226). Holzkamm also contests Hickerson's claim that the Chippewa earlier had an arrangement with the Dakota to act as fur trade middlemen in exchange for access to Dakota hunting grounds; he cites various evidence that the Dakota were not dependent on Chippewa traders for European trade goods (1983: 228-229). He believes that Dakota westward movements were influenced not so much by the expanding French fur trade frontier and related pressures from the Chippewa, as by the Dakotas' own interests in combining fur trade activity with their growing participation in equestrian buffalo hunting on the Plains. Their increasing emphasis on horses complemented their accumulating of trade goods with which to purchase horses (Holzkamm 1983: 231-232).

While Hickerson pursued the historical-ecological factors in Chippewa/ Dakota relations, Gary Anderson and Holzkamm, besides probing the documents more deeply, have drawn attention to Dakota motivations and perceptions of the situation. Part of the elegance of Hickerson's interpretation resided in his dualistic focus on two confronting parties interacting across a zone of interest to both, without the complications of other powerful intervening variables. But the Dakotas' growing (and willing) involvement with Plains economic life casts a somewhat different light on their relations with the Chippewa, just as a new look at the Lake Superior Chippewa resource base leads to a reassessment of the role of hunting compared to other means of subsistence.

A reexamination of the "debatable zone" by Bruce A. Cox suggests that the complexity of interactions within that area was also greater than Hickerson's analysis allowed. Cox calls attention to the numbers of Canadians and Métis in and around the zone; they too were using resources and complicating the patterns of Chippewa-Dakota relations. The numbers of American whites began to increase rapidly in the region after 1810. As well, he cites indications that the Menominee Indians were a more significant presence in the zone than Hickerson allowed; in sum, it was not so well protected from hunting and use by others. The Chippewa and Dakota belligerents themselves hunted there under the terms of recurring seasonal winter truces (Cox 1986: 4-8).

Cox concludes by urging that "an elaborate functional explanation of native warfare on the upper Mississippi" (1986: 17) is not needed; rather we may learn much by attending to how the parties themselves explained and justified the conflict. Both sides knew that boundaries, as such, could not be defended;

the priority was to protect their villages. This could best be done through the existence of buffer zones that "served to contain conflict once it had begun" (1986: 16). As for the Chippewa view of why intermittent warfare continued, he urges that we treat more seriously such sources as the Chippewa chief who in 1820 told Lewis Cass that "They fought because their fathers fought before them" (1986: 9, 17), and the others who described the causes of ongoing conflict "in terms of grievance and retaliation" (this volume, p. 98). Concerns with blood revenge and honor were real and compelling on both sides, and require attention along with the issues of ecology and the evolving fur trade frontier that Hickerson brings forward.

Speaking more broadly, the fact that four of the eight chapters of *The Chippewa and Their Neighbors* are devoted to warfare and the debatable zone conveys an impression that Chippewa culture and history were characterized by a heavy emphasis on military activity and the hunt. As noted in earlier sections of this review, much of the newer literature offers counterweights to this emphasis, calling attention to other resources besides large game and other activities besides those of adult male warriors. With these perspectives in mind, it is revealing to compare two major nineteenth-century sources on the Chippewa, one extensively used by Hickerson and the other not cited. William W. Warren's *History of the Ojibway Nation* (1885), mentioned above, celebrates his people's history, with particular attention to its chiefs, warriors, and conflicts with the Dakota. Its richly detailed text shares the limitations of perspective that usually characterize nationalistic and military-political histories, and is otherwise flawed as Gary Anderson observed. But it offers a wealth of material for Hickerson's analysis.

J.G. Kohl's *Kitchi-Gami: Life among the Lake Superior Ojibway* (1985, first published in English in 1860), which was not cited in this volume, presents portraits of Chippewa life and people that throw a very different light on his subjects. As an independent visitor who quickly developed unusual empathy with his hosts, Kohl was deeply interested in their religion, mythology, historical traditions, values, and daily life; he placed little emphasis, relatively speaking, on warfare and big game as central Chippewa preoccupations. Warren and Kohl were of course writing with different interests and for different purposes; but serious students of Chippewa/Ojibwa history and culture may find the contrasts between them suggestive. Since these two sources are more available than most, their comparison may readily be undertaken, and helps in reassessing both Hickerson's presentation and his subject matter.

The Chippewa and Their Neighbors does not go beyond the 1840s, and the nine decades from that period to the start of serious anthropological fieldwork have not been subjected to much ethnohistorical analysis. Three studies are of interest, however, for pursuing some of Hickerson's themes in this post-treaty period of heavy white settlement and resource development. About half of E.J. Danziger's history, *The Chippewas of Lake Superior* (1978), is devoted to the period between the 1840s and 1970s. Patricia A. Shifferd (1976) has examined economic change among the northern Wisconsin Chippewa from 1854 to 1900; her analysis recalls James G.E. Smith's in finding considerable cultural and social continuity through the hardships of this period; "by continuing their traditional risk-spreading behavior the people were able to maintain their social system" (1976: 38). James A. Clifton's (1987) study of the Lake Superior Chippewas' responses to governmental efforts at their forced removal in the 1850s is a careful examination of their tactics and their many problems in this period.

The Chippewa and Their Neighbors, as this essay suggests, retains its power to stir discussion and debate, and to focus our attention on issues that continue to require further research and discussion. In this book, as in his other writings on the Chippewa, Harold Hickerson laid open a series of questions and problems and a methodology for approaching them — that of ethnohistory — which was still a relative novelty in 1970. With hindsight, we may find fault in numerous aspects of his approach, discover gaps in his research (which he would have admitted), and query his conclusions. But on reflection, ethnohistorians also owe him a great debt for helping to build a new field of study that now produces some of the most insightful and thought-provoking work in both anthropology and history. We hope that this book, in the new edition, continues to be a stimulus to students and researchers. With the passage of time, it takes on a double value — as a contribution to methodology and to its subject, and as a historical document in its own right, a landmark in the history of ethnohistory.

Bibliographical Supplement
1988

Anderson, Gary C., 1984. *Kinsmen of Another Kind: Dakota-White Relations in the Upper Mississippi Valley, 1650-1862*. Lincoln: University of Nebraska Press.

_____, 1986. *Little Crow: Spokesman for the Sioux*. St. Paul: Minnesota Historical Society Press.

Arthurs, David, 1986. Archaeological Investigations at the Long Sault site (Manitou Mounds). Conservation Archaeology Report, Northwestern Region, No. 7. Ontario: Ministry of Citizenship and Culture.

Axtell, James, 1981. *The European and the Indian: Essays in the Ethnohistory of Colonial North America*. New York: Oxford University Press.

Benton-Banai, Edward, 1979. *The Mishomis Book: The Voice of the Ojibway*. St. Paul: Indian Country Press.

Berkhofer, Robert, 1978. *The White Man's Indian: Images of the American Indian from Columbus to the Present*. New York: Knopf.

Bishop, Charles A., 1974. *The Northern Ojibwa and the Fur Trade: An Historical and Ecological Study*. Toronto: Holt, Rinehart and Winston of Canada.

_____, 1976. The Emergence of the Northern Ojibwa: Social and Economic Consequences. *American Ethnologist* 3:39-54.

_____, 1978. Cultural and Biological Adaptations to Deprivation: The Northern Ojibwa Case. In Charles D. Laughlin, Jr., and Ivan A. Brady, eds., *Extinction and Survival in Human Populations*, pp. 208-230. New York: Columbia University Press.

_____, 1986. Territoriality among Northeastern Algonquians. *Anthropologica* 28(1-2): 37-63.

Bishop, Charles A., and Toby Morantz, ed. 1986. Who Owns the Beaver? Northern Algonquian Land Tenure Reconsidered. *Anthropologica* 28(1-2). Special issue.

Black-Rogers, Mary, 1986. Varieties of "Starving": Semantics and Survival in the Subarctic Fur Trade, 1750-1850. *Ethnohistory* 33:353-383.

_____, 1988. Dan Raincloud: "Keeping our Indian Way." In James A. Clifton, ed., *Being and Becoming Indian: Biographic Studies of North American Frontiers*. In press. Chicago: Dorsey Press.

Broker, Ignatia, 1983. *Night Flying Woman*. St. Paul: Minnesota Historical Society Press.

Brown, Jennifer S.H., 1980. *Strangers in Blood: Fur Trade Company Families in Indian Country*. Vancouver: University of British Columbia Press.

_____, 1987. People of Myth, People of History: A Look at Recent Writings on the Metis. *Acadiensis* 17:150-162.

Brown, Jennifer S.H., and Robert Brightman, 1988. *The Orders of the Dreamed: George Nelson on Cree and Northern Ojibwa Religion and Myth, 1823.* Winnipeg: University of Manitoba Press/St. Paul: Minnesota Historical Society Press.

Buffalohead, Priscilla K., 1983. Farmers, Warriors, Traders: A Fresh Look at Ojibway Women. *Minnesota History* 48: 236-244.

Cleland, Charles E., 1982. The Inland Shore Fishery of the Northern Great Lakes: Its Development and Importance in Prehistory. *American Antiquity* 47: 761-784.

Clifton, James A., 1978. Merchant, Soldier, Broker, Chief: A Corrected Obituary of Captain Billy Caldwell. *Journal of the Illinois State Historical Society* 71: 185-210.

_____, 1987. Wisconsin Death March: Explaining the Extremes in Old Northwest Indian Removal. *Transactions of the Wisconsin Academy of Sciences, Arts and Letters,* vol. 75.

_____, ed., 1988. *Being and Becoming Indian: Biographic Studies of North American Frontiers.* Chicago: Dorsey Press.

Conway, Thor, 1987. Archaeological Evidence for Algonkian Shamanism. Report on file with Ministry of Culture and Communication, Sault Ste. Marie, Ontario.

Cox, Bruce Alden, 1986. Debating the "Debatable Zone": A Re-examination of Explanations of Dakota-Algonquian Conflict. Department of Sociology and Anthropology Working Paper 86-7. Ottawa: Carleton University.

Dahlberg, Frances, ed., 1981. *Woman the Gatherer.* New Haven: Yale University Press.

Danziger, Edmund Jefferson, 1978. *The Chippewas of Lake Superior.* Norman: University of Oklahoma Press.

Dawson, Kenneth C.A., 1982. The Northern Ojibwa of Ontario. In Margaret G. Hanna and Brian Kooyman, eds., *Approaches to Algonquian Archaeology,* pp. 81-96. Calgary: Archaeology Association of the University of Calgary.

Deleary, Nicholas, 1986. The Midewiwin, an Aborginal Institution: A Traditional, Culture-based Perspective. Paper presented at the Eighteenth Algonquian Conference, Winnipeg.

Dewdney, Selwyn, 1975. *The Sacred Scrolls of the Southern Ojibway.* Toronto: University of Toronto Press.

Dewdney, Selwyn, and Kenneth E. Kidd, 1962. *Indian Rock Paintings of the Great Lakes.* Toronto: University of Toronto Press.

Dobyns, Henry F., 1976. *Native American Historical Demography: A Critical Bibliography.* Bloomington: Indiana University Press.

_____, 1983. *Their Number Become Thinned: Native American Population Dynamics in Eastern North America.* Knoxville: University of Tennessee Press.

_____, 1984. Native American Population Collapse and Recovery. In W.R. Swagerty, ed., *Scholars and the Indian Experience: Critical Reviews of Recent Writing in the Social Sciences.* Bloomington: Indiana University Press.

Edmunds, R. David, 1984. *Tecumseh and the Quest for Indian Leadership.* Boston: Little, Brown.

Feit, Harvey A., 1987. Waswanipi Cree Management of Land and Wildlife: Cree Ethno-Ecology Revisited. In Bruce Alden Cox, ed., *Native People, Native Lands: Canadian Indians, Inuit and Metis,* pp. 75-91. Ottawa: Carleton University Press.

Green, Rayna, 1983. *Native American Women: A Contextual Bibliography.* Bloomington: Indiana University Press.

Hamell, George, 1982. Trading in Metaphors: the Magic of Beads. In C. Hayes, ed., *Proceedings of the 1982 Glass Trade Bead Conference.* Rochester, NY: Rochester Museum and Science Center.

Hamilton, Scott, 1985. Competition and Warfare: Functional versus Historical Explanations. *Canadian Journal of Native Studies* 5: 93-113.

Harris, R. Cole, ed., and Geoffrey J. Matthews, cartographer/designer, 1987. *Historical*

Atlas of Canada, vol. 1, *From the Beginning to 1800*. Toronto: University of Toronto Press.

Helm, June, 1976. *The Indians of the Subarctic: A Critical Bibliography*. Bloomington: Indiana University Press.

———, ed., 1981. *Subarctic. Handbook of North American Indians*, vol. 6. Washington, DC: Smithsonian Institution.

Helm, June, and Beryl C. Gillespie, 1981. Dogrib Oral Tradition as History: War and Peace in the 1820s. *Journal of Anthropological Research* 37: 8-27.

Hickerson, Harold, 1973. Fur Trade Colonialism and the North American Indian. *Journal of Ethnic Studies* 1: 15-44.

———, 1974. *Ethnohistory of Chippewa in Central Minnesota*. New York: Garland Series in North American Indian Ethnohistory.

Holzkamm, Tim E., 1983. Eastern Dakota Population Movements and the European Fur Trade: One More Time. *Plains Anthropologist* 28-101: 225-233.

Holzkamm, Tim E., Victor P. Lytwyn, and Leo G. Waisberg, 1988. The Ojibway Sturgeon Fishery of the Rainy River: A Regional Resource in the Fur Trade Economy. *Canadian Geographer*, forthcoming.

Kidd, Kenneth E., 1981. A Radiocarbon Date on a Midewiwin Scroll from Burntside Lake, Ontario. *Ontario Archaeology* 35:41-43.

Kohl, Johann Georg, 1985. *Kitchi-Gami: Life Among the Lake Superior Ojibway*. St. Paul: Minnesota Historical Society Press (1st English ed. 1860).

Krech, Shepard, III, ed., 1981. *Indians, Animals, and the Fur Trade: A Critique of Keepers of the Game*. Athens: University of Georgia Press.

Krupat, Arnold, 1983. The Indian Autobiography: Origins, Type, and Function. In Brian Swann, ed., *Smoothing the Ground: Essays on Native American Oral Literature*, pp. 261-282. Berkeley: University of California Press.

Long, John S., 1987. *Manitu*, Power, Books and Wiihtikow: Some Factors in the Adoption of Christianity by Nineteenth-Century Western James Bay Cree. *Native Studies Review* 3: 1-30.

McClellan, Catharine, 1987. *Part of the Land, Part of the Water: A History of the Yukon Indians*. Vancouver: Douglas and McIntyre.

McCormack, Patricia A., 1984. Becoming Trappers: The Transformation to a Fur Trade Mode of Production. In Thomas C. Buckley, ed., *Rendezvous: Selected Papers of the Fourth North American Fur Trade Conference*, 1981. St. Paul: North American Fur Trade Conference.

Martin, Calvin, 1978. *Keepers of the Game: Indian-Animal Relationships and the Fur Trade*. Berkeley: University of California Press.

Moodie, D. Wayne, 1988. Manomin: Historical Geographical Perspectives on the Ojibway Production of Wild Rice. Paper presented at Conference on Aboriginal Resource Use in Canada: Historical and Legal Aspects. St. John's College, University of Manitoba, Winnipeg.

Morantz, Toby, 1984. Oral and Recorded History in James Bay. In William Cowan, ed., *Papers of the Fifteenth Algonquian Conference*, pp. 171-192. Ottawa: Carleton University.

Peers, Laura Lynn, 1987. An Ethnohistory of the Western Ojibwa, 1730-1830. Master's thesis, University of Winnipeg.

Peterson, Jacqueline, 1978. Prelude to Red River: A Social Portrait of the Great Lakes Metis. *Ethnohistory* 25: 41-68.

Peterson, Jacqueline, and John Anfinson, 1984. The Indian and the Fur Trade. In W.R. Swagerty, ed., *Scholars and the Indian Experience: Critical Reviews of Recent Writing in the Social Sciences*. Bloomington: Indiana University Press.

Peterson, Jacqueline, and Jennifer S.H. Brown, eds., 1985. *The New Peoples: Being and*

Becoming Metis in North America. Winnipeg, University of Manitoba Press/ Lincoln: University of Nebraska Press.

Ray, Arthur J., 1974. *Indians in the Fur Trade: Their Role as Trappers, Hunters, and Middlemen in the Lands Southwest of Hudson Bay, 1660-1870.* Toronto, University of Toronto Press.

———, 1980. Indians as Consumers in the Eighteenth Century. In Carol M. Judd and A.J. Ray, eds., *Old Trails and New Directions: Papers of the Third North American Fur Trade Conference.* Toronto: University of Toronto Press.

Ray, Arthur J., and Donald B. Freeman, 1978. *"Give Us Good Measure": An Economic Analysis of Relations between the Indians and the Hudson's Bay Company before 1763.* Toronto: University of Toronto Press.

Rogers, Edward S., 1967. CA Comment on Harold Hickerson, Some Implications of the Theory of the Particularity, or "Atomism", of Northern Algonkians. *Current Anthropology* 8: 333-334.

———, 1973. Review of Hickerson, *The Chippewa and Their Neighbors.* Michigan *History* 57: 83-86.

———, 1983. Cultural Adaptations: The Northern Ojibwa of the Boreal Forest 1670-1980. In A. Theodore Steegmann, Jr., ed., *Boreal Forest Adaptations: The Northern Algonkians,* pp. 85-142. New York: Plenum Press.

Rogers, Edward S., and Mary Black Rogers, 1982. Who were the Cranes? Groups and Group Identity in Northern Ontario. In Margaret G. Hanna and Brian Kooyman, eds., *Approaches to Algonquian Archaeology,* pp. 147-188. Calgary: Archaeology Association of the University of Calgary.

Shifferd, Patricia A., 1976. A Study in Economic Change: The Chippewa of Northern Wisconsin 1854-1900. *Western Canadian Journal of Anthropology* 6: 16-41.

Siebert, Frank T., Jr., 1967. The Original Home of the Proto-Algonquian People. National Museum of Canada, Contributions to Anthropology: Linguistics I, Bull. 214: 13-47. Ottawa.

Smith, Donald B., 1987. *Sacred Feathers: The Reverend Peter Jones (Kahkewaquonaby) and the Mississauga Indians.* Toronto: University of Toronto Press.

Smith, James G.E., 1973. Leadership among the Southwestern Ojibwa. Publications in Ethnology, no. 7. Ottawa: National Museums of Canada.

———, 1974. Proscription of Cross-Cousin Marriage among the Southwestern Ojibwa. *American Ethnologist* 1:751-762.

———, 1988. Early Ojibwa Social Organization and the Problem of Clan. Unpublished paper.

Snow, Dean R., 1976. The Archaeological Implications of the Proto-Algonquian Urheimat. In William Cowan, ed., *Papers of the Seventh Algonquian Conference, 1975,* pp. 339-346. Ottawa: Carleton University.

Snow, Dean R., and Kim M. Lanphear, 1988. European Contact and Indian Depopulation in the Northeast: The Timing of the First Epidemics. *Ethnohistory* 35: 15-33.

Stocking, George W., Jr., ed., 1983. *Observers Observed: Essays on Ethnographic Fieldwork.* Madison: University of Wisconsin Press.

Tanner, Adrian, 1979. *Bringing Home Animals: Religious Ideology and Mode of Production of the Mistassini Cree Hunters.* New York: St. Martin's Press.

Tanner, Helen Hornbeck, 1976. *The Ojibwas: A Critical Bibliography.* Bloomington: Indiana University Press.

———, 1987. *Atlas of Great Lakes Indian History.* Norman: University of Oklahoma Press.

Thistle, Paul C., 1986. *Indian-European Trade Relations in the Lower Saskatchewan River Region to 1840.* Winnipeg: University of Manitoba Press.

Trigger, Bruce G., 1969. *The Huron Farmers of the North.* New York: Holt, Rinehart and Winston.

―――, 1976. *The Children of Aataentsic: A History of the Huron People to 1660.* 2 vols. Montreal: McGill-Queen's University Press.

―――, ed., 1978. *Northeast. Handbook of North American Indians,* vol. 15. Washington, DC: Smithsonian Institution.

―――, 1985. *Natives and Newcomers: Canada's "Heroic Age" Reconsidered.* Kingston and Montreal: McGill-Queen's University Press.

―――, 1986. Ethnohistory: The Unfinished Edifice. *Ethnohistory* 33: 253-267.

Van Kirk, Sylvia, 1980. *"Many Tender Ties": Women in Fur-Trade Society, 1670-1870.* Winnipeg: Watson and Dwyer.

Vecsey, Christopher, 1983. *Traditional Ojibwa Religion and its Historical Changes.* Philadelphia: American Philosophical Society.

―――, 1984. Midewiwin Myths of Origin. In William Cowan, ed., *Papers of the Fifteenth Algonquian Conference,* pp. 445-467. Ottawa: Carleton University.

Warren, William W., 1984. *History of the Ojibway People.* Introduction by W. Roger Buffalohead. St. Paul: Minnesota Historical Society Press.

White, Bruce M., 1982. "Give Us a Little Milk." *Minnesota History* 48: 60-71.